BIBLE
TRAVEL GUIDE

FOR STUDENTS

BIBLE TRAVEL GUIDE

FOR STUDENTS

Tyndale House Publishers, Inc.
Carol Stream, Illinois

Visit Tyndale online at www.tyndale.com.

TYNDALE and Tyndale's quill logo are registered trademarks of Tyndale House Publishers, Inc.

Bible Travel Guide for Students

Copyright © 1999, 2016 by The Barton-Veerman Company. All rights reserved.

Previously published in 2008 as *Student's Bible Handbook* by Tyndale House Publishers, Inc. under ISBN 978-1-4143-1859-2.

Cover illustration of map copyright © Tyndale House Publishers, Inc. All rights reserved.

Designed by Jennifer Phelps

Edited by Stephanie Rische

Scripture quotations are taken from the *Holy Bible*, New Living Translation, copyright © 1996, 2004, 2015 by Tyndale House Foundation. Used by permission of Tyndale House Publishers, Inc., Carol Stream, Illinois 60188. All rights reserved.

Some of the material used in this book was adapted from these other Tyndale products: the *Life Application Study Bible*, the *Student's Life Application Bible*, and the *Life Application Commentary* series, all produced for Tyndale House by The Livingstone Corporation.

Library of Congress Cataloging-in-Publication Data
Names: Tyndale House Publishers.
Title: Bible travel guide for students.
Other titles: Student's Bible handbook.
Description: Carol Stream, Illinois : Tyndale House Publishers, Inc., 2016. |
    Includes index.
Identifiers: LCCN 2015036647 | ISBN 9781496411808 (sc)
Subjects: LCSH: Bible—Introductions.
Classification: LCC BS475.3 .S77 2016 | DDC 220.6/1—dc23 LC record available
    at http://lccn.loc.gov/2015036647

Printed in the United States of America

22	21	20	19	18	17	16
7	6	5	4	3	2	1

CONTENTS

INTRODUCTION & USER'S GUIDE

Welcome to the Bible Travel Guide for Students! This guide will help lead you through the sometimes confusing world of God's Word. It will serve as your atlas to the Bible. But remember, looking at a map can be interesting but not nearly as exciting as visiting the actual place. Checking your route and finding out what you may discover are good ways to prepare for a journey, but they shouldn't replace the journey itself. Opening, reading, and studying your Bible will transport you into the adventure. Take the *Bible Travel Guide for Students* with you as you explore God's Word!

Make the Most of This Guide
You have probably picked up this book for one of two reasons:

1. You would like to be able to read and understand the Bible on your own. Whether your Bible is old and dusty or new and shiny, you want to start owning it. You have decided you don't just want other people's comments about God's Word. You want to check it out for yourself.
2. You are teaching others about the Bible and want a helpful source of basic information.

In either case you will find this guide useful. It will keep the big picture in front of you as you read God's Word.

Packing List
The material in the *Bible Travel Guide for Students* is organized in biblical order. Each book in the Bible has a fascinating individual history. Part of understanding and applying the Bible involves

becoming familiar with that background. You will find the following essential features packed here to guide you through each Bible book.

Snapshot This easy-to-read section will inform you about the impact and importance of each Bible book. Each Snapshot will help you see how the message of a given book is relevant to your own needs and concerns. This feature also gives you the following information about each Bible book:

- "Purpose" answers the question, Why was this book originally written?
- "Author" identifies the human author when possible.
- "To Whom Written" identifies the original audience of the book.
- "Date Written"/"Date of Events" locates the book on the timeline of history.
- "Setting" notes important historical events that impacted the writer and original audience.
- "Key People" highlights the people who stand out most in the book.
- "Key Places" points out where the events recorded in the book occurred or where the audience of the book lived.
- "Special Features" notes unusual facts that will help you get a sense of each book's uniqueness.

Itinerary This section gives a narrated outline of each Bible book.

Notebook This section describes the major themes in each Bible book and supplies several questions to help you dig into each theme, whether in the context of personal or group study.

Postcard This section concludes each book's summary by challenging you to personally apply the important lessons from that portion of God's Word.

Each of these features will facilitate your study whether you are pursuing it alone or with a group. At first you may find that you have a lot of knowledge gaps to fill. Every insight will seem crucial. As you become familiar with the territory, certain features will stand out for you as particularly helpful. When preparing a study for a group, the questions in the "Notebook" sections will provide a starting point. Both the "Snapshots" and "Itinerary" will give you an overview of the book that you can share with others or simply absorb as you begin to read that part of God's Word. Consider all the features as part of the baggage you are taking as you explore the world of the Bible. Some of the items you will naturally use more than others.

Traveling Companions

This guide also includes a suggested reading plan and a special index that will act as experienced companions during your Bible explorations. This unique Bible reading plan will give you a guided overview of all of Scripture. You won't read the entire Bible the first time through, but you will visit all the major events, stories, and lessons in God's Word. When following the reading plan, use the provocative question included with each reading to help you make a personal application of God's Word to your life. You will also find the "Where to Find It" Index, which tells you where to locate key stories and events in the Bible and then specifically in the life and teachings of Jesus Christ.

Have an exciting, lifelong adventure in God's Word. The journey leads to an eternity with your heavenly Father. As for this guide? Don't leave home without it!

INTRODUCING . . . THE BIBLE

As you probably already know, the Bible is a unique book. It repeatedly calls itself the Word of God. Although the Bible came to us through many authors who wrote over many centuries, it presents and displays the thoughts, plans, and character of one mind—God's. Working through the talents, styles, and experiences of many people, God's Spirit made sure that the final product was God's Word to the world.

The Bible is unusual in another way. Between the covers we actually find a library of sixty-six volumes. They vary in length and style. Although we call them all books, some of the individual volumes in the Bible fit other categories: letters (for example, the letter of Paul to the Romans); anthologies of poetry (Psalms); collections of wise sayings (Proverbs). If you don't have a church background, one of your first goals ought to be to simply know the names of the books of the Bible.

The Bible books are grouped in two large sections: the Old Testament (thirty-nine books) and the New Testament (twenty-seven books). The Old Testament books were written during the centuries before Jesus Christ. The New Testament books begin with the four biographies of Jesus (the Gospels) and record the first years of the Christian church. The Old Testament and the New Testament can be subdivided further into thematic sections:

- *The Basics* (In the Old Testament, Genesis to Deuteronomy, also known as the Pentateuch because of its five books, frequently referred to as the Law elsewhere in the Bible; in

the New Testament, Matthew to John, the four biographies of Jesus)
- *History* (Joshua to Esther in the Old Testament; Acts in the New Testament)
- *Crucial Issues for Thought* (Job to Song of Songs in the Old Testament)
- *Teaching Letters* (Romans to Jude in the New Testament)
- *Prophetic Writings* (Isaiah to Malachi in the Old Testament; Revelation in the New Testament)

Don't be surprised if you find parts of the Bible beyond your understanding. Most of it isn't easy reading. God meant it to offer you enough challenge for a lifetime, so you won't grasp everything even after years of study. What you do understand, however, will change your life! The more you persist in exploring God's Word, the more you will find God speaking in your life. James described the adventure this way: "But if you look carefully into the perfect law that sets you free, and if you do what it says and don't forget what you heard, then God will bless you for doing it" (James 1:25).

OLD
TESTAMENT

GENESIS

 Snapshot of Genesis

Have you ever turned on a TV program a few minutes late? Chances are you turned it off before the show was over because you couldn't figure out what was going on. To understand a television program, you have to see the beginning.

Now think of the Bible. If you want to find out what's going on in this big book—to get the whole picture—it helps to start with Genesis. Why? Because Genesis is the book of beginnings. It explains how just about everything got started. If you don't understand how this world began, it will be harder to figure out why and how God is going to end everything.

In Genesis we marvel at the awesome creation of the entire universe by the spoken word of God. And we get our first glimpse into God's character. We see that though everything else has a definite beginning, God is eternal. He always has been and always will be. We notice God's creativeness and power; we see his hatred and judgment of sin; we view his incredible love for his people even when they constantly disobey him.

Genesis is the book of beginnings: the beginning of the universe, of people, of sin, of salvation, and of an understanding of God. Take time to read Genesis. You will be amazed at how fascinating it is. Later, you may be interested to see how often other books in the Bible refer to something first mentioned in Genesis— the book of beginnings.

PURPOSE:
To record God's creation of the world and his desire to have a people set apart to worship him

AUTHOR:
Moses

TO WHOM WRITTEN:
The people of Israel and to all believers everywhere

DATE WRITTEN:
1450–1410 BC

SETTING:
The region presently known as the Middle East

KEY PEOPLE:
Adam, Eve, Noah, Abraham, Sarah, Isaac, Rebekah, Jacob, Joseph

SPECIAL FEATURE:
Genesis contains the record of the origins of the human race.

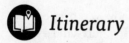 *Itinerary*

The Story of Creation (1:1–2:4)
God. That's where Genesis begins. All at once we see God creating the world in a majestic display of power and purpose culminating with a man and woman made like himself. In the first section of this book, God sets the stage for all of history.

The Story of Adam (2:4–5:32)
The second section highlights Adam and Eve and their immediate descendants. Before long, sin enters the world, and Satan is unmasked. Bathed in innocence, creation is shattered by the Fall (the willful disobedience of Adam and Eve). Fellowship with God is broken, and evil begins weaving its destructive web. We read how, in rapid succession, Adam and Eve are expelled from the beautiful Garden, their first son turns murderer, and evil breeds evil.

The Story of Noah (6:1–11:32)
God takes radical action in the third section. Into a world flooded with evil, he sends a watery judgment that destroys everyone on earth except for a small family led by Noah, the only godly person

left. Unfortunately, sin also survives the Flood and immediately continues its destructive work.

The Story of Abraham (12:1–25:18)

In section 4 we meet Abraham, whom God chooses as the first father of the covenant people. God's plan begins to unfold. His ultimate purpose is not to judge people but to save them. Abraham experiences periods of sharp testing, but he remains faithful to God. Through Abraham we learn what it means to live by faith.

The Story of Isaac (25:19–28:9)

Section 5 takes up the story with Abraham's son Isaac. God keeps his promise to Abraham and gives him a son. Isaac does not demand his own way. He does not resist when he is about to be sacrificed, and he gladly accepts a wife chosen for him by others. Like Isaac, we must learn to put God's will ahead of our own.

The Story of Jacob (28:10–36:43)

Isaac's son Jacob is the central figure in section 6. Jacob lives a tenacious life. He faithfully serves Laban fourteen years for a woman he loves. Later, he wrestles with God. Although Jacob makes many mistakes, his persistence teaches us about lifelong service for our Lord.

The Story of Joseph (37:1–50:26)

Genesis closes with a fascinating account of Joseph's life. Joseph overcomes disastrous setbacks—family betrayal, slavery, sexual harassment, prison—by maintaining a calm reliance on God. Through Joseph's life we learn that suffering, no matter how unfair, can develop strong character in us.

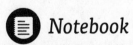 *Notebook*

BEGINNINGS (1:1–2:25)

The name of this book means "beginning." Genesis introduces God as Creator of all that exists: the universe in general and life in particular. God announces the creation of human beings, with whom God shares his own image.

Genesis also describes the initial fall and persistent descent of human beings into sin. The moral infection passes from parent to child in each generation. But God also begins to work out the marvelous plan of salvation, which offers hope to the human race.

- What aspects of God's character are revealed in the first three chapters of Genesis?
- How much significance and value did God give humans by making in his image? In what ways does that fact affect your life?
- What difference does it make when we think about the universe having been created by a personal Creator as opposed to thinking about ourselves as the product of mindless, purposeless, impersonal chance?

SIN AND DISOBEDIENCE (3:1-24; 6:5-22; 18:17–19:26)
Sin is destructive. It destroys the goodness of God's creation, ruining the life God intended. Sin results from human beings choosing to go their own way rather than obeying God. Sin leads to sin. Only God can reverse the consequences of sinful choices and provide an antidote for sin.

No person can escape the effects of sin. Each one is born with a sinful nature! Without God providing salvation, we would all be condemned to death because of sin. But God offers life that is good and glorifying to himself. The person who chooses neither to trust nor obey God misses out on the goodness and glory of God.

- How was the creation affected by Adam and Eve's sin?
- Does a person ever get away with sin? Explain.
- What are some of the common reasons people give for sinning even though they know that they are disobeying God?
- How have you learned to resist temptation?

PROMISES (6:18; 9:8-17; 12:1-3; 17:1-27)
In contrast to human sinfulness, Genesis also reveals the faithful, loving, and promise-keeping nature of God. For example, God promised to protect and provide for his people. God entered into special promises, called "covenants," or binding agreements. Through these covenants, God guaranteed his relationship with people.

One of God's core character traits is truthfulness. He can be trusted to keep his promises. God has not left the world in the dark about who he is and what his plans are. He has given us a written record. While we may not always know the details of what God will do, we can be confident that he will do what he has promised.

- What promise did God make to Noah following the Flood (see 9:8-17)?
- What were the details of the covenant between God and Abraham (see 12:1-3)?
- How do these promises inform your understanding of God?
- Which of God's promises do you claim in your own life?

OBEDIENCE AND PROSPERITY (45:1-11)

Choosing to obey God results in enjoying his goodness and glory. Everyone who makes the choice to obey will prosper. Appearances and experiences may temporarily seem to indicate differently, but those who honor God will eventually see their lives deeply benefited by God.

If a person wants to choose life, that person must put his or her faith in God. Growing in one's faith means discovering God's directions and obeying them. It also involves trusting that God will provide for all of life's needs. God is not boring, nor is he a spoiler of fun. God created life to be enjoyed and really lived! Wouldn't the Creator know best how we should live?

- In spite of his "failures," how would you defend the idea that Joseph was a truly successful person?
- Joseph had to choose what to do with his hurt and bitterness from being rejected and betrayed by his brothers. Based on 45:1-11, what did he do with those feelings?
- What are the basic guidelines you live by? If you haven't done so, write them down. How do they match the life of someone like Joseph?
- What would it take for you to be able to judge your teenage years a success?

Postcard

In spite of all the years between ourselves and our original parents, we are really not that different from Adam and Eve. The differences that do come to mind are superficial. We can understand a lot about ourselves by looking at our first parents' lives and the lives of other early people. In what ways are you living for God today?

 ## Tour Map of Genesis

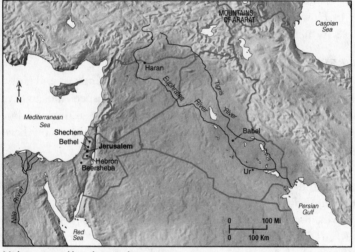

Modern names and boundaries are shown in gray.

EXODUS

 Snapshot of Exodus

"I promise!" she exclaimed. But soon her words were forgotten in the rush and excitement of school.

Remember when you promised to do something for a friend but then forgot? Or what about when someone made an important promise to you and then didn't come through? Promises are part of life—from innocent childhood pledges to earnest romantic commitments. We promise to do something, be somewhere, or give something. And when others make promises to us, we expect them to keep their word. If not, we become angry, disappointed, and even heartbroken.

The book of Exodus is all about promises: God's promises to his people. We, too, are God's people. Just as God was faithful to Israel in keeping promises made to them, he will keep every promise he has made to us: promises to love us no matter what, to care for and protect us, to help with temptation we can't handle, to comfort and teach us, and to bring us to heaven someday.

Do you know the promises of God? Do you realize the things God has said he will do for you and to you? If you do, you understand how incredible those promises are. If you don't, you may have no idea of the many ways God has promised to be there for you. Each and every promise God makes, he keeps—to the Israelites and to you.

PURPOSE:
To record the events of Israel's deliverance from Egypt and to trace its development as a nation

AUTHOR:
Moses

TO WHOM WRITTEN:
The people of Israel and all believers everywhere

DATE WRITTEN:
1450–1410 BC, approximately the same time as Genesis

SETTING:
Egypt. God's people, once highly favored in the land, are now slaves. Their God of great miracles is about to set them free.

KEY PEOPLE:
Moses, Miriam, Pharaoh, Pharaoh's daughter, Jethro, Aaron, Joshua, Bezalel

KEY PLACES:
Egypt, Goshen, Nile River, Midian, Red Sea, Sinai Peninsula, Mount Sinai

SPECIAL FEATURES:
Exodus relates more miracles than any other Old Testament book and is noted for containing the Ten Commandments.

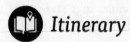 *Itinerary*

Israel in Egypt (1:1–12:30)
The first section of Exodus describes events from Moses' birth to the eve of the great exit from slavery that gives the book its name. Between the end of Genesis and the opening words of Exodus, four hundred years have passed. Jacob's family has grown into a large nation. They have remained in the Egyptian region of Goshen, where they still live as shepherds. Their growing population attracts the concern of a new pharaoh, who has no respect for the contributions of Joseph. The Egyptian ruler enslaves the people and eventually institutes a policy of killing the newborn males. Thanks

to the courage of midwives, the resourcefulness of a mother and sister, the tenderness of an Egyptian princess, and the faithfulness of God, Moses' life is saved.

Although raised as an Egyptian prince, Moses knows his heritage, and eventually, he sides with his own people. After killing a cruel Egyptian taskmaster, Moses becomes a fugitive in the desert. There God enrolls him in a forty-year wilderness training experience. Moses leads sheep around the desert in preparation for leading a nation through the same harsh territory.

When God decides the time is right, he speaks to Moses out of a burning bush and gives him orders to return to Egypt and lead his people back to the land promised to their forefather Abraham. Reluctantly Moses returns for a showdown with the pharaoh. The crushing and punishing ten plagues of judgment on the Egyptians lead to the release of God's chosen people from their bondage.

Israel in the Wilderness (12:31–18:27)

The second section of Exodus begins on the night in which the pharaoh's will is broken and the people begin their march to the Promised Land. God further insures their departure by parting the Red Sea for their passage. Finding themselves out of slavery but in the desert, the people quickly begin to grumble. Thirst, hunger, and heat make them forget how bad things were in Egypt. They complain against God and Moses, but God continues to provide what they need to survive.

Israel at Sinai (19:1–40:38)

The third section of Exodus finds the people at Mount Sinai. Here God gives them the stone tablets with the Ten Commandments. Their rebellion continues. God remains faithful, giving them instructions regarding the Tabernacle, where worship will be centered. Moses directs the building of the Tabernacle. God's presence, in the form of a pillar of fire by night and a cloud by day, rests on the Tabernacle and determines when the nation will remain camped and when they will move.

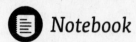 *Notebook*

SLAVERY/CAPTIVITY (1:1–3:22)

The Israelites were slaves for over four hundred years. Pharaoh, the king of Egypt, treated them cruelly.

Physical slavery is like slavery to sin. The longer you are a slave, the more difficult it becomes to break free. Gaining freedom from sin requires God's power and the guidance of godly leaders.

- How did the Hebrews feel about being enslaved to the Egyptians?
- To what degree is it fair to use slavery to describe the effects of sin in our life?
- What are some examples of how people become enslaved to specific sins?
- How has God's power enabled you to escape sin and live in freedom?
- What would be your counsel to someone who recognizes that he or she is in slavery or in danger of becoming a captive to sin?

RESCUE/REDEMPTION (12:23-27)

God rescued Israel through the leader Moses and through mighty miracles. God gave the Passover celebration as an annual reminder of the miraculous escape from bondage.

Every person needs to experience the deliverance from sin that God provides. That escape is just as supernatural as the escape of the Israelites! Jesus Christ celebrated the Passover with his disciples at the Last Supper and then completed God's plan for our redemption by dying in our place on the cross.

- Describe the characteristics that were required for a Passover lamb (12:3-10).
- Why was the lamb important?
- In what way can Jesus be described as our Passover Lamb (John 1:29)?
- How would you answer the question, Why did Jesus have to die?
- How has the fact that you have been redeemed by Christ affected your life?

GUIDANCE (3:1–4:17)

God guided Israel out of slavery using the plagues, Moses' heroic courage, the miracle of parting the Red Sea, God's presence in the cloud column and the pillar of fire, and the Ten Commandments.

God demonstrates his power through the guidance of his Word, wise leaders, and the wisdom that comes from Christian friends working together. God can be trusted to give the guidance needed to follow his will.

- At first Moses had difficulty following God's guidance. What questions did Moses ask God when they met at the burning bush? How did God respond (3:1–4:17)?
- Think about a time when you, like Moses, felt inadequate or unwilling to obey God's will in your life. What decisions did you make? If God had spoken aloud to you in that situation, how do you think you would have reacted?
- What resources has God provided to help you learn how to follow his will for you?
- What decisions are you facing now or in the near future that will require you to rely on God's resources?
- What specific lessons have you learned about God's guidance that you are prepared to apply to your choices?

TEN COMMANDMENTS (20:1-17)

God's rule system had three interwoven parts. The Ten Commandments were the first part, containing the absolutes of spiritual and moral life. The civil law was the second part, giving the people rules to manage their lives. The ceremonial law was the third part, showing the patterns for building the Tabernacle and for regular worship.

God was teaching Israel the importance of choice and responsibility. When the people obeyed God's law and cooperated with his rules, he blessed them; when they forgot or disobeyed, he punished them or allowed disasters to come upon them. God's moral laws, as given in Exodus, have been reflected in the legal systems of many great countries, past and present.

- The law was given to the people of Israel to show them their sin and their need for redemption. How does the law point people to Christ?

- There were some severe and immediate consequences for those who disobeyed the law. What are some of the long-term consequences facing young people who go against God's moral law (the Ten Commandments)?
- To what degree do you find people assuming that God's moral law no longer applies?
- Why does God want you to obey his moral law?

THE NATION/GOD'S PEOPLE

God chose and established the nation of Israel as the source and channel of truth and salvation to all the world. His relationship to his people was loving, yet firm. God was their ultimate leader in government, social concerns, and worship.

The nation of Israel models for us our need to depend upon God. Whether we are rebellious or obedient, God remains our only source of absolute, eternal truth and life.

- What lessons about the character of God do you think were most important for the people of Israel to learn?
- Which of these aspects of God's character affect your own present relationship with God?
- In what specific areas are you satisfied with your dependence on God, and in what areas do you know you need to increase your trust? At home? At school? With close friends?
- Based on your observations of God's relationship to Israel in Exodus, how can you know that God can be trusted in the important areas you just considered?

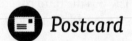 *Postcard*

Picture your life as a journey from the bondage of sin, through life and lessons in the wilderness, to a destination in the Promised Land. What phase of the journey are you in right now? What will be your next step?

Tour Map of Exodus

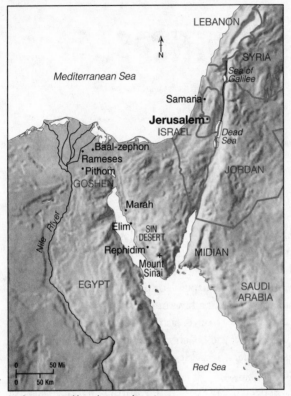

Modern names and boundaries are shown in gray.

LEVITICUS

 Snapshot of Leviticus

The coach was Jason's father. At practice Jason tried hard to pay attention, but one day he knew he was doomed. Patti, the cutest girl on the cheerleading squad, stopped by. Soon she sat next to Jason, and they began to whisper—until Jason's dad looked their way. Jason paid attention for a few minutes, but soon he and Patti were whispering again . . . until Jason's father intruded. "Jason!" he demanded. "You are the coach's son, and I expect you to pay attention!" Jason understood. He remained attentive for the rest of the practice.

The coach expected Jason to listen during practice because Jason was his son. Jason's father felt that Jason's actions reflected on him, so Jason should pay attention—even if no one else did.

The Israelites were in a similar situation. God demanded they pay attention because they were his chosen people, his children. God told them, "You must be holy because I, the LORD your God, am holy" (19:2). Holy means set apart, good, and different. That's why God gave his children the book of Leviticus. It contains laws of holiness, things they needed to do to remain holy. God also gave them the Day of Atonement so they could be forgiven.

The book of Leviticus is important to us, too. Our Day of Atonement is the day Jesus died. His death covers everything we do wrong.

As you read Leviticus, consider your relationship with God. And where it's needed, ask him for forgiveness.

PURPOSE:
A handbook for the Levites, outlining their priestly duties in worship, and a guidebook of holy living for the Hebrews

AUTHOR:
Moses

TO WHOM WRITTEN:
The people of Israel and all of God's people everywhere

DATE OF EVENTS:
1445–1444 BC

SETTING:
At the foot of Mount Sinai. God teaches the Israelites how to live as holy people.

KEY PEOPLE:
Moses, Aaron, Nadab, Abihu, Eleazar, Ithamar

SPECIAL FEATURES:
Holiness is mentioned more often (152 times) than in any other book of the Bible. Also, when asked to name the greatest commandment (Mark 12:28-34), Jesus used a phrase from Leviticus in his answer: "Love your neighbor as yourself" (19:18).

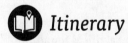 *Itinerary*

Worshiping a Holy God (1:1–17:16)
Leviticus records the various instructions God gives his people during part of their lengthy stay at the foot of Mount Sinai. These instructions fall into two sections. In the first section, God provides specific directions for the kind of worship that is pleasing to him. These instructions teach about the nature of God and can help people develop a right attitude toward worship. Through the offerings we learn of the seriousness of sin and the importance of bringing our sins to God for forgiveness.

Living a Holy Life (18:1–27:34)
In section 2 God gives clear standards to the Israelites for living holy lives. They are to be separate and distinct from the pagan nations around them. In the same way, all believers should be separated from sin and dedicated to God. God still wants to remove sin from the lives of his people.

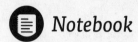

Notebook

SACRIFICES/OFFERINGS (1:1–7:38)

God instituted five kinds of offerings/sacrifices to accomplish two main purposes: (1) to express praise, gratitude, and devotion to God; and (2) to visualize the way in which God atones, covers, and removes guilt and sin.

The instructions in Leviticus about worship point out the costly aspects of worship. God doesn't need anything we might offer him. We simply benefit greatly from giving back to God part of what he has given to us. Why? Because we need to learn to depend on God rather than on the securities of this life.

The instructions about sacrifice reveal the terrible debt created by sin. Sin deserves the death penalty, but even that would only be punishment, not payment for the debt of sin. Because men and women cannot remove their own sins, God told the people to offer animals as substitutes for their lives and as atonement (wiping away) of the debts. These instructions also turned out to be a hint of God's permanent solution to the debt and guilt of sin. Jesus' death, the ultimate sacrifice, did away with this temporary system by paying the penalty for our sins once and for all time.

- What differences are there between the sacrifices found in the book of Leviticus and the sacrifice provided by Jesus? (Check the book of Hebrews in the New Testament for a detailed comparison between the ancient sacrificial system and God's final solution for sin.)
- The worship offerings helped people express praise, thankfulness, and devotion. What similar kinds of offerings can we bring today as we worship God?
- What specific character traits or actions of God create in you the greatest desire to worship him?
- How have you understood and personally applied Jesus' sacrifice to your own life?

HEALTHY LIVING (11:1–15:33)

God called Israel to obey him and to be different from the surrounding nations. God even gave them specific civil rules relating to food, disease, and sex. Through these rules God planned to preserve them from disease and genetic problems as well as to teach them spiritual principles.

We still are to be different morally and spiritually from unbelievers. Principles for healthy living are as important today as in the day of Moses. God is concerned not just about our inner spirit but also about our outer body because it, too, was created to glorify him.

- In what ways do people abuse their bodies?
- Based on what Leviticus reveals about God's view of our body, why is he against such abuse?
- What biblical principles relate to how we should treat our body?
- How do you expect these principles to affect your health?
- Do you agree or disagree with this statement? "Taking care of your body's health is an important part of Christian discipleship." Explain your answer.
- What aspect of the way you treat your body have you found most challenged by God's rules in Leviticus? What changes do you plan to make?

HOLY LIVING (18:1–20:27)

Holy means "separated" or "devoted." God removed his people from Egypt; then he had to remove Egypt from his people. God called his people to be committed to his ways, leaving behind the old lifestyles they had lived in Egypt.

God calls us to devote every area of our life to him. This requires learning to live in obedience to him daily so that we reflect his holiness in the world. While we may not be required to worship as the Israelites did, we are to be committed to leaving behind those things that belong to "Egypt" in our lifestyle.

- How would your friends at school describe a "holy" person?
- How is their definition of holiness similar to and different from the definition you are learning from the Scriptures?
- What would a biblical holy life look like at your school?
- What areas of your life still belong to "Egypt" and keep you from personal holiness? How are you seeking God's help and taking action in these areas?

SPIRITUAL LEADERSHIP (21:1–22:16)

The Levites and priests taught the people how to worship. God set them apart to oversee the moral, civil, and ceremonial laws of the people. They supervised the health, justice, and welfare of the nation on God's behalf.

The Levites served by showing Israel the way to God. Understanding their role enables us to better understand Jesus as our High Priest and how God wants us to live as priests today.

- What attitudes do you think the people had toward the Levites?
- The high priest led God's people into God's presence. In what ways does Jesus fulfill our need for a high priest? (The book of Hebrews in the New Testament includes many insights into Jesus' fulfillment of the Old Testament patterns.)
- Although Jesus was the legitimate and eternal High Priest (Philippians 2:5-11), what significance do you find in the fact that he chose to live as a servant, like a Levite?
- How do you visualize and experience Jesus' ongoing role in your life? In what areas do you find yourself relying most on him?
- In what specific ways will you spend time with Jesus today?

 Postcard

Decide on a gift or action that you can give or do this week that will most express your gratitude and worship toward God. Describe from your own experience how God has been involved in "getting you out of Egypt and getting Egypt out of you."

NUMBERS

📷 *Snapshot of Numbers*

Two weary travelers who had been walking all day wanted to get out of the heat, and rest. They noticed a huge tree with branches that formed a canopy of shade. They stumbled to the shade of the tree, spread their blankets, and were soon blissfully asleep. When they awoke, one of the travelers, feeling refreshed, gazed into the branches and complained, "What a useless tree. There's no fruit!" He had forgotten about the wonderful shade. That traveler was a lot like Israel in the time of Numbers.

The Israelites were sitting in God's "shade." The future looked great. God was leading them, and they were about to enter the Promised Land. Then they began to complain about everything. They decided that they would rather be back in Egypt as slaves than where they were. Finally God got fed up and banished them to the wilderness, refusing to let them enter the Promised Land. Though God still considered these complainers his people, he postponed his promise to them and left them to wander in their ungratefulness.

Are we much different from the Israelites? God has done, is doing, and will do so much for us. Yet we complain. "God, what are you doing?" "God, you don't care!" "God, I hate you!" We don't trust him, although he has proven himself trustworthy. Do you trust God, or do you complain? You are sitting under the "shade" of God's love—don't complain. God was leading the Israelites even when they thought he wasn't, and he is leading you.

PURPOSE:
To tell the story of how Israel prepared to enter the Promised Land, how they sinned and were punished, and how they prepared to try again

AUTHOR:
Moses

TO WHOM WRITTEN:
The people of Israel and God's people everywhere

DATE WRITTEN:
1450–1410 BC

SETTING:
The vast wilderness of the Sinai region, as well as the lands just south and east of Canaan (present-day Israel)

KEY PEOPLE:
Moses, Aaron, Miriam, Joshua, Caleb, Eleazar, Korah, Balaam

SPECIAL FEATURE:
Two unique events are reported in the pages of Numbers: the story of the bronze serpent Moses raises on a pole (21:4-9) and the account of Balaam and his speaking donkey (22:21-41).

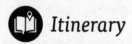 *Itinerary*

Although Numbers gets its name from the census of the people of Israel, the book gives us a journal of the travels of God's people. The journey involves four major stages.

Preparing for the Journey (1:1–10:10)
In the first stage, the people of Israel are still at Mount Sinai, preparing for the trip to the Promised Land. Moses counts the people. God provides special instructions for the journey.

First Approach to the Promised Land (10:11–14:45)
In the second stage, the people leave Mount Sinai, where they have camped for a year. As they approach Canaan, their complaining continues. Moses sends twelve spies into the land. They return with a ten-to-two negative report on the possibilities of victory. Only Caleb and Joshua urge the people to advance. The vote of the nation rejects God's promise to make them victorious. As a result God sends them back into the desert for forty years.

Wandering in the Wilderness (15:1–21:35)

In stage 3, conditions remain bleak. Complaints and rebellion lead to numerous deaths. The generation that saw God perform the miracles to free Israel from Egypt dies in the desert. A new generation comes to adulthood.

Second Approach to the Promised Land (22:1–36:13)

The fourth stage of Numbers reports the last days in the desert and the final events leading up to the second approach to the Promised Land. Another census is taken of the people. God's final instructions regarding life in their new land are given.

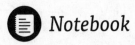 *Notebook*

CENSUS (1:1–4:49; 26:1-65)

Moses counted the people twice. The first census organized the people into marching units for better defense. The second census prepared them to conquer the country east of the Jordan.

People have to be organized, trained, and led to be effective in making a difference in their world. Before beginning a great task, it is always wise to count the potential cost and identify the members of the team. Preparation for being effective for God in this world also includes removing any barriers in our relationships with others so that we can work with God's people to accomplish his will.

- Musical groups are examples of how people can work together to produce something greater than they could do as individuals. What other efforts require teamwork in order for people to reach their goals or produce effects that they could not accomplish alone?
- In what ways is a church an example of teamwork?
- In your church or youth group, what can you accomplish with God through working together that could not be done if you did not practice teamwork?
- What actions or attitudes might cause this group of people to fail to be a team?
- What actions or attitudes will help this group of people become successful as a team?

- In what specific ways can you contribute to the success of this group?

REBELLION (10:11–14:45)

At Kadesh Moses sent twelve men into Canaan to survey the land and check on the enemies' fortifications. When the spies returned, ten said that they should give up and go back to Egypt. As a result the people refused to go into the land. They rebelled against God's will. That decision was not a sudden change of attitude. It was the final step in a long journey of complaining and resentment against Moses and God.

Rebellion against God is always serious. It is not something to take lightly, because God's punishment for sin is often severe. Usually rebellion is not an abrupt, radical departure from God as much as it is a result of a pattern of drifting, often characterized by griping and criticizing.

- About what do adults most often criticize or gripe?
- About what do your friends most often criticize or gripe?
- In what situations have you found yourself complaining to God about something or someone? What were the results of that kind of praying?
- When have you felt unhappy with your circumstances? Perhaps you wondered if God really was taking care of you. How did you work through those feelings?
- What appropriate responses can people practice when they feel frustrated or angry because they do not understand why God is allowing life to be the way it is? Why is it important to avoid criticizing God or griping? How can you express your feelings without becoming rebellious?

WANDERING (15:1–21:35)

Because they rebelled, the Israelites wandered forty years in the wilderness. This shows how strongly God feels about sinful rebellion. During that time God trained a new generation to follow him while those who still had wrong attitudes died.

God judges sin because he is holy and cannot tolerate sinfulness. The Israelites serve as a negative example of how God punishes sin and a positive example of how he uses even the punishment as an environment to further his purposes in the lives of individuals and nations.

- What happens to Christians who drift away from God?
- If you saw a friend rebelling against God, what would you tell him or her as a warning about the consequences of rebellion? What if that friend replied, "It's okay. God will forgive me"?
- How can you prepare yourself to avoid drifting and instead become a godly person?

CANAAN (13:1-33; 33:50–36:13)

Canaan was the Promised Land. It was the land that God had promised Abraham, Isaac, and Jacob—the land of the covenant (Genesis 17:7-8). Canaan was to be the dwelling place of God's people.

Because God is holy, he punishes sin severely. Because he is Lord, however, God graciously offers forgiveness of sins. Just as God's holy law and loving grace led Israel to the Promised Land, God wants to lead us into his purpose and destiny for our life.

- What did you learn about God as you read about him leading his people toward Canaan?
- Based on those insights, what kind of relationship does God want to have with you?
- What are some of your dreams for the future? In what ways do you see God's participation in those dreams?
- How would you complete these thoughts for your own life? (a) God's purpose for my life is _____. (b) I can trust God with this purpose because _____.

▣ *Postcard*

Numbers is about trusting God with big choices! We won't trust God with big choices if we haven't learned to trust him with little ones. List the various choices you are facing right now (big and little). Pray about those decisions and ask God for guidance and for greater trust on your part.

Tour Map of Numbers

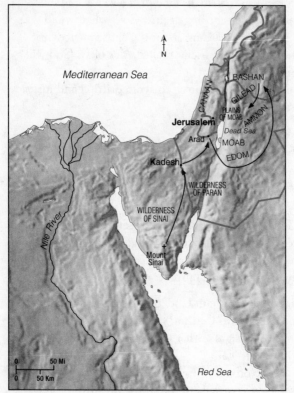

Modern names and boundaries are shown in gray.

DEUTERONOMY

 Snapshot of Deuteronomy

Do you have a "memories drawer," a place where you keep various reminders from your past? Maybe you have a wall, or even a box filled with mementos of happy occasions. Some people save petals from prom flowers. Others keep ticket stubs from movies, ball games, or concerts. Some store especially meaningful letters or old pictures.

If you are like most people, these treasures become even more meaningful to you when you are going through tough times, when you're sad or lonely or scared about the future. There is something comforting in remembering the good times you've had. Your keepsakes help you believe that everything will be okay.

Deuteronomy is a book of memories. God had made a covenant, or promise, with the Hebrew slaves who had first come out of Egypt, pledging to take them into the Promised Land. But the Israelites had refused to obey or trust God. So he left them to wander in the wilderness until they died.

Meanwhile, a new generation grew up, and God, through Moses, reminded them of the covenant. Moses recounted to the people the mighty acts that God had done for Israel. Then he let them know that, based on the past, they must trust, obey, and love God as they advanced on their new homeland. Only such an attitude would enable them to conquer the Promised Land.

As you read Deuteronomy, let God remind you of the ways he

has helped you in the past. Then, when you are fearful, you will entrust yourself to him.

PURPOSE:
To remind the Israelites of all God has done and to encourage them to rededicate their lives to him

AUTHOR:
Moses (except for the final summary, which was probably recorded by Joshua after Moses' death)

TO WHOM WRITTEN:
Israel (the new generation entering the Promised Land) and all of God's people, everywhere

DATE WRITTEN:
About 1407 BC

SETTING:
The east side of the Jordan River, in view of the Promised Land

KEY PEOPLE:
Moses, Joshua

SPECIAL FEATURES:
The name of this book means "second law," or the repetition of the original one. Deuteronomy 5 records Moses' review of the Ten Commandments. During his ministry Jesus quoted from and referred to Deuteronomy more often than any other Old Testament book. Deuteronomy also includes the heart of the great commandment: "Listen, O Israel! The LORD is our God, the LORD alone. And you must love the LORD your God with all your heart, all your soul, and all your strength" (6:4-5).

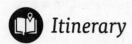 *Itinerary*

Deuteronomy begins with a painful observation. The people of Israel are camped on the border of Canaan. Normally the trip from Mount Sinai to the border takes eleven days; the Israelites have made the journey in forty years. Old Moses, having lived almost 120 years, has arranged for three extended messages that he wants to deliver to the people as his own responsibilities come to an end.

What God Has Done for Us: Moses' First Address (1:1–4:43)
Moses' first message reviews the mighty acts God has accomplished for the people of Israel. Moses knows how easily the people forget what God has done. Moses begins his story with the earlier

approach of the land. Then he recounts the forty years of humbling and training. Remembering God's special involvement in the high and low points of life gives us hope and encouragement for the future.

Principles for Godly Living: Moses' Second Address (4:44–29:1)

Moses' second message focuses on the principles for godly living. Obeying God's laws has brought blessings to the Israelites, and disobeying has brought misfortune. This is part of the written agreement between God and his people. This principle holds true: obedience and disobedience carry inevitable consequences in this life and the next.

A Call for Commitment to God: Moses' Third Address (29:2–30:20)

Moses' third message challenges the people to commit themselves and their future to God. As with the ancient Israelites, so with us; God still calls us to be committed to love him with all our heart, soul, mind, and strength.

The Change in Leadership: Moses' Last Days (31:1–34:12)

Deuteronomy also includes a postscript, a record of Moses' final days. Although Moses has made some serious mistakes, he has lived his life with integrity. He has carried out God's commands. Now he will die in God's care. We, too, may make some serious mistakes, but with God's help even these should not stop us from living with integrity and godly commitment.

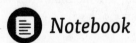 *Notebook*

HISTORY (29:2-29)

In the writings of Moses, culminating in Deuteronomy, we learn that God has entrusted us with a written record of his Word. History, as the saying goes, is his-story. As Moses reviewed the history of Israel, he reminded the people not to forget. If they forgot, they would repeat earlier mistakes and fail to receive God's benefits.

By studying God's promises and mighty acts, we can learn about his character. We come to know God more intimately through understanding how he has acted in the past. We can learn to do his will and avoid Israel's mistakes.

- What stands out for you about the character of God as he is revealed through the pages of Deuteronomy?
- How would Moses' review of history prepare the people to live for God in the Promised Land?
- At this point in your life, what would be the high and low points of your personal history with God?
- What have you learned about God from your own experiences? Which of those insights will have a major impact as you live for God in the future?

LAWS (5:1–6:9)

The people of Israel could never say that God had not given them any idea of how to live. God was very specific! Moses reviewed those rules and principles so that the legal contract between God and his people could be renewed for those who would be entering the Promised Land.

Commitment to God and his truth cannot be taken for granted. Each person and each generation must respond in person to God's call and his invitation to trust and obedience.

- What was God's stated purpose in giving his people the law? (Refer also to the book of Exodus.)
- Why did Moses review the law for the people?
- Why is it important to read, study, and be reminded of God's commands?
- What difference does it make that you have the Bible available to you for making decisions about God's will?

LOVE (8:1-18)

God's faithful and patient love is portrayed more often than his punishments. God reveals his love in keeping his promises to people even when they are disobedient. God seeks the love of his people displayed in their wholehearted devotion to his will, not just by a strict legalistic following of the law.

God's love forms the foundation for our trust in him. We can be confident that the one who loves us perfectly can be trusted with our life. Therefore, we can trust that the commands he gives us are good and are designed to help us live fully in our relationships with him and others.

- What words best describe God's love?
- How has God's love for you helped make you the person you are today?
- What evidence do you have that some of your friends need to know more of God's love? What qualities of God's love do they most need to experience?
- Suppose one of those friends replied, "But I have sinned too much for God to still love me." Based on your observations of God's love for the Israelites, how would you respond to such a statement? How would your understanding of God's love for you affect your response?
- In what specific ways could you show God's love to one or two of the friends you mentioned above?

CHOICES (30:11-20)

God reminded his people that in order to enjoy the blessings of his will for them, they would have to continue in obedience. Personal choices to obey could bring benefits to their lives; rebellion would bring disaster.

Our choices make a difference. Choosing to follow God produces good results in our life and in our relationships. Choosing to abandon God's ways brings harmful results to us and to others.

- Respond to the following statement: you always have a choice; it always makes a difference.
- How do you think and feel when a friend makes a choice that leads to bad consequences in his or her life?
- What conclusions do you draw when a friend makes a wrong choice according to God's instructions, but it seems as though he or she is not experiencing any negative consequences?
- Is it possible for a person to make a choice against God's will and get away with it? Explain.
- What are some of the choices facing you in the present or in the near future? Complete this statement: I will choose to obey what I believe to be God's way in my life because

_____.

TEACHING (6:1-9)

God commanded the Israelites to teach their children his ways. They were to use ritual, instruction, and memorization to make sure that their children understood God's principles and passed them on to the next generation.

God's truth must be passed on to future generations. It is not, however, just the traditions or commands that are to be passed on. Rather, we are to teach each new generation to know and love God personally.

- What people from previous generations have been most responsible for passing on God's Word to you?
- How were those from the previous generation able to teach you about knowing and loving God?
- What are some of the most important lessons you have learned from older Christians?
- What habits, traditions, and biblical values in your life today do you think will most likely impact your own children or others in the next generation?
- Consider what specific responsibilities you could accept as an older Christian in the life of someone younger than you (for example, volunteer as a leader for Bible school, become a Sunday school teacher for children, or spend time with a child in your community who needs a big brother or sister). Take the next step!

 Postcard

Deuteronomy turned out to be Moses' last words. He had his whole life to reflect upon. In all likelihood you are at the start of yours. But it is also true that tomorrow is never guaranteed. If those around you do not know what you believe or the ways in which you have seen God work in your life, don't let too many more days go by without telling them in some way. Write out your spiritual autobiography. Establish a record of your walk with God.

JOSHUA

 Snapshot of Joshua

What characteristics are important in leaders? If you were chosen to be captain of the football team, head cheerleader, or student body president, what would most help you succeed? Strength? Intelligence? Cleverness? Good people skills? Good looks? Enthusiasm? Commitment?

God called Joshua to be Israel's leader as the Israelites were about to enter the Promised Land. Joshua was unsure about his own leadership capabilities, but God told him, "No one will be able to stand their ground against you as long as you live. For I will be with you as I was with Moses. I will not fail you or abandon you" (1:5). Then God explained the qualities Joshua needed in order to be a good leader for his people.

The first quality was obedience to God's law: "Be strong and very courageous. Be careful to obey all the instructions Moses gave you. Do not deviate from them, turning either to the right or to the left. Then you will be successful in everything you do" (1:7).

The second leadership quality was total dependence on God. God instructed Joshua to study and meditate on God's Word day and night. There he would learn how God had taken care of Israel in the past; then Joshua could continue to depend on him and lead his people to do the same.

Listen to the wisdom of this book. God does not demand that you be strong, clever, efficient, or good looking as the basis for being a good leader. Instead, God wants you to obey his Word and depend on his power. Then, if God has called you, he will use you.

PURPOSE:
To give the history of Israel's conquest of the Promised Land

AUTHOR:
Joshua, except for the ending, which may have been written by the high priest Phinehas, an eyewitness to the events recounted there

TO WHOM WRITTEN:
The people of Israel and the followers of God

DATE WRITTEN:
For the most part before 1375 BC

SETTING:
Canaan, also called the Promised Land, which occupied the same general geographical territory of modern-day Israel

KEY PEOPLE:
Joshua, Rahab, Achan, Phinehas, Eleazar

SPECIAL FEATURE:
Out of over a million people who left Egypt, Joshua and Caleb were the only two adults who lived to enter the Promised Land.

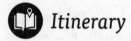 *Itinerary*

Entering the Promised Land (1:1–5:12)

The story of Joshua begins in the Israelites' camp on the border of the Promised Land. After wandering for forty years in the wilderness, a new generation is ready to enter Canaan. But first God has to prepare both Joshua and the nation by teaching them the importance of courageous and consistent faith. The nation then miraculously crosses the Jordan River to begin the long-awaited conquest of the Promised Land. Like Joshua and the Israelites, we, too, need faith to begin and continue living the Christian life.

Conquering the Promised Land (5:13–12:24)

After fording the Jordan River, the Israelites begin to conquer Canaan. Mighty Jericho falls first. Then Israel suffers its first defeat because of one person's disobedience. After the people remove the sin from their community, they strike again—this time with success. Soon great kings unite and attack from the north and south, but they are defeated because God is helping Israel. Evil cannot be tolerated in the Promised Land, nor can it be tolerated in our life.

We, like Israel, must ruthlessly remove sin from our life before it takes control of us.

Dividing the Promised Land (13:1–24:33)

After seven years of battle, Israel gains control of the land, which is then divided and assigned to the twelve tribes of the nation. Joshua dismisses the army, for it is each tribe's responsibility to clear out the remaining enemies from its own area. Joshua continues to encourage the people to remain faithful to God so they can remain in the land. The Promised Land is Israel's earthly inheritance. But Israel also has a spiritual inheritance, which we can share as we live lives of faithfulness to God.

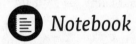 *Notebook*

SUCCESS (1:5-9; 10:1-15; 23:4-11)

God gave success to the Israelites when they obeyed his master plan, not when they followed their own desires. Victory came when they trusted him rather than their military power, money, muscle, or mental capacity.

God's work done in God's way will bring success. The standard for success is not to be set by the society around us but by God's Word. We must adjust our mind to God's way of thinking in order to see his standard for success.

- Think of an adult whom your parents view as successful. What is it about that person that makes him or her a success in your parents' minds?
- What types of people are considered successful in your school?
- Based upon the majority of commercials you see on television or in magazines, what is the media's image of a successful person?
- What seems to be God's definition of success for Joshua? (See chapter 1.)
- In what ways was Joshua a success according to God's point of view? What experiences and qualities in Joshua's life most contributed to this success?
- What can you do to develop some of the qualities that Joshua had so that you will indeed become successful?

FAITH (3:1-17; 6:6-21; 14:6-15; 22:10-34)

The Israelites demonstrated their faith by trusting God daily to save and guide them. By taking note of how God fulfilled his promises in the past, they developed strong confidence that he would be faithful in the future.

Our strength to do God's work comes from trusting him. His promises reassure us of his love. We can be confident that God will be there to guide us in the decisions and struggles we face.

- What factors helped the Israelites' faith grow as they moved to conquer the Promised Land?
- What is happening in your life now that is contributing to the growth of your faith?
- What else needs to happen to help your faith grow? What does God want you to do to increase your faith?

GUIDANCE (1:1-9; 6:1-5; 7:1–8:8; 20:1-9)

God gave instructions to the Israelites for every aspect of their lives. His law guided their daily living, and his specific marching orders gave them victory in battle.

Guidance from God for daily living can be found in his Word. By staying in touch with God, we will have the wisdom needed to meet life's great challenges.

- Describe a time in your life when you felt you needed God's guidance. (It may be right now!)
- How did you see God's guidance during that time? What were the results?
- What makes it difficult at times for us to know God's will for specific areas of our life?
- The more you know of God, the more you will know of his will. What resources has God given you for knowing more about him and his will for you?
- At times all Christians need God's guidance. How can you specifically prepare for those times before they occur? What can you do to seek God's guidance when they do occur?

LEADERSHIP (1:1-9; 5:13-15; 8:30-35; 23:1–24:28)

Joshua was an example of an excellent leader. He was confident in God's strength, courageous in the face of opposition, and willing to seek God's advice.

To be a strong leader like Joshua, we must be ready to listen and to move quickly when God speaks. Once we have his instructions, we must carry them out. Strong leaders are characterized by their commitment to follow God first.

- What were Joshua's strengths as a leader?
- What types of challenges did Joshua face as a leader of the people?
- All Christians have opportunities to be leaders for Christ. A person does not have to hold an office or title in order to be a leader. What type of challenges are facing you as you try to lead friends closer to Christ in your church? School? Neighborhood?
- What are your strengths as one of God's leaders? What qualities do you need to develop as you become an adult so that, like Joshua, you will spend your life leading others closer to God?

CONQUEST (10:40-43; 11:16-23; 23:4-11; 24:2-13)

God commanded his people to conquer the Canaanites and take all their land. Completing this mission would have fulfilled God's promise to Abraham and brought judgment on the evil people living there. Unfortunately, Israel never finished the job. The people were faithful in accomplishing the mission at first, but their commitment faltered.

Loving God means more than being enthusiastic about him. Discipleship is more than spiritual highs. We must complete all the work that God gives us and apply his instructions to every part of our life.

- What was the difference in the lives of the Israelites when they were successful and victorious as opposed to when they failed?
- What can you learn from the Israelites' examples of success and failure?
- Christians should look at a life of faith as a long-term process in which the goal is to finish stronger than they were when they began. Based on this study of Joshua and the Israelites' entry into the Promised Land, how can you assure yourself of overcoming the obstacles that lie ahead?

Postcard

Leaving a mark like Joshua's may involve an entire nation, but it begins at home and in a person's private life. Joshua challenged the nation: "But if you refuse to serve the LORD, then choose today whom you will serve. . . . But as for me and my family, we will serve the LORD" (24:15). What do you need to change and what do you need to keep doing in order to lead like Joshua?

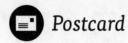 *Tour Map of Joshua*

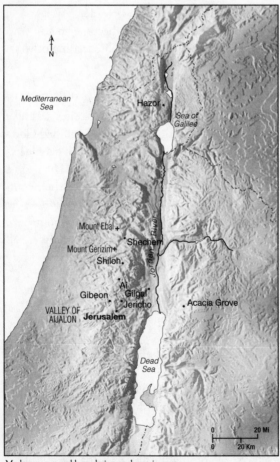

Modern names and boundaries are shown in gray.

JUDGES

 Snapshot of Judges

Superman, Batman, Wonder Woman, Spiderman— superheroes. The world longs for them—always arriving in the nick of time to ward off evil, beat up bad guys, prevent corruption, and promote truth, justice, and goodness. Unfortunately, superheroes don't exist. And eventually, every human being will let us down.

The book of Judges is about heroes—twelve people God used to deliver Israel from its enemies. No way were they superheroes. Some didn't want the job. One was even a murderer. But God used them to rescue Israel.

Judges talks about the horrible results of sin but also about God's mercy. The people of Israel had become evil. Judges describes them this way: "In those days Israel had no king; all the people did whatever seemed right in their own eyes" (17:6). They intermarried with wicked people and worshiped strange gods. When the stench of their actions became unbearable to God, he would raise up a neighboring nation to conquer them. Then the people would repent and turn back to God . . . and he would send a "judge" to rescue them.

Let the book of Judges remind you that God uses normal people to do his work; let it remind you of the effects of sin; and let it remind you that, above all, God is merciful to sinful people when they ask for forgiveness.

PURPOSE:
To show that God's judgment against sin is certain and that his forgiveness of sin and restoration of fellowship is just as certain for those who repent

AUTHOR:
Probably Samuel

TO WHOM WRITTEN:
Succeeding generations of the people of God

DATE WRITTEN:
Between 1050 and 1045 BC

SETTING:
The land of Canaan, later called Israel. God has helped the Israelites conquer Canaan, which had been inhabited by many wicked nations. But the Israelites are in danger of losing the Promised Land because they continue to compromise their convictions and disobey God.

KEY PEOPLE:
Othniel, Ehud, Deborah, Gideon, Abimelech, Jephthah, Samson, Delilah

SPECIAL FEATURE:
Records Israel's first civil war

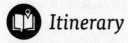 Itinerary

The Military Failure of Israel (1:1–3:6)
The book of Judges can be viewed as three consecutive scenes. The first scene provides a review of the history of Israel's conquest of Canaan. The Israelites conquer the land in general but not in many specific areas. Instead of driving out the inhabitants of the land, the Israelites often move in among them and quickly begin to live like them. Following Joshua's death, a cycle of disobedience, punishment, repentance, rescue, and restoration becomes routine for God's people. In their experiences we find many warnings about the danger of compromising with wickedness.

The Rescue of Israel by the Judges (3:7–16:31)
Scene 2 describes the details of God's rescue missions. Twelve judges, some of whom act at the same time, serve as God's rescuers. Repeatedly we see the nation of Israel sinning against God and, then, God allowing the people and the land to suffer. Sin always

has consequences. Knowing that others have experienced the painful results of disobedience should be a strong incentive for us to live a consistent life of faithfulness to God.

The Moral Failure of Israel (17:1–21:25)
The final scene allows us to see how bad things can get when people live only for themselves.

 Notebook

DECLINE/COMPROMISE (2:10-23; 3:7, 12; 4:1; 6:1; 10:6)
The people faced decline and failure because they compromised their high spiritual purpose in many ways. They abandoned their mission to drive all the people out of the land, and they adopted the customs of the people living around them.

Society offers many rewards to those who compromise their faith: wealth, acceptance, recognition, power, and influence. But when God gives us a mission, it must not be polluted by a desire for approval from social groups.

- In what ways have you seen people compromise their faith and values for wealth, pleasure, power, and acceptance?
- When did you compromise your faith or values? At that time how were you feeling? Why did you make the choice you made? How did you feel after you realized the price you had paid?
- The Israelites began living entirely different lifestyles following a few major compromises. Why does it get easier and easier to compromise after you have done it for a while?
- Why does it get easier not to compromise if you continually make decisions based on your faith and values?
- Consider the temptations that you face in school, at work, or with friends. Given the many opportunities you have to make choices that would compromise your faith and values, it takes a serious commitment not to compromise. Fill in the following statement of faith with some specific areas where you must choose not to compromise: I will not compromise my faith and values in the area of _____ because of my commitment to trust God with my life.

DECAY/APOSTASY (2:11-23; 3:7, 12; 4:1; 6:1; 8:33-35; 10:6; 13:1; 21:25)

Israel's moral downfall had its roots in the fierce independence that each tribe cherished. This led the people to do whatever seemed right to them individually (21:25). There was no unity in government or in worship. Law and order broke down. Finally idol worship and human-made religion led to the complete abandonment of faith in God.

We can expect things to fall apart when we value anything more highly than God. If we value our own independence more than God, we worship an idol, and soon our life will become a temple to the god of self. We must constantly keep God first in our life and in all our desires.

- The Israelites had difficulty giving up their idols. What are the idols in contemporary society? In what ways do people worship these idols?
- What are the top three "idols" among people your age? What about these "idols" attracts people to them?
- All idols are false representations of God's truth. How does knowing and obeying God's truth keep you from idols?
- What is there in your life that you are tempted to put in God's place?
- What do you know about God that causes you to believe that you should have him first in your life? How can this be accomplished?

DEFEAT/OPPRESSION (2:11-23; 3:8, 12-14; 4:2-3; 6:1-6; 10:7-9; 13:1)

God used evil oppressors to punish the Israelites for their sin, to bring them to the point of repentance, and to test their allegiance to him.

Rebelling against God leads to disaster. God may use oppression to bring wandering hearts back to him. At those times God's love displays its tough side.

- Why did God allow the Israelites' enemies to defeat them?
- How did these defeats affect the people?
- Why does it often take painful experiences to turn people

away from their rebellion against God? What does this teach you about human nature?

- In what ways are you currently expressing your commitment to Christ? In what areas are you expressing rebellion? Besides the fact that this may result in painful experiences, why should you turn away from rebellion and turn toward God?

REPENTANCE (3:9, 15; 4:3; 6:6-7; 10:10-16)

Decline, decay, and defeat caused the people to cry out for help. They vowed to turn from idolatry and to turn to God for mercy and deliverance.

Idolatry gains a foothold in our heart when we make anything more important than God. We must identify modern idols in our heart, renounce them, and turn to God for his love and mercy.

- What did the people feel when they repented of their sin and rebellion? What led to those feelings?
- Is repentance an emotion or an action? Why?
- To repent means literally "to turn from," that is, to change direction. Describe a time in your life when you turned from a sin or sinful attitude and redirected your life toward God. What did you do? What was the evidence of your repentance?
- Looking back at the last question under DEFEAT/ OPPRESSION, perhaps you see the need to repent today. What are some new directions you can take that will lead you back toward the Lord, who lovingly draws you?

DELIVERANCE/HEROES (2:16-18; 3:9-11, 15-30; 4:4-23; 6:7–8:21; 11:1-40; 13:2–16:31)

Because Israel repented, God raised up heroes to deliver his people from their path of sin and the oppression it brought. He used many kinds of people to accomplish this purpose. These were certainly not perfect people. But God made good use of their lives anyway.

God's love and mercy are available to all who trust in him. Anyone who is dedicated to God can be used for his service. Real heroes recognize the futility of human effort without God's leading.

- What qualities did the judges possess that enabled them to make a difference for God?
- What are the differences between the superstars that our society idolizes and the people God uses as heroes?
- What people have made the biggest positive impact in your life? In what ways could they be described as God's heroes?
- What qualities would God's hero need in your school? At your church? In your community?
- God wants to make a difference in you. He wants you to be a hero for his plan in the world. What qualities do you possess that he could use to make an impact in others' lives?
- To make a difference in the world, we must begin by seeking a difference in our own life. Changing the world starts with us. In what areas do you need to grow so that you will be better prepared to be God's hero?

✉ Postcard

Identify at least one area of your life in which you are most tempted to "go with the flow"—to "do whatever seems right in your own eyes." What is God's uncompromising view of that activity or attitude? Are you willing to stand with God even though it may mean that you have to stand alone at times?

Tour Map of Judges

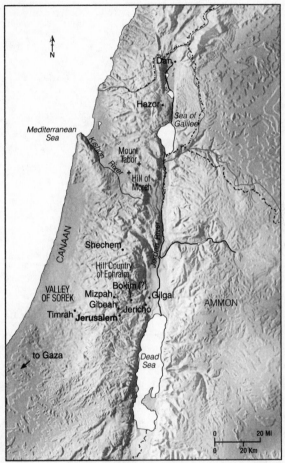

Modern names and boundaries are shown in gray.

RUTH

 Snapshot of Ruth

"Mom, that food looks awful!"

"Dad, you always make me take out the garbage."

"She's the worst teacher ever!"

"My allowance isn't enough."

"I hate the way I look."

Sound familiar? Everyone likes to complain. When things don't go exactly as we think they should, we are quick to let others know that we feel cheated and angry.

In the book of Ruth, we read of Naomi's complaints. Her husband and two sons had recently died, and she decided to blame God. She figured that because God had caused her loved ones' deaths, he deserved her anger.

But God didn't deserve her anger. And Naomi learned that God wasn't to be blamed for her family members' deaths; instead, he was to be thanked for his kindness.

We tend to complain against God. If something in life is wrong, we conclude that it must be his fault. The book of Ruth reminds us strongly and clearly that this is not the case. God is not to be blamed for our problems but praised for his goodness.

Read the book of Ruth—a story of relationships, rescue, and romance—and thank God for his goodness in your life.

PURPOSE:

To show how three people remained strong in character and true to God even when the society around them was collapsing

AUTHOR:
Unknown. Some think it was Samuel, but internal evidence suggests that the book was written after Samuel's death.

DATE WRITTEN:
Sometime after the period of the judges (1375–1050 BC)

SETTING:
In Moab and the town of Bethlehem during a dark time in Israel's history when people lived to please themselves, not God (Judges 17:6)

KEY PEOPLE:
Ruth, Naomi, Boaz

SPECIAL FEATURE:
This short book introduces one of the non-Israelite women (Ruth) in the family lineage of Jesus Christ.

 Itinerary

Ruth Remains Loyal to Naomi (1:1-22)

The four chapters that make up the book of Ruth follow four stages of her story. In the first stage, a famine in the land of Israel causes a man to move his wife and two sons east of the Jordan River, into the land of Moab. Later the man dies. During the ten years that follow, both boys marry local girls. Eventually the boys die, leaving their widows and their mother, Naomi, alone. She decides to move back to Israel. One of her daughters-in-law, Ruth, insists on going with her.

Ruth Gleans in Boaz's Field (2:1-23)

The second stage takes place in Bethlehem. With little to keep her and Naomi alive, Ruth begins to glean in the field of Boaz, a wealthy farmer. During harvest the poor are allowed to gather the grain missed by the harvesters.

Ruth Follows Naomi's Plan (3:1-18)

In the third stage, Naomi realizes Boaz is a distant relative. She thinks that if he marries Ruth, perhaps both she and Ruth will be safe. Naomi proposes a plan to Ruth, and the younger woman accepts. It turns out that Boaz has also noticed Ruth and is open to marriage.

Ruth and Boaz Are Married (4:1-22)

The final stage begins as Boaz negotiates with another relative concerning Naomi's land. The fact that Ruth will come with the land causes the other relative to give up his purchase rights. Boaz and Ruth are married. Their first child is a boy named Obed, who eventually becomes the grandfather of King David.

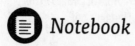 *Notebook*

FAITHFULNESS (1:6-18; 4:13-15)

Ruth's faithfulness to Naomi as a daughter-in-law and friend is a great example of love and loyalty. Ruth, Naomi, and Boaz were also faithful to God and his laws. Throughout the story we see how God is faithful in return.

Ruth's life was guided by faithfulness toward God, and that was exhibited in her loyalty to the people she knew. We, too, should imitate God's faithfulness by being loyal and loving in our relationships.

- Describe the relationship Ruth had with Naomi. How did this relationship reflect Ruth's relationship with God?
- What have you learned through other people about God's love? When and how did you learn these things?
- How does growing in your relationship with God enable you to have deeper relationships with the important people in your life?
- Who are your important friends? What are some specific ways you could show them more of God's love?

KINDNESS (1:16-18; 2:8-20)

Ruth showed great kindness to Naomi. And Boaz showed kindness to Ruth—a despised Moabite woman with no money. God showed his kindness to Ruth, Naomi, and Boaz by bringing them together for his purposes.

Just as Boaz showed his kindness by buying back land to guarantee Ruth and Naomi's inheritance, so Christ showed his kindness by purchasing us to guarantee our eternal life. God's kindness in providing a Redeemer for our life should motivate us to love and honor him.

- What makes kindness such an important quality?
- What have you learned about the kindness of God from the life of Ruth? From the life of Jesus?
- What could a person learn about God's kindness from seeing your relationships with your friends? Your family?
- In what ways could you display more of this kindness in your important relationships?

INTEGRITY (3:7-15, 18; 4:1-12)

Ruth showed high moral character by her loyalty to Naomi, by her clean break from her former land and customs, and by her hard work in the field. Boaz showed integrity in his moral standards, in his honesty, and by following through on his commitments.

When we have experienced God's faithfulness and kindness, we should respond by living godly lives. Just as Ruth's and Boaz's values contrasted with those of the culture portrayed in Judges, so should our life stand out from the world around us.

- What people do you know or know about who have integrity?
- What people do you know or know about who lack integrity?
- What is the connection between being a witness for Jesus Christ and being a person of integrity?
- In what specific areas might Christians be tempted to compromise their integrity as followers of Christ?
- What can you do to help maintain your integrity?

PROTECTION (2:8-9, 20-22; 4:13-17)

We see God's care and protection of Naomi and Ruth. His supreme control over circumstances brought them safety and security. God guides the minds and activities of people to fulfill his purposes.

No matter how devastating our present situation may be, we can hope in God. His resources are infinite. We must believe that God can work in any person's life, whether that person is a king or a stranger in a foreign land.

- Think of a time when, as a child, you were frightened, and an adult comforted you. What was it about that person that calmed your fears? How did you feel toward that person?
- Every person has fears. What are some of the things that cause you to feel afraid or insecure?

- What qualities do you find in God that tend to calm your fears and bring you a sense of security?
- What fears do you have about the present? About the future?
- To whom can you go to be reminded of God's secure love?
- Think of someone you know who is in a very difficult, possibly scary, time in his or her life. Based on your understanding of God and the way he uses us to communicate his protection, how can you help this person?

PROSPERITY/BLESSING (2:11-12; 4:1-17)

Ruth and Naomi came to Bethlehem as poor widows, but they soon became prosperous through Ruth's marriage to Boaz. Ruth became a mother (and eventually the great-grandmother of King David). Yet the greatest blessing was not the money, the marriage, or the children; it was the quality of love and respect between Ruth, Boaz, and Naomi.

We tend to think of blessings in terms of prosperity rather than the high-quality relationships that God makes possible for us. Regardless of our economic situation, we can love and respect the people whom God has brought into our life. In so doing we give and receive blessings.

- What does the word *rich* mean to you?
- What is dangerous about always comparing what one has with what others have?
- What should be your attitude about gaining riches?
- Some Christians have extensive possessions, while others have very little. Who is more blessed by God? Explain.
- What do you think is God's will for you concerning gaining possessions and becoming rich?
- What does it mean for you to be blessed by God?

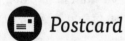 *Postcard*

In many ways Ruth was a person participating in a much larger plan than her own life. You are too. Like Ruth, you are only responsible for your part. God is in charge—the Master Planner. Up until now what has been your most significant lesson in learning to cooperate with God's plan?

1 SAMUEL

 Snapshot of 1 Samuel

"Susan, is that you?"

"Yeah," she replied. "Who is this?"

"Oh, my name is Eric," said the voice. "You don't know me, but I see you at school a lot."

Susan was popular and was dating the captain of the basketball team, Allen. "Why did you call me?" she asked.

Eric said he just wanted to talk. So they did, for an hour that night, and for several hours over the next few weeks—about everything they could think of.

Susan started looking forward to Eric's calls. She wanted to meet him, but he always refused. She wondered what he looked like. So far, she had dated only popular guys.

Soon Susan realized that Eric's status didn't really matter. He had become a good friend. She started to understand that though we often judge people by what we see on the outside, what really matters is what's on the inside.

First Samuel tells about the first two kings of Israel. Saul was tall, handsome, and brave. He looked like a king. David, on the other hand, didn't look like a leader, much less a king. He was young and small.

Yet Saul proved he wasn't worthy to be king, while David became a great king.

As you read 1 Samuel, watch the rise and fall of Saul and the rise of David. Remember that while people judge by outward appearances, God looks at thoughts and intentions (16:7).

PURPOSE:

To record the life of Samuel, Israel's last judge; the reign and decline of Saul, Israel's first king; and the choice and training of David, Israel's greatest king

AUTHOR:

Probably Samuel, but 1 Samuel also includes writings from the prophets Nathan and Gad (1 Chronicles 29:29)

SETTING:

The book begins in the days of the judges and describes Israel's transition from a theocracy (being led by God) to a monarchy (being led by a king).

KEY PEOPLE:

Eli, Hannah, Samuel, Saul, Jonathan, David

SPECIAL FEATURE:

Probably the best-known event from 1 Samuel is the contest between young David and the Philistine giant Goliath. The giant's size and weapons were no match for David's confidence in God and marksmanship with a sling (17:1-58).

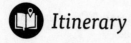 *Itinerary*

Eli and Samuel (1:1–7:17)

The story of 1 Samuel revolves around four powerful relationships. Two of them involve Samuel directly, while the other two are part of David's life. The first relationship, between Samuel and Eli, brings together a young child and an old priest. Eli becomes Samuel's mentor as a result of Hannah's promise to give her firstborn into God's service. Samuel grows up in Israel as the nation is being harassed and attacked by the Philistines. Although Eli has two sons of his own, their wickedness brings punishment and eventually death, leading to Samuel's development as priest, prophet, and judge over Israel. Samuel's faithful character provides an excellent model for any young person seeking to live a godly life.

Samuel and Saul (8:1–15:35)

The second relationship, between Samuel and Saul, begins as a result of the nation's rebellion against the rule of God and their demand for a king. God has Samuel identify and declare Saul the first king of Israel. Saul looks like the ideal king candidate—strong, tall, and modest. God's Spirit comes upon Saul, and Samuel serves as his counselor. But Saul deliberately disobeys God and becomes an evil king. We must not base our hopes or future on our own potential. Instead, we must consistently obey God in all areas of life. God evaluates obedience, not potential.

Saul and David (16:1–31:13)

The third relationship, between Saul and David, is a volatile mix between one leader's descent into wickedness and another leader's growth into power. Although Saul's failure leads to David's anointment as Israel's next king, David has to wait years before this promise is realized. Meanwhile, David's reputation grows in the wake of his heroic defeat of the giant Goliath. Perhaps David's greatest test of integrity is his willingness to wait for God's timing rather than his own political power regarding his rise to the throne. As in David's life, the difficult circumstances in life and the times of waiting often refine, teach, and prepare us for future responsibilities that God has for us.

David and Jonathan (18:1–31:13)

The fourth relationship, between David and Saul's son Jonathan, turns into a great friendship. Jonathan is caught between his respect and love for his father and his commitment and admiration for David. Jonathan retains his integrity with both men by displaying an even greater allegiance to God and the truth. God's guidance does provide answers when we find ourselves in relationship conflicts.

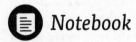 *Notebook*

KING (8:1-21; 10:17-27; 12:1-25; 15:10-11, 22-23, 34-35; 16:1-13; 24:1-22)
Because Israel had corrupt priests and judges, the people wanted a king. They wanted to be organized like the surrounding nations. Although it was against his original purpose, God answered the people's request and gave them Saul.

Unfortunately, establishing a monarchy did not solve Israel's problems. God wants each person to give the genuine devotion of his or her mind and heart to him—not to some earthly king. No government or set of laws can substitute for the rule of God.

- Why, do you think, does the Bible describe God as the King? Why is Jesus called King of kings?
- What does it mean to say that Jesus Christ is Lord in a person's life?
- How do you feel about having God as your King? If you consider Jesus to be Lord, what difference does it make in your daily life?

GOD'S CONTROL (1:9–2:11; 3:19-21; 5:1–7:17; 8:1-21; 12:1-25; 15:10-31; 24:1-15)

Israel prospered as long as the people regarded God as their true King. When the leaders strayed from God and his law, God intervened in their lives and overruled their actions. This way, God maintained ultimate control.

God is always at work in this world, even when we can't see what he is doing. No matter what kinds of pressures we must endure or how many changes we must face, ultimately God is in control. When we grow confident of God's sovereignty, we can face the difficult situations in our life with boldness.

- As King, God is in control of the world. When have you felt that God was not in control? How did you feel? What were your options? How did you choose to deal with the situation?
- God is in control, even when you do not feel that he is. How can you be sure this is true?
- What difference does it make for you that God controls the world?
- In what areas of your life do you feel the need to know that he is in control? How will you deal with those times when it seems as though he is not in control? How can you prepare yourself for those times?

LEADERSHIP (2:12-17, 22-25, 35-36; 3:19-21; 8:1-21; 12:1-25; 14:1-15; 16:1-13; 17:19-51)

God guided his people using different types of leaders: judges, priests, prophets, and kings. Those chosen for these different offices, such as Eli, Samuel, Saul, and David, portrayed different styles of leadership. Yet the success of each leader depended on his devotion to God.

When Eli, Samuel, Saul, and David disobeyed God, they faced tragic consequences. Sin affected what they achieved for God as well as how they raised their children. Being a true leader means letting God guide your activities, values, and goals—including your family relationships.

- What were the strengths and weaknesses of the following leaders: Eli, Samuel, Saul, and David?
- Taking the best from each leader, what qualities characterize godly leadership?
- Taking the worst from each leader, what qualities characterize leadership that isn't godly?
- What characteristics of godly leadership have developed most in you?
- Each person has a chance to be a leader by leading others toward Christ. Describe the kind of leader you want to be for God.

OBEDIENCE (12:14-25; 15:1-31; 28:16-19)

To God, "obedience is better than sacrifice" (15:22). God wanted his people to obey, serve, and follow him with their whole hearts rather than maintaining a superficial commitment based on traditions or ceremonies.

Although we don't have to perform all the Jewish sacrifices, we may still rely on outward observances to substitute for inward commitment. God wants all our work and worship to be motivated by genuine, heartfelt devotion to him.

- Express 15:22 in your own words.
- In what ways can being "religious" interfere with a person's relationship with God?
- What is the connection in your life between loving God and obeying God?
- What is the connection between obedience and sacrifice?

GOD'S FAITHFULNESS (2:1-10; 7:1-17; 12:6-25; 20:12-17)

God faithfully kept the promises he made to Israel. He responded to his people with tender mercy and swift justice. In showing mercy

God faithfully acted in the best interest of his people. In showing justice he was faithful to his word and perfect moral nature.

God's mercy is seen in the way he withholds the punishment for our sins. Because God is faithful, he can be counted on to show us mercy. Yet God is also just and will not tolerate rebellion. His faithfulness and unselfish love should inspire us to dedicate ourselves to him completely. We must never take this precious mercy for granted.

- What do you learn about God's mercy from his relationships with the following people: Eli, Samuel, Saul, David, and the nation of Israel?
- What do you learn about God's justice from those same relationships?
- How are both loving mercy and holy justice examples of God's faithfulness?
- How should Christians respond to God's faithfulness? Why?
- Complete these statements: (a) Because God is faithful, I know that _____. (b) Because God is faithful, I will_____.

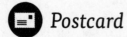 *Postcard*

First Samuel records the completed lives of several people: Eli, Samuel, Saul, and Jonathan. Take some time to reflect on where your life is going. If it ended today, would you be content with the summary of your life? What changes in your relationship with God would improve the big picture?

2 SAMUEL

 Snapshot of 2 Samuel

Genuine heroes are hard to find—those men and women who excel in their careers and in life. They are people we watch carefully and even copy. The problem is that whenever we put them on pedestals, they all seem to fall. Under the magnifying glass of public scrutiny, people's shortcomings and weaknesses become painfully obvious, and we become very disappointed.

That's the way it is with any human being. All of us sin and fall . . . all the time. But somehow we expect our heroes to be bigger than life, to be perfect.

David was the essence of a hero. Strong, brave, handsome, forceful, and committed. He had reached the top of the world. He was king, his enemies were defeated, and the people loved him. But David was human, too, and at the pinnacle of his success, he fell, committing lust, adultery, and murder.

With modern heroes, that would be the end of the story—another one bites the dust. But with David there was more. Recognizing his sin, he turned back to God and led the nation God's way. His comeback complete, he again became a "man after [God's] own heart" (1 Samuel 13:14; Acts 13:22).

Do you need a hero? David would be a good one. Not for his glory or accomplishments—and certainly not for his sin—but for his humble repentance and his determination to do things God's way.

PURPOSE:
To record the history of David's reign and foreshadow Christ, who will be the ideal leader of a new and perfect Kingdom (7:5-16)

AUTHOR:
Unknown. Some have suggested that Nathan's son Zabud may have been the author (1 Kings 4:5). The book also includes the writings of Nathan and Gad (1 Chronicles 29:29).

DATE WRITTEN:
930 BC, soon after David's reign (1010–970 BC)

SETTING:
The land of Israel under David's rule

KEY PEOPLE:
David, Joab, Bathsheba, Nathan, Absalom

SPECIAL FEATURE:
This book was named after the prophet who anointed David and guided him in godly living.

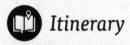 **Itinerary**

David's Successes (1:1–10:19)

The story of David's life can be told in two contrasting panoramas. The first follows young David rising through successes to the throne of Israel. David takes the fractured kingdom Saul left behind and builds a strong, united nation. His reign lasts forty years. David displays a remarkable heart for God. He governs God's people by God's principles, and God blesses him with spiritual, military, and political successes. But David's rise reveals an important lesson: success doesn't insulate us from sin. Even godly success doesn't insure against failing and falling. We never outgrow our need for God's daily help. David's turning point comes when it seems everything is perfect.

David's Struggles (11:1–24:25)

The second panoramic view of David's life begins during a spring evening while the king, with too much time on his hands and not enough on his mind, takes a walk on the palace roof. A glimpse of a woman bathing leads to a rapidly descending series of decisions involving lust, adultery, betrayal, murder, and even apparent success. Then Nathan shows up at David's door with God's shattering confrontation. David's repentance and God's forgiveness highlight the last chapters of 2 Samuel, but the consequences of David's sins create havoc in his family and kingdom. God is always ready to forgive, but we must live with the consequences of our actions. Covering up our sin often multiplies sin's painful results.

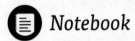 *Notebook*

KINGDOM GROWTH (5:1–6:14; 8:1-18; 10:1-19)
Under David's leadership Israel grew rapidly. With the growth came many changes—from tribal independence to centralized government, from the leadership of judges to a monarchy, and from decentralized worship to worship at Jerusalem.

No matter how much growth or how many changes we experience, God will meet our needs if we love him and highly regard his principles.

- What do you think life was like in Israel during the high points of David's reign?
- How did God supply his blessing through David?
- What are some of the "high points" of your life? How did God bless you during those times?
- Why do some people seem to forget God when things are going great?
- What are some biblical principles that you can use to guide you when everything seems to be going great?

PERSONAL GREATNESS (1:1–2:7; 3:31-39; 4:9-12; 5:6-10; 7:1-29; 9:1-12; 12:13-25; 19:15-40; 22:1–23:7; 24:10-25)
David's popularity and influence increased greatly. He realized that the Lord was behind this success because he wanted to pour out his kindness on Israel.

God graciously favors us because of what Christ has done. God does not regard personal greatness as something to be used selfishly but as an instrument to carry out his work among his people. The greatness we should desire is to love others as God loves us. We should never use or take advantage of someone for our own benefit.

- When God exalted David, how did David respond? How did others respond?
- What attitude should we have toward those who are raised up by God to be our leaders?

- What qualities would be seen by God as qualities of greatness?
- What would it take for you to achieve true greatness?

JUSTICE (1:14-16; 2:4-7; 3:31-39; 4:9-12; 8:15; 9:1-12; 12:1-25; 16:5-14; 19:15-40)

King David showed justice, mercy, and fairness to Saul's family, his own enemies, rebels, allies, and close friends alike. His just rule was grounded in his faith and knowledge of God.

Although David was the most just of all Israel's kings, he was still imperfect. His use of justice offered hope for a heavenly, ideal Kingdom. This hope will never be satisfied in the hearts of human beings until Christ, the Son of David, comes to rule in perfect justice forever.

- How was God's justice revealed in David's life?
- What difference does it make whether or not you live according to God's will?
- How should you respond when another Christian indicates concern about the justice of a decision you are making?
- As an individual Christian, what can you do to work for justice in the world?

CONSEQUENCES OF SIN (3:26-39; 4:9-12; 12:1-25)

David's sin with Bathsheba had disastrous consequences for both his family and the nation. David's prosperity and ease led him from triumph to temptation to trouble.

Temptation quite often comes when a person's life has no direction. Sometimes we may think that sinful pleasures will bring a sense of life and adventure, but sin creates a cycle of suffering that is not worth the fleeting pleasure or rush it offers.

- What led to David's choosing to sin with Bathsheba?
- What happened as a result of that choice and other sinful choices that followed?
- What causes Christians to choose sin even though they know what is right?
- Suppose you sinned against God knowingly, and then nothing seemed to go wrong in your life. Could it then be said that you had "gotten away with it"? Explain.
- Based on this study of 2 Samuel, what needs to be changed in your life in order to avoid the types of mistakes that David made?

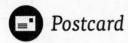

Postcard

Obedience for a lifetime has to be lived out one day at a time. Note as you read 2 Samuel how often impulsive decisions for the moment led to lifelong results. Ask God for a growing wisdom to depend on him for even what appear to be small decisions.

Tour Map of 2 Samuel

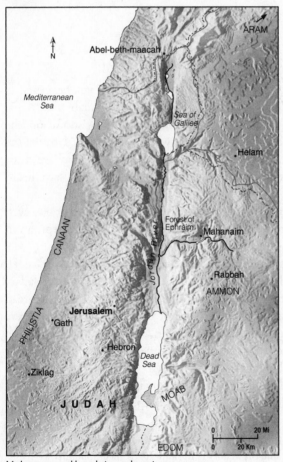

Modern names and boundaries are shown in gray.

1 KINGS

 Snapshot of 1 Kings

Here's a quick quiz. What do you think of when you hear each of these names: Solomon? Elijah? Ahab? Jezebel? Nadab?

The usual response for Solomon would be "wisdom" or "the Temple." For Elijah you might answer "prophet" or "defeated the Baal worshipers on the mountain." Ahab and Jezebel are most certainly associated with evil. And you may not even have heard of Nadab.

It's amazing what people remember about other people, even after they're gone. Whether good or evil, a person's reputation often remains long after his or her death.

First Kings tells the stories of many of the leaders of Israel. Some, like Solomon, take chapters to relate. Others, like Nadab, just take a line or two. No matter what the length, when we read these accounts, we gain a snapshot of what these people were like—their characters and their lives. As we read, we can learn what it takes to be someone who is remembered for good and not for evil, for following God and not self.

What would your friends and acquaintances say if given your name in a similar quiz? What kind of a reputation are you building?

PURPOSE:

To contrast the lives of those who live for God with the lives of those who refuse to do so, using the history of the kings of Israel and Judah

AUTHOR:

Unknown. Possibly Jeremiah or a group of prophets

SETTING:
The once great nation of Israel turns into a divided land both physically and spiritually.

KEY PEOPLE:
David, Solomon, Rehoboam, Jeroboam, Elijah, Ahab, Jezebel

SPECIAL FEATURE:
The books of 1 Kings and 2 Kings were originally one book.

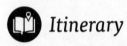 ## Itinerary

The United Kingdom (1:1–11:43)
The book of 1 Kings divides neatly into two halves. The first half focuses on the life of Solomon, the wisest king in the history of Israel. Solomon is a botanist, zoologist, architect, poet, and philosopher. Unfortunately, he does not exercise wisdom in his personal life, as he marries often to insure political alliances. Then Solomon's many wives introduce false gods and false worship in Israel. It is good for us to have wisdom, but that is not enough. The highest goal in life is to obey the Lord. Patient obedience to God should characterize our life.

The Divided Kingdom (12:1–22:53)
The second half of 1 Kings traces the tragic division of the kingdom and the cycle of good and evil kings who rule the split kingdom. When the northern kingdom of Israel is being led by wicked kings, God raises up a prophet to proclaim his messages. Elijah single-handedly challenges the priesthood of the state religion and has them removed in a single day. Through the dividing of the kingdom and the sending of Elijah, God deals with the people's sin in powerful ways. Sin in our life is graciously forgiven by God. However, the sin of an unrepentant person will be handled harshly. We must turn from sin and turn to God to be saved from judgment.

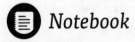 ## Notebook

THE KING (2:1-12; 3:1-28; 4:20-34; 9:1–11:13)
Solomon's wisdom, power, and achievements brought honor to the Israelite nation and to God. All the kings of Israel and Judah were

told to obey God and to govern according to his laws. But their tendency to abandon God's Word and to worship other gods led them to change the religion and government to meet their personal desires. This neglect of God's law led to their downfall.

Wisdom, power, and achievement do not ultimately come from any human source; they are from God. No matter how we lead or govern, we won't do well if we ignore God's guidelines. Whether or not we are in a position of leadership, we can be successful by listening to and obeying God's Word.

- What qualities characterized the kings whose reigns were successful? Those whose reigns failed?
- Which of these qualities were evident in Solomon's life?
- How did each king's relationship with God affect the people?
- What qualities will you look for in those whom you follow as Christian teachers, pastors, and disciplers?

THE TEMPLE (5:1–6:38; 7:13–8:66)
Solomon's Temple was a beautiful setting for worship and prayer. It was the place of God's special presence, and it housed the Ark of the Covenant, which contained the Ten Commandments.

A beautiful house of worship doesn't always indicate that the people gathered there are truly worshiping God. God wants to live in people's hearts, not just meet them in a sanctuary. We need to worship God daily as individuals and once or twice a week with others.

- Why was building the Temple so important to Solomon?
- Solomon was successful in building the Temple, but in other ways he failed to glorify God. What do you learn about worshiping God as you read about Solomon's life and reign?
- Many people believe that being a "good Christian" means going to church every week. Do you agree or disagree? Why?
- What are some specific ways that you can enter the temple to worship God, whether you are inside or outside of a church building? Commit yourself to personally worshiping God at least once a day during the coming week.

OTHER GODS (11:1-8; 12:25–13:34; 14:22-24; 16:29-33; 18:1-40)
Although the Israelites had God's law and had experienced his presence among them, they became attracted to other gods. When

this happened, their hearts became cold to God's law, resulting in the ruin of families and government and eventually leading to the destruction of the nation.

Through the years the people took on the qualities of the false gods they worshiped. They became cruel, power hungry, and sexually perverse. We tend to become what we worship. Unless we serve the one true God, we will become slaves to whatever takes his place.

- In what ways did the Israelites worship false gods? What were the results of this worship?
- What are some of the false gods of our society?
- What are some similarities between the results of the Israelites' false worship and the "worship" of false gods in modern culture? What are some differences?
- Why do Christians still need to beware of the attraction of false gods?
- What will you do to ensure that you never fall into the trap of false worship?

PROPHETIC MESSAGE (11:9-13, 29-39; 12:21-24; 13:1-33; 14:1-18; 16:1-4; 17:1-7; 18:1-40; 20:35-43; 21:17-29; 22:1-28) The prophet's responsibility was to confront and correct any deviation from God's law. Elijah brought a bolt of judgment against Israel. His messages and miracles warned the evil and rebellious kings and people.

The Bible, sermons that teach the truth, and the wise counsel of believers provide strong warnings. Anyone who points out how we may be moving away from God's Word is a blessing. Changing our life in order to obey God often takes painful discipline and hard work. We should seek people who will be honest with us about our weaknesses.

- What judgments did Elijah announce?
- What do you learn about God's will for his people from these judgments?
- In what ways do these judgments apply to contemporary churches? To Christians today?
- What is happening in your relationship with God that you know is in his will?

SIN/REPENTANCE (13:4-6; 21:27-29)

Each king had God's Word, a prophet, and the lessons of the past to draw him back to God. All the people had the same resources. Whenever they turned away from their sin and returned to God, he heard their prayers and forgave them.

God hears us when we pray. We have the assurance of forgiveness if we are willing to trust him and turn from sin. When God forgives us, he provides a fresh start and a new desire to live for him.

- How did God respond to the kings who repented?
- Contrast those kings' lives with the lives of those who chose to continue in their rebellion. How did God respond to those rebellious kings?
- How does this study direct you about how you should deal with sin when God reveals it to you?
- Spend a few moments reflecting on your life as it compares to God's will. What sins do you need to confess to God? List them. After listing and praying over each item, destroy the list as a symbol of the fresh start that God provides his people when they turn from their sins and to him.

 *Postcard*

Spend a few minutes reading and reflecting on Proverbs 3:5-6. First Kings is filled with examples of people who obeyed and those who violated this wise absolute. Identify some areas of your life in which you need to apply the wisdom of Solomon with more consistency.

2 KINGS

 Snapshot of 2 Kings

"He used to be such a nice guy. But since he became president, he thinks he owns the school!"

"We used to be friends. But she turned into a snob about a week after making cheerleader!"

Maybe you have heard, thought, or even spoken lines like that. It's amazing, isn't it, how some people change when they get a little power or an important position? Suddenly they're in the spotlight, and you're not good enough or popular enough or rich enough to be seen with them. Someone else put it this way: "Power corrupts."

Of course, it doesn't always happen that way. Now and then someone who has made it to the top will remember who he or she is and the people who put him or her there. But with so many examples on the other side (politicians, businesspeople, athletes, entertainment stars, etc.), it's clear that such people are the exceptions.

Second Kings tells about the leaders of the two nations of Israel and Judah. These kings could have used their power to help their people and lead them God's way. But of the twelve northern kings (of Israel) and the sixteen southern kings (of Judah) whose stories are recorded in 2 Kings, only two (Hezekiah and Josiah) are called good.

As you read, learn from the negative examples of the kings, and determine to be God's person even if you win the race, get elected, or gain the prize.

PURPOSE:
To demonstrate the fate that awaits all who refuse to make God their true leader

AUTHOR:
Unknown. Possibly Jeremiah or a group of prophets

SETTING:
The once-united nation of Israel has been divided into two kingdoms, Israel and Judah, for over a century.

KEY PEOPLE:
Elijah, Elisha, the woman from Shunem, Naaman, Jezebel, Jehu, Joash, Hezekiah, Sennacherib, Isaiah, Manasseh, Josiah, Jehoiakim, Zedekiah, Nebuchadnezzar

SPECIAL FEATURE:
The seventeen prophetic books at the end of the Old Testament give great insights into the time period of 2 Kings.

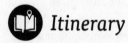 *Itinerary*

The Divided Kingdom (1:1–17:41)

Without taking a pause, 2 Kings continues the narrative of 1 and 2 Samuel and 1 Kings, documenting Israel's and Judah's journey toward destruction. For much of the book, the two nations compete to outdo each other in wickedness. Beginning with Israel, the story scene shifts back and forth between north and south. The contest ends with the defeat and deportation of the northern kingdom. Although Israel has the power and witness of the prophet Elisha, the nation turns from God and is exiled to Assyria. In their place Assyria fills the land with mixed peoples from other conquered nations. The expression "the ten lost tribes of Israel" comes from this time; these exiles never return to the Promised Land.

The Surviving Kingdom (18:1–25:30)

The last chapters of 2 Kings record the downfall of Judah, the southern kingdom. Although the defeat of Israel should have been a vivid warning to Judah, the nation continues moving away from God. A few bright spots of hope appear, however. Kings Hezekiah and Josiah each make valiant attempts to stem the tide of evil. They repair the Temple, celebrate the Passover, and call the people to repentance. They remove and destroy pagan idols and other symbols. But their efforts touch the hearts of few people. As soon as the good kings are gone, the people return to their pursuit of evil. They insist on living their own way instead of God's. Each individual must believe and live for God in his or her family, church, and nation. Second Kings vividly illustrates the results of a nation's failure to respond to God.

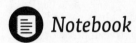 *Notebook*

ELISHA (2:1-25; 4:1–8:15)
The purpose of Elisha's ministry was to restore respect for God and his message. Elisha stood firmly against the evil kings of Israel. By faith, with courage and prayer, he revealed not only God's judgment on sin, but also his mercy, love, and tenderness toward faithful people.

Elisha's mighty miracles showed that God controls not only great armies but also events in everyday life. God's care is not reserved for kings and leaders but is for all who are willing to follow him. He can perform miracles in your life.

- If you were writing a letter of reference for Elisha, how would you describe him?
- What evidence do you find that Elisha had a heart willing to serve God?
- What two people do you know who display evidence of hearts that are willing to serve God?
- What people in your life need to see evidence of this willing heart in you? What can you do to be an example for them? What will you do to be God's living testimony of power to them?

IDOLATRY (1:1-6, 16; 3:1-3; 10:25-31; 13:1-3, 10-12; 14:23-27; 15:8-9, 17-18, 27-28; 16:1-4; 17:7-23; 21:1-16, 19-21; 24:18-20)
Every evil king in both Israel and Judah encouraged idolatry. These false gods represented war, cruelty, power, and sex, and the people began to take on their characteristics. Although they had God's law, priests, and prophets to guide them, the evil kings sought false priests and prophets whom they could control and manipulate to their own advantage.

An idol is anything we regard more highly than God. An idol can be an idea, ability, possession, or person. We condemn Israel and Judah for foolishly worshiping idols, but we also worship other gods: power, money, physical attractiveness, and so on. Behind idol worship is the desire to control one's destiny, pleasure, and other people. Even those who believe in God must resist the lure of these attractive idols.

- Idols led to great destruction when the kings turned to them. What could have been so attractive about worshiping these idols? What did the kings hope to gain?
- What important things in life can only be supplied by the one true God?
- With this knowledge in mind, what do you think attracts so many young people to idolatry, to replacing the worship of God with the worship of power, pleasure, or possessions?
- How could you specifically communicate to those around you (without just making an announcement or handing them a Bible) the truth about who God is and that he alone should be worshiped?

EVIL KINGS/GOOD KINGS Israel—Ahaziah (1:18), Joram (3:1), Jehu (9:13), Jehoahaz (13:1), Jehoash (13:10), Jeroboam II (14:16), Zechariah (14:29), Shallum (15:10), Menahem (15:14), Pekahiah (15:22), Pekah (15:25), Hoshea (15:30); Judah—Jehoram (8:16), Ahaziah (8:24), Queen Athaliah (11:1), Joash (11:2, 21), Amaziah (14:1), Azariah, Uzziah (15:1), Jotham (15:32), Ahaz (16:1), Hezekiah (16:20), Manasseh (21:1), Amon (21:18), Josiah (21:26), Jehoahaz (23:30), Jehoiakim (23:34), Jehoiachin (24:6), Zedekiah (24:17)
Only 20 percent of all the kings of both kingdoms followed God. The evil kings were shortsighted, thinking that they could control their nation's destiny by importing other religions and idols, forming alliances with heathen nations, and enriching themselves. The good kings had to spend most of their time undoing the evil done by their predecessors.

Although the evil kings led the people into sin, they were not the only ones responsible for the downfall of the nation. The priests, princes, heads of families, and military leaders all had to cooperate with the proposed evil plans and practices in order for them to be carried out. We cannot discharge our responsibility to obey God by blaming our leaders.

- What qualities did the good kings have in common?
- What qualities did the evil kings have in common?
- What other historical leaders made a good difference in the lives of their followers? What leaders made an evil difference in the lives of their followers?
- What are several ways that a Christian young person can be a person of influence in the home, church, school, and community?
- What choices have you decided to make that will make a positive, God-glorifying difference in the lives of those you lead?

GOD'S PATIENCE (8:19; 17:7-13; 22:8-20)

As recorded in Deuteronomy, God told his people that if they obeyed him, they would live successfully; if they disobeyed, they would be judged and punished. God had been patient with his people for hundreds of years. He had sent many prophets, including Elisha, to guide them, and he had given ample warning of coming destruction. But even God's patience has limits.

God is patient with people today. In his mercy he still gives many opportunities to hear his message, turn from sin, and believe in him. But his patience does not mean that he is indifferent to how we live or that we are free to ignore his warnings. His patience should make us want to come to him now.

- What does it mean to have patience?
- What evidence do you see of God's patience with the Israelites?
- What evidence do you see of God's patience with you?
- Suppose a Christian friend seems to have the attitude that since God is so patient, we do not have to be so concerned about whether or not we sin. Based on 2 Kings, how would you correct the error in this friend's thinking?
- In view of God's patience, how will you choose to live your life?

JUDGMENT (1:1-17; 5:20-27; 9:1-13; 13:3; 15:1-5; 17:18-23; 19:1-37; 21:10-15; 23:24-27; 24:1-4, 18-20)

Both kingdoms were destroyed as punishment for their sins. After King Solomon's reign, Israel lasted 209 years before the Assyrians conquered the nation; Judah lasted 345 years before the Babylonians took Jerusalem. After repeated warnings to his people, God used these evil nations as instruments for his justice.

When we reject God's commands and purpose for our life, the consequences are severe. He will not ignore unbelief or rebellion. To avoid the penalty for sin, we must believe in Christ and accept his sacrificial death on our behalf, or we will be judged and punished. Having accepted Christ, we must still remain sensitive and responsive to God's will.

- Would you describe God's discipline of his people as gentle, mild, serious, or severe? Explain.
- What does this judgment reveal to you about God?
- What does the death of Jesus on the cross reveal about God's love? What does Jesus' death reveal about God's holiness?
- As a Christian who has been redeemed by Christ, how should you respond to the fact that God is a God of judgment?
- What *effect* does God's holiness have on your daily choices? On the relationships you have with others? On the way you approach God?

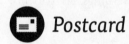 *Postcard*

You can probably think of a number of clues that show what direction a nation is headed in relation to God. But what are the most persistent positive or negative habits in your own life that indicate the direction you are headed in relation to God?

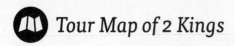

Tour Map of 2 Kings

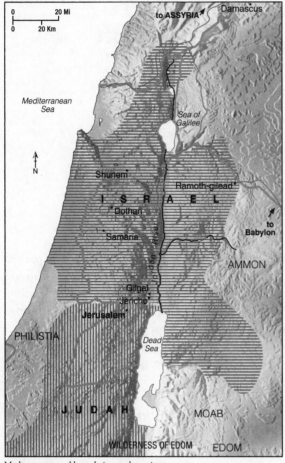

Modern names and boundaries are shown in gray.

1 CHRONICLES

 Snapshot of 1 Chronicles

"I promise that we will demolish them tonight!"

The coach's voice booms over the PA system in the packed gymnasium. With those words the student body begins to clap and yell wildly. Somewhere in the back, a few people start chanting, "Beat the Raiders! Beat the Raiders!" More people join in until soon everyone is screaming in unison.

Pep rallies can draw a school together. And for those few moments, all differences are forgotten as the crowd focuses on the one objective: winning the big game.

First Chronicles can be considered a written pep rally. Writing for the Jews who had returned to their homeland, the author attempts to form a sense of national conscience and to awaken a sense of national pride and unity.

Beginning with Adam, 1 Chronicles relates the exciting history of Israel. By recalling the past, the author hopes to spur the Israelites on to a great future. But 1 Chronicles is more than a history lesson. It is a recounting of the spiritual strength of the nation. That, the author writes, is the hope for the greatness of the new Israel. Only as the nation unites in its worship of God can it regain the importance and vitality it once had.

We, too, have a great spiritual heritage, built by men and women who have contributed to any spiritual vitality we see today. As you read 1 Chronicles, trace your spiritual heritage and commit yourself to doing your part to pass on God's truth to the next generation.

PURPOSE:
To unify God's people, to trace the Davidic line, and to teach that genuine worship ought to be the center of individual and national life

AUTHOR:
Ezra, according to Jewish tradition

TO WHOM WRITTEN:
Israel and God's people everywhere

DATE WRITTEN:
Approximately 430 BC, recording events that occurred about 1000–960 BC

SETTING:
First Chronicles parallels 2 Samuel and serves as a commentary on it. Written after the Exile from a priestly point of view, 1 Chronicles emphasizes the religious history of Judah and Israel.

KEY PEOPLE:
David, David's warriors, Nathan, Solomon

KEY PLACES:
Hebron, Jerusalem, the Temple

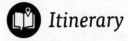 *Itinerary*

The Genealogies of Israel (1:1–9:44)
First Chronicles begins with a quick review of all of Israel's history, going back as far as Adam and traveling forward as far as the return of God's people from exile in Babylon. These chapters are filled with genealogical data on the development of the people whom God chose as his own. Some of the names mentioned remind us of stories of great faith, and others, of tragic failure. About most of the people named, however, we know nothing. God knows the details of their lives even as he knows the details of ours. God remembers.

The Reign of David (10:1–29:30)
The last two-thirds of 1 Chronicles highlights the reign of David. The king loves the Lord and wants to build a temple to replace the tent that has been Israel's place of worship for so many years. But God denies his request. David's greatest contribution to the

Temple will not be the construction but the preparation. He gathers money and materials for his son Solomon to use. He does what he can. We may be unable to see the results of our labors for God in our lifetime, but David's example helps us understand that we serve God so he will see his results, not so we will see ours.

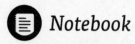 *Notebook*

GOD'S PEOPLE (9:1; 11:1-2; 16:7-36; 17:20-22)
By retelling Israel's history through the genealogies and the stories of the kings, the writer of 1 Chronicles laid the true spiritual foundation for the nation. God kept his promises, and we are reminded of them in the historical records of his people, leaders, prophets, priests, and kings.

Israel's past formed a reliable basis for rebuilding the nation after the Exile. God's promises are written in the Bible; we can know God and trust him to keep his word. Like Israel, we can have no higher goal in life than serving God. Like Israel, we will find God to be trustworthy and faithful.

- As you review Israel's history, what qualities of God are most evident? What do you learn about the people themselves?
- There were definite differences in the lives of the people when they were submissive to God's will, as opposed to times when they ignored or rebelled against God. In what ways do you see a similar pattern developing in your life?
- Think about the next ten years. How important is doing God's will in your future? Explain this importance.
- Now think about the next generation. If God blesses you with children, what spiritual heritage do you want to give to them? How can you begin in the present to prepare that future heritage?

DAVID (11:1–29:30)
The story of David's life and his relationship with God showed that he was God's appointed leader. David's devotion to God, the law, the Temple, true worship, the people, and justice set the standard for what God's chosen king should have been.

Jesus Christ came to earth as a descendant of David. One day Christ will rule as King over all the earth. His strength and justice will fulfill God's ideal for the king. He is our hope.

- What do you remember about David?
- From looking at David's life, what do you learn about God? About living in God's will?
- Why do most people seem to live based merely on what they want rather than seeking God's purposes in their lives?
- What do you think God wants to accomplish in and through you? What can you do to see that God's purpose is accomplished in your life?

TRUE WORSHIP (6:49; 13:1-14; 15:1–17:27; 21:18-30; 28:2-21; 29:10-20)

David brought the Ark of the Covenant to the Tabernacle at Jerusalem in order to restore true worship to the people. God chose priests and Levites to guide the people in faithful worship. This worship was to be a central part of the Israelites' daily lives.

When we acknowledge and focus on God as the true King, we experience worship. This worship is to be the center of our life, with the rest of our thoughts and activities organized around God's kingship. Today every believer is a priest in the sense that each of us, in Christ, can personally enter into worship. Thus we believers also can encourage one another to deeper worship.

- In what ways did the Israelites worship God?
- How do you worship God?
- In your worship, what is the importance of the church? Other Christians? The Bible?
- In what ways can Christians be "priests" for one another? Picture your Christian friends. What can you do to be a "priest" for one of them?

📧 *Postcard*

David made a lot of mistakes along the way. His sins were many, but his opportunities for sin were probably greater than most of us will ever experience. Yet what kept David going was his unwavering trust in God's willingness to forgive. David didn't assume that he would be forgiven as an excuse for sin; he simply lived confidently, knowing that if and when he did sin, God would not turn his back on his confession and repentance. Do you tend to be like most people and avoid admitting your sins even to God, or are you more like David, who readily faced up to his failures and found God's grace?

2 CHRONICLES

 Snapshot of 2 Chronicles

"Mom, I promise I'll never be late again! Please!"

The mother desperately wanted to believe her daughter. But no matter how strong the daughter's promises were to get in on time, she was always late.

"Honey," the mother began, "I'm sorry. But for the rest of the weekend you're grounded." The mother had been more than fair; now she had to mete out punishment.

Many times during Israel's history, God would send messengers to the country's leaders, threatening punishment for their disobedience. Each time, the leaders would beg for one more chance, promising to do better and to obey God this time. But each time they would break those promises. Finally, God allowed them to be conquered and taken into captivity.

Second Chronicles was written after the return of some of the Jews from that captivity. The author reminded these people of their forefathers' sins and the results. Only by truly submitting to God could Israel regain its strength as a nation. "Then if my people who are called by my name will humble themselves and pray and seek my face and turn from their wicked ways, I will hear from heaven and will forgive their sins and restore their land" (7:14).

Second Chronicles was written for you, too. God punishes those who ignore him, but he blesses those who obey. Read this book, and dedicate yourself to following after God.

PURPOSE:
To unify the nation of Israel around true worship of Jehovah by show-ing his standard for judging kings. The righteous kings of Judah and the religious revivals under their rule are highlighted, and the sins of the evil kings are exposed.

AUTHOR:
Ezra, according to Jewish tradition

TO WHOM WRITTEN:
Israel, Judah, and God's people everywhere

DATE WRITTEN:
Approximately 430 BC, recording events from the beginning of Solomon's reign (970 BC) to the beginning of the Babylonian captivity (586 BC)

SETTING:
Second Chronicles parallels 1 and 2 Kings and serves as their commentary.

KEY PEOPLE:
Solomon, the queen of Sheba, Rehoboam, Asa, Jehoshaphat, Jehoram, Joash, Uzziah, Ahaz, Hezekiah, Manasseh, Josiah

KEY PLACES:
Jerusalem, the Temple

SPECIAL FEATURE:
Includes a detailed record of the Temple's construction

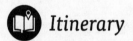 *Itinerary*

The Reign of Solomon (1:1–9:31)
Second Chronicles begins with an overview of Solomon's reign. Solomon achieves much in business and government through his application of wisdom. Also, Solomon is the man God uses to build the glorious Temple in Jerusalem. This magnificent building is a visual reminder of God's presence and the religious center of the nation. It symbolizes the unity of all the tribes, the presence of God among them, and the high calling of God's people.

Reading about the construction of the Temple and under-standing its importance in Jewish life allow us to reflect on what is central in our life. We may achieve greatness in many areas, but we must focus our efforts in helping to nurture God's people and in bringing others into God's Kingdom. God and his work should be our first priority.

The Kingdom of Judah (10:1–36:23)

The second part of 2 Chronicles follows the ups and downs of twenty kings in David's lineage. During their reigns, the nation of Judah wavers between obedience to God and apostasy (turning from the truth). The king's response to God usually determines the nation's spiritual climate. That in turn determines whether God will punish or bless his people.

Likewise, our personal history is shaped by our response to God. Just as Judah's failure to repent brought them captivity in Babylon, so the abuse of our high calling by sinful living will ultimately bring us catastrophe and destruction.

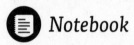 *Notebook*

TEMPLE (2:1–5:14; 6:7–7:22)

The Temple was the symbol of God's presence and the place set aside for worship and prayer. Built by Solomon from the plans God had given to David, the Temple was the nation's spiritual center.

- How did the people feel about the Temple? What caused them to feel this way?
- What did the Temple provide for the nation?
- Because Christians are the temple of God, what attitude should they have toward each other?
- What attitudes keep the body of Christ from fulfilling its intended role as the temple?
- Toward what Christian(s) do you have a negative attitude? How could you improve your attitude and restore that relationship(s)?

PEACE (1:1-17; 8:1–9:28; 15:12-19; 20:27-30; 26:4-5; 32:20-23)

As Solomon and his descendants were faithful to God, they received God's blessings. They experienced victory in battle, success in government, and peace with other nations. Peace comes from loyalty to God and his law.

Only God can bring true peace, and he is greater than any enemy, army, or national alliance. Israel's peace and survival as a nation depended on its faithfulness to God. Our obedience to

God as individuals and as a nation is also vital to our individual and national peace today.

- What causes nations to go to war? Families to break apart? Friends to fight?
- What do the above causes have in common?
- What was the source of Israel's peace?
- What does it mean to "be at peace"?
- Jesus said, "God blesses those who work for peace" (Matthew 5:9). How can a person "work for peace"?
- What can you do to work for peace?

PRAYER (1:1-13; 6:1-42; 7:11-22; 12:5-12; 13:13-18; 14:9-13; 20:1-30; 32:20-23; 33:10-13, 19)

After Solomon died, the kingdom divided. When a king led the Israelites into idolatry, the nation suffered. When a king and his people prayed to God for deliverance and they turned from their sinful ways, God delivered them.

God still answers prayer. God promises to hear, heal, and forgive those who humble themselves, seek him, turn from their sin, and pray. When we pray, we should be seeking to know and experience God's will for our life.

- What were the attitudes of the king and the people as they went to God in prayer?
- How did the people put their prayers into action?
- What attitudes do you think are most important for you to have when you pray?
- What are five of your most important prayer requests? What can you expect from God when you share these with him?
- Take ten minutes to bring your requests and your life before God. Approach your prayers not as a time to share your list with God but as a time to understand more of your Father's love, provision, and grace for you.

REFORM (14:1-7; 15:1-19; 17:3-10; 19:1-11; 23:16–24:16; 29:3–31:21; 33:14-17; 34:3–35:19)

Although idolatry and injustice were common, some kings led the people back to God and, in doing so, reformed society. This involved destroying idols, obeying the law, and restoring the priesthood.

God still brings about personal, community, and national reformation. When that happens, we suddenly become aware that we have drifted far from God's direction. Sometimes the required changes are drastic. But reforms of any kind don't become permanent changes unless they are followed through with consistent obedience to God.

- Changes in society begin with people coming back to God. What caused the people to return to God? What did they do next?
- What changes need to take place in the world? In your community? In your school?
- Christian young people can be agents of change in the world, but to do so they must have a desire for a relationship with God and a commitment to obey him. What changes would happen if a group of committed Christian friends were to begin to work together in your school? In your community?
- Seek God's will in your own life and in the lives of your Christian friends. How might you share your vision with them of how, with God's help, you could join together to create positive change?

COLLAPSE (10:1–36:23)

In 586 BC the Babylonians completely destroyed Solomon's beautiful Temple. The Israelites had abandoned God. Therefore God allowed them to be carried away into captivity. The collapse of the nation came at the end of painful centuries of moral and spiritual decay. There were many efforts and opportunities for correction. But the continual trend led to the eventual consequences.

Although our disobedience may not be as obvious as Israel's, quite often our commitment to God is casual or even phony. When we forget that all our power, wisdom, and wealth come from God and not from ourselves, we are in danger of suffering the same spiritual and moral collapse that Israel experienced.

- What decisions led to Judah's collapse?
- What causes leaders who claim to be serving God to turn away from him and become immoral?
- In what specific ways could you prevent such failure in your life?

- How can you be a person who changes your world, rather than someone who is changed by it?

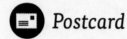 *Postcard*

Most of 2 Chronicles illustrates the benefits and consequences of obeying or violating the principles God spelled out in 7:14. The verse includes four personal or group actions that must be taken in the face of sin (humility, prayer, seeking God's face, and turning from wicked ways). It also spells out three actions God promised to take in response to repentance (God will hear, forgive, and heal). Spend some time prayerfully exploring your own life using these principles, and then apply them to the various groups (including your nation) of which you are a part.

EZRA

Snapshot of Ezra

When a celebrity commits suicide, we can't believe it. After all, we think, he or she had everything: millions of fans, talent, good looks, a beautiful spouse, fame, and fortune. What more could anyone want? From all surface appearances, the person's life seemed perfect. Inside, however (where it really counts), he or she was filled with loneliness, depression, and turmoil.

Ezra, a devoted priest and scribe, knew what was important. He was concerned for the Jews living in Jerusalem. Years earlier, under Zerubbabel's leadership, a group of Jews had been given permission to leave Babylon and return to rebuild the Temple. Though the returnees had met with some opposition, eventually they had been successful. The Temple had been completed and dedicated. Everything looked good on the outside.

But when Ezra reached Jerusalem, he wept. The people looked obedient because they had rebuilt the Temple, but their personal and spiritual lives were in shambles. The inside had fallen apart. Ezra realized that if this went unchanged, the new nation of Israel would be committing spiritual suicide.

How does your "inside life" match with your outside? Read Ezra, and decide to be a person who follows God in every area.

PURPOSE:
To show God's faithfulness and the way he kept his promise to restore his people to their land

AUTHOR:
Not stated in the text, but probably Ezra

TO WHOM WRITTEN:
Judah and all God's people

DATE WRITTEN:
Around 450 BC, recording events from about 538–450 BC (omitting 516–458 BC); possibly begun in Babylon and finished later in Jerusalem

SETTING:
Ezra follows 2 Chronicles as a history of the Jews, recording their return to the Promised Land after their captivity.

KEY PEOPLE:
Cyrus, Zerubbabel, Haggai, Zechariah, Darius I, Artaxerxes I, Ezra

KEY PLACES:
Babylon, Jerusalem

SPECIAL FEATURES:
Ezra and Nehemiah originally were one book in the Hebrew Bible. With Esther, they comprise the postcaptivity historical books. The postcaptivity prophetic books are Haggai, Zechariah, and Malachi. Haggai and Zechariah should be studied with Ezra because these prophets ministered during the period of the reconstruction.

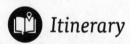 # Itinerary

Ezra picks up the story of God's people from the events at the end of 2 Chronicles. Cyrus, king of Persia, announces a resettlement plan for Jerusalem. Permission to rebuild the Temple has been granted. Volunteer settlers gather.

The Return Led by Zerubbabel (1:1–6:22)
The first group to travel back to Judah is led by Zerubbabel. When they arrive, they quickly set about laying the foundation of the Temple, only to be stopped by their enemies. God's work in the world is not without opposition. We must not get discouraged and quit, as the returning Israelites do at first. Instead, we must continue boldly in the face of difficulties, as they did later with the encouragement from God's prophets.

The Return Led by Ezra (7:1–10:44)
The second group returns under the leadership of Ezra. Eighty years have passed since Zerubbabel's efforts. Ezra finds a discouraged population that has begun to intermarry with people

from the surrounding pagan nations. These marriages pollute the religious purity of the people and endanger the future of the nation. Ezra is forced to take drastic action to confront the people. They still have work to do and lives to live for God. We see in their experience the temptations and the dangers that threaten our walk with God when we accept the practices of unbelievers.

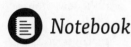

Notebook

JEWS RETURN (1:1–2:70; 7:1–8:36)

By returning to the land of Israel from Babylon, the Jews showed their faith in God's promise to restore them as his people. They returned not only to their homeland but also to the place where their forefathers had promised to follow God.

God shows his mercy to every generation. He compassionately restores his people. No matter how difficult our present "captivity," we are never far from his love and mercy. He restores us when we return to him.

- If you were one of those who returned to the homeland after being released from captivity, how would you feel? What would you think about as you returned to your home?
- Undoubtedly this generation of Jews had heard about the sins that had led to their forefathers' captivity. What type of commitment to God do you think they carried with them as they returned to Jerusalem? How should they have used their new freedom to worship?
- In what sense were you a slave to sin until you received Christ's forgiveness? How are you using your freedom in Christ to worship God?
- In what ways can you creatively (1) worship God in your freedom and (2) communicate this freedom to those still enslaved by sin?

OPPOSITION (4:1-24; 5:3–6:15)

Opposition came soon after the altar was built and the Temple foundation was laid. For more than six years, the enemies of the Jews used deceit to hinder the building. Finally, there was a decree to stop construction altogether. This opposition severely tested the Jews' wavering faith.

There will always be people who oppose God's work. The life of faith is never easy, but God can overcome all opposition. We must not falter or withdraw from our enemies; we need to stay active and patient. God is with us in every circumstance.

- Why and how did some people try to keep the Jews from building the Temple?
- Why do some people strongly oppose Christianity and Christians? Give some examples of how they do this.
- When have you thought about giving up your Christian witness because you felt alone or opposed? How did you work through those feelings so that you would not give up?
- If a Christian friend were facing tough opposition from kids at school, what could you do to encourage that friend to remain true to Christ?
- Who are some people you know who need encouragement because of obstacles or opposition they are facing? List specific ways you can encourage them. How will you do this in the next week?
- If you were (or are) facing opposition, to whom could you go for encouragement?

GOD'S WORD (1:1; 3:2-5; 7:6-10; 9:1–10:11)
When the people returned to the Promised Land, they were also returning to the influence of God's Word. The prophets Haggai and Zechariah helped encourage them, while Ezra's preaching of Scripture built them up. God's Word gave them what they needed to do God's work.

We also need the encouragement and direction of God's Word. We must never waver in our commitment to hear and obey his Word and to keep it in our life daily.

- What main message did God give through Haggai? Through Zechariah? Through Ezra?
- What difference did it make whether or not the people obeyed the prophets' messages?
- What important lessons have you learned through reading and studying God's Word?

- What difference has obeying (or not obeying) God's Word made in your life?
- Based on this study, what would you tell a new Christian about the importance of the Bible in the Christian life?

FAITH/ACTION (3:1-9; 8:15-35; 9:1–10:17)
Israel's leaders motivated the people to complete the Temple. But over the years, many of them had intermarried with idol worshipers and had adopted heathen practices. Only when their faith was tested and strengthened did they remove these sins from their lives.

Faith led God's people to complete the Temple and to remove sin from their society. As we trust God with our heart and mind, we also must put our faith into action.

- As recorded in this book, how did the Jews put their faith into action?
- What decisions have you made as a result of your faith in God in the last year? The last month? The last week?
- What decisions are you facing right now that will give you the opportunity to act on your faith?
- The people supported each other in their commitment to put their faith into action. To whom can you turn for support in the decisions you listed in the previous question?

📧 Postcard

If you are like most people, you can think of areas in your life to which you need to "return and rebuild." Broken relationships, unfinished business, shattered promises—something you see or hear today may remind you of one of them. As you read Ezra, think about the insights you might gain regarding the limits, challenges, disappointments, and cost of returning and rebuilding in your life. Put those insights into practice!

NEHEMIAH

 Snapshot of Nehemiah

Are you a leader? Most people think they are leaders, but real leadership is proven in adversity, in working through tough problems and painful situations. When tough times come, many would-be leaders find themselves falling apart.

Nehemiah was a proven leader. He left a secure position in the government of Persia to return to his homeland and rebuild the walls of Jerusalem. He succeeded, too, despite incredible obstacles and opposition. The book of Nehemiah tells his story.

We often dream of the glory and the praise of leadership, but we tend to forget about the turmoil and difficulty that leadership can carry. God uses men and women with the same tenacity as Nehemiah. Unfortunately, few people are like Nehemiah. Read the book to see true leadership in action. And ask God to help you become a leader like Nehemiah.

PURPOSE:

Nehemiah, the last of the Old Testament historical books, contains the history of the third return of the Jews to Jerusalem after their captivity. It explains how the people built the walls and renewed their faith.

AUTHOR:

Much of the book is written in the first person, suggesting Nehemiah as the author. Nehemiah probably wrote the book, with Ezra serving as editor.

TO WHOM WRITTEN:
Judah and God's people everywhere

DATE WRITTEN:
Approximately 445–432 BC

SETTING:
Zerubbabel led the first return to Jerusalem in 538 BC. In 458 BC, Ezra led the second return. Finally, in 445 BC, Nehemiah returns with the third group of exiles to rebuild the city walls.

KEY PEOPLE:
Nehemiah, Ezra, Sanballat, Tobiah

KEY PLACE:
Jerusalem

SPECIAL FEATURE:
Shows the fulfillment of the prophecies of Zechariah and Daniel concerning the rebuilding of Jerusalem's walls

 *Itinerary*

Rebuilding the Wall (1:1–7:73)
The book of Nehemiah records one man's efforts to serve God in two great reconstruction projects. The first rebuilding project involves the wall around Jerusalem. Nehemiah's life is an example of leadership and organization. After giving up a comfortable and wealthy position in Persia, he returns to his fractured homeland and rallies the people to rebuild Jerusalem's wall. In the face of opposition, Nehemiah uses wise measures to keep the people safe and to keep the project moving. His actions demonstrate how prayer, perseverance, and sacrifice will allow us to accomplish more for the sake of God's Kingdom.

Reforming the People (8:1–13:31)
The second rebuilding project involves the reformation of God's people. After the wall is rebuilt, Ezra reads the law to the people, bringing about national repentance. Nehemiah and Ezra are very different types of people, yet God uses them both to lead the nation. Remember, there is a place for you in God's work even if you differ from most other people. God uses each person in a unique way to accomplish his purposes.

📄 *Notebook*

VISION (2:11-20; 4:14-22; 6:10-13)

Although the Jews completed the Temple in 515 BC, the city walls remained in shambles for the next seventy years. A city's walls represented power, protection, and beauty. Jerusalem also needed walls to protect the Temple from attack. God put the desire in Nehemiah's heart to rebuild the city walls, and he gave Nehemiah a vision for the work.

Does God have a vision for us? Are there "walls" that need to be built today? God still wants his people to be united and trained to do his work. As we recognize deep needs in our world, God can give us the vision and desire to "build." Look for construction projects that you can complete for God.

- Nehemiah's vision for doing what God wanted began with his relationship with God. Based on the first chapter, how would you describe that relationship?
- What qualities can you find in Nehemiah that could serve as your example of what it means to be God's visionary?
- How can you prepare yourself now to be a person who not only has a vision for God's will, but who also is used by God to fulfill that vision?
- You may not be ready for a task as large as Nehemiah's, but what small tasks are available to you that would be "building" for God's people? What can you do to begin your "construction project" in the coming days?

PRAYER (1:4-11; 2:4; 4:4-5, 9; 5:19; 6:9; 8:6–9:38; 13:14, 22, 29, 31)

Both Nehemiah and Ezra responded to problems with prayer. When Nehemiah began his work, he recognized the problem, prayed right away, and then acted to solve the problem.

Prayer still is God's way to solve problems. Prayer and action go hand in hand. Through prayer God guides our preparation, teamwork, and efforts to carry out his will. Without prayer we are limited to our own finite resources.

- How was prayer part of Nehemiah's preparation for doing God's work?

- How is prayer connected to a person's attitudes and actions?
- How would you complete this sentence? I can prepare myself to be God's builder by beginning with a prayer that includes _____.
- For what do you need to pray concerning the "construction project" you listed previously under "Vision"? Write it out.

LEADERSHIP (1:2-4; 2:11-20; 4:12-23; 5:1-13; 6:2-9; 7:1-3; 8:9-12; 12:31-43; 13:6-31)

Nehemiah was an excellent leader. He was spiritually ready to heed God's call. He used careful planning, teamwork, problem solving, and courage to get the work done. Although Nehemiah had tremendous faith, he never avoided the extra work necessary for good leadership.

Being God's leader is not just getting recognition, holding a position, or being the boss. It requires planning, hard work, courage, and perseverance. And there is no substitute for doing the difficult work. In order to lead others, you need to follow God's direction.

- What are a few specific examples of Nehemiah's excellent leadership?
- Based upon your study of Nehemiah and your experience with leaders you have known personally, what are the qualities that make a strong leader?
- Evaluate yourself based on your list from the previous question. Which qualities are your strengths? Which are your weaknesses?
- In what ways could you use your strengths to influence others for Christ? How can you develop those strengths and overcome your weaknesses?

PROBLEMS (1:2-7; 2:9-10; 4:1-23; 5:1-13; 6:1-19; 7:4-5; 13:1-31)

After the work began, Nehemiah faced scorn, slander, and threats from enemies, as well as fear, conflict, and discouragement from his own workers. Although these problems were difficult, they did not stop Nehemiah from finishing the work.

When difficulties come, it is easy to get discouraged. Remember, however, that triumphs come through troubles. When problems arise, we must face them squarely and press on to complete God's work. We do not have to retreat; our God is a God of absolute victory.

- How would you have felt had you been Nehemiah when he faced all of his problems? What would you have wanted to do when you were threatened and slandered?
- Nehemiah overcame these problems. What seems to have been the key to his not giving in or giving up?
- Choose one problem you have faced in the past or are now facing in your attempts to obey God. Based on Nehemiah's example, what will you do to be an overcomer rather than being a person who is overcome?

REPENTANCE (1:4-11; 5:8-13; 9:1–10:39; 13:1-31)
Although God had enabled the people to build the wall, the work wasn't complete until they rebuilt their lives. Ezra taught the people God's Word. As they listened, they recognized the sin in their lives, admitted it, and took steps to remove it.

Recognizing and admitting sin is not enough. Being serious about God must result in a changed life, or it is merely enthusiasm. God does not want halfhearted measures. After removing sin from our life, we must place God at the center of all we do.

- According to Nehemiah, is this statement true or false? God is not just concerned that we take care of big tasks; he wants our entire life surrendered to him. Explain your answer based only on the book of Nehemiah.
- What "little things" in your life are important to God although no one else may ever notice them?
- The people in Jerusalem responded to the new wall with a recommitment to God in all of life. After reading chapters 10 and 11, write out some statements of your own recommitment to live all of your life, from the heart, for God.

✉ *Postcard*

Nehemiah certainly had his share of problems. Most of them involved people. He had plenty of enemies as well as friends whom he needed to confront. Notice how often Nehemiah dealt with his problems in prayer before he dealt with them in public. In fact, many of Nehemiah's problems got settled in prayer. How often do you discuss your problems with God? What would it take to increase that practice?

ESTHER

 Snapshot of Esther

Overflowing with fans, the gymnasium rocks with excitement. It's the crucial moment—the one anticipated all season—but joy mixes with fear and tension. Only one point behind, the team could find its season ending abruptly. Two seconds remain in the game, and their player stands at the free-throw line. Cheers erupt as the ball swishes through the hoop. Then silence engulfs the stands as he approaches the line for the second shot. Everything seems to be on the line: the play-offs, the dreams, the season. But the shooter's training pays off. He makes the basket, wins the game, and becomes the hero! He came through when it counted.

In Persia Esther also faced a crucial moment, but the stakes were much higher—the lives of thousands. All the Jews in Persia were scheduled to be killed, and Esther, the queen and a Jew, was the only one who could save them. She could make the difference. She could have avoided the responsibility or looked for an easy out. But Esther knew God had placed her in an influential position "for just such a time as this" (4:14). She seized the moment and took action regardless of the consequences (4:16). Because of Esther lives were spared, the victory won.

Read Esther and commit yourself to act for God when he gives you the opportunity. Remember, he places you where you can make a difference "for just such a time as this."

PURPOSE:
To demonstrate God's sovereignty and his loving care for his people

AUTHOR:
Unknown—possibly Mordecai (9:29). Some have suggested Ezra or Nehemiah because of the similarity of the writing style.

TO WHOM WRITTEN:
Judah and all of God's people everywhere

DATE WRITTEN:
Approximately 483–471 BC (Esther became queen in 479 BC.)

SETTING:
Although Esther follows Nehemiah in the order of Bible books, its events are about thirty years prior to those recorded in Nehemiah. The story is set in the Persian empire, and most of the action takes place in the king's palace in Susa, the Persian capital.

KEY PEOPLE:
Esther, Mordecai, King Xerxes I, Haman

KEY PLACE:
The king's palace in Susa, Persia

SPECIAL FEATURES:
Esther is one of only two books in the Bible that are named for women (Ruth is the other). The book is unusual in that, in the original version, God's name doesn't appear in it. This caused some early church leaders to question its inclusion in the Bible. But God's presence is clear throughout the book.

Itinerary

The book of Esther is an exciting and exotic journey into a beautiful woman's life of service to God. Romance, danger, intrigue, betrayal, rescue—all these and more fill the story. Esther's life is an example of God's divine guidance and care. God's control and power are seen throughout this book. Although we may question certain circumstances, we must have faith that God is in control, working through both the pleasant and difficult times so that we can serve him effectively.

Notebook

IN CONTROL (2:5-23; 4:4-17; 6:1–9:19)
The book of Esther tells of circumstances that were essential for the survival of God's people in Persia. These circumstances were

not the result of chance but of God's grand design. God is in control of every area of life.

With God in charge, we can take courage. He can guide us through the circumstances we face in our life. We should expect God to display his power in carrying out his will.

- Esther showed great courage in the face of frightening circumstances. How would you have felt in Esther's situation, risking your life for your people?
- How did Esther's decisions reflect a trust in God's control of her life?
- Think of a time when things worked out just the opposite of the way you had wanted and expected them to. How did you feel toward God?
- What choices in your life show you believe that God is in control?
- In what areas of your life do you want to learn to trust God's control more? How can you begin to do this today?

RACISM (2:10, 19-20; 3:2-13; 4:13-14; 5:9-14; 7:1-7; 8:7-14; 9:1-4, 13-19)
The Jews in Persia had been a minority since their deportation from Judah one hundred years earlier. Haman was a descendant of King Agag, an enemy of the Jews. Lust for power and pride drove Haman to hate Mordecai, Esther's cousin. Haman convinced the king to kill all the Jews.

Racial hatred is always sinful. We must never condone it in any form. Every person on earth has intrinsic worth because God created human beings in his image. Therefore, God's people must stand against racism whenever and wherever it occurs. We must learn to see others as God sees them rather than through the often cloudy lenses of our own cultural glasses.

- In the story of Esther, what were the results of racial hatred?
- What results of racial hatred do you remember in history? In the present world?
- What people in your school or community suffer because of racial hatred?
- What can Christians in your school and community do to show how God's love overcomes racial hatred?

DELIVERANCE (2:21-23; 3:12–4:17; 6:1-13; 8:1–9:32)
In March the Jews celebrate the Feast of Purim, which symbolizes God's deliverance. Purim means dice, such as those used by Haman to set the date for the extermination of all Jews from Persia. But God overruled, using Queen Esther to intercede on behalf of the Jews.

Because God controls history, he is never frustrated by any turn of events or by any human action. He is able to save us from the evil in this world and deliver us from sin and death. Because we trust God, we should not fear what people may do to us; instead, we should be confident in God's control.

- Haman planned the destruction of the Jews. What did he learn about God when he tried to carry out his plan?
- Where else in the Bible did God deliver his people?
- In what specific situations has God delivered you?
- What does this study of deliverance teach you about placing your confidence in God? What difference can this confidence make in your life?

ACTION (4:1–5:8; 8:1-17)
Faced with death, Esther and Mordecai set aside their own fears and took action. Mordecai took great risks to talk with Esther about the situation; Esther risked her life by asking King Xerxes to save the Jews. They did not allow fear to paralyze them.

When outnumbered and powerless, it is natural to feel helpless. Instead, Esther and Mordecai resisted and acted with courage. It is not enough to know that God is in control; we must also courageously follow God's guidance.

- How did Esther show herself to be a woman of action?
- What was Esther's view of God?
- Why can you tell a person's view of God more by how he or she acts than what he or she says?
- How would you describe your view of God based on your actions this past week? What strengths do you see? Weaknesses?

WISDOM (2:10-20; 4:1-14; 8:9-17; 9:20-28; 10:3)
The Jews were a minority in a hostile world. It took great wisdom for Mordecai to survive. Serving as a faithful official of the king,

Mordecai took steps to understand and work with the Persian law. Yet he did not compromise his integrity.

It takes great wisdom to survive in a nonbelieving world. In a setting that is mostly hostile to Christianity, we can demonstrate wisdom by giving respect to what is true and good and by standing against what is wrong. An important step in becoming mature is learning to distinguish good from evil. God will help us in that process through the Word, his Spirit, and the body of Christ, the church.

- How does Mordecai provide an example of godly wisdom in an ungodly environment?
- In what ways does God want believers to be active in non-Christian environments? What makes this difficult?
- What situations or relationships do you face where you need godly wisdom in order to not compromise your faith?
- What sources does God give you for getting the godly wisdom you need?
- What specific wisdom will you seek from God through the Word, prayer, and godly advice in order to be a more effective witness for Christ?

 Postcard

God is capable of doing much with you in your circumstances and with the skills and character he has given you. The first step in receiving guidance from God is not asking, Where can I go to serve God? Instead, it is asking, How can I serve God better right where I am? Have you answered that question lately?

JOB

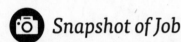 *Snapshot of Job*

"Why me, God?" Have you ever thought, whispered, or screamed that question? Have you ever thought that God was against you personally? At one time or another, everyone does—even people in the Bible. That is not surprising. What is surprising is God's answer.

Job loved God, and everything was going great in his life. He had money, land, possessions, and a large, wonderful family. But one day Job's world fell apart. He lost everything . . . except his life, a bitter wife, and accusing "friends." As you might imagine, Job asked why. Why him? Why now? The book of Job tells this story, and it gives God's reply. And after God spoke, Job was silent.

Job is a book about success, tragedy, friends, and faith. As you read Job, allow God to begin changing your ideas about suffering. Learn to trust God even when you don't understand.

PURPOSE:
To demonstrate God's sovereignty and the meaning of true faith. It addresses the question, Why do the righteous suffer?

AUTHOR:
Possibly Job himself. Some have suggested Moses, Solomon, or Elihu.

TO WHOM WRITTEN:
Israel and God's people everywhere

DATE WRITTEN:
Unknown. The events recorded probably occurred during the time of the patriarchs, approximately 2000–1800 BC.

SETTING:
The land of Uz, probably located northeast of Palestine, near desert land between Damascus and the Euphrates River

KEY PEOPLE:
Job, Eliphaz the Temanite, Bildad the Shuhite, Zophar the Naamathite, Elihu the Buzite

SPECIAL FEATURES:
Job is the first of the poetic books in the Hebrew Bible. Many believe this was the first book of the Bible to be written. Job gives us insights into the work of Satan. Ezekiel 14:14, 20 and James 5:11 mention Job as a historical character.

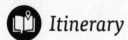 *Itinerary*

The book of Job presents a case study in one of the most difficult questions that people ask: What's the reason for terrible suffering? Answers to the problem of pain always seem clearer when we aren't suffering. Job suffered. He suffered because he loved God. That may not make sense, but Job had to live with that reality anyway.

Job Is Tested (1:1–2:13)
Job's story begins with three rapid scenes: (1) an inventory of Job's prosperous life; (2) a conversation between the Lord and Satan; and (3) the destruction of Job's life. Suddenly, Job loses his possessions, his children, and his health. He does not understand why he is suffering. Why has God allowed Job's children to die? That's a good question. Although God knows the answer, he may not reveal it to his people while they live. In the meantime we must always be ready for testing in our life.

Three Friends Answer Job (3:1–31:40)
The long aftermath of the tragedy is filled with Job's questions and the answers from Job's friends, who wrongly assume that suffering always comes as a result of sin. With this in mind, they try to persuade Job to repent of his sin. But the three friends are mistaken. Suffering is not always a direct result of personal sin.

A Young Man Answers Job (32:1–37:24)
Job's intense conversation with his friends is interrupted by a young observer, Elihu. Elihu criticizes Job's friends for being unable to

answer Job, and he offers another possible reason for Job's suffering: pride. According to Elihu, God must be allowing Job to suffer in order to humble him. Elihu's words carry weight because suffering can purify people's faith and clarify their view of themselves and God. But Elihu's answer is not enough to make sense of Job's experience. The more we think we must have or do have an answer for everything that happens, the less we will understand the importance of trusting God.

God Answers Job (38:1–41:34)
After the friends have their say, God speaks up. He responds to Job without answering his questions. God makes three points very clear to Job: (1) I, your Creator, don't have to answer you; (2) You wouldn't understand if I answered you; and (3) You will have to trust me even though I don't answer you.

Job Is Restored (42:1-17)
Job's story ends with his personal restoration. Job learned that when nothing else is left, he has God, and that is enough. Through suffering we learn that God is enough for our life and our future. We must love God regardless of whether he allows blessing or suffering. Testing is difficult but often can deepen one's relationship with God. Those who endure the testing of their faith will, eventually, experience God's great rewards.

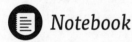 *Notebook*

SUFFERING (1:13-22; 2:7-13; 3:1-26)
Through no fault of his own, Job lost his wealth, children, and health. Even Job's friends were convinced that he had brought this suffering upon himself. For Job the greatest trial was not the pain or loss; it was his inability to understand why God was allowing him to suffer.

Suffering can be, but is not always, a penalty for sin. In the same way, prosperity is not always a reward for being good. Those who love God are not exempt from trouble. Although we may not be able to understand fully the pain we experience, it can lead us to rediscover God. He is always present, even in suffering.

- If you had been in Job's position, what would you have been thinking about yourself? About God?

- What was Job's attitude toward God throughout his suffering? In light of Job's personal pain, what does this tell you about his relationship with God?
- Who do you know that maintained a strong faith in God even when he or she was suffering? What did you learn by watching him or her?
- How does Job's example give you hope as you live in a world that often includes suffering, even for God's children?

SATAN'S ATTACKS (1:6-19; 2:1-7)

Satan tried to drive a wedge between Job and God by getting Job to believe that God's governing of the world was not just and good. Satan had to ask God for permission to take Job's wealth, children, and health away. Satan was limited to what God allowed.

We must learn to recognize Satan's attacks, but we should not fear them. Satan cannot exceed the limits that God sets. Don't let any experience separate you from God. Although you can't control how or when Satan may attack, you can always choose how you will respond when those attacks come.

- What have you learned about Satan from the book of Job?
- Many people think of God and Satan as opposing equals, sort of like the "force" from the Star Wars movies, which had a powerful good side and an equally powerful dark side. What do you read in Job that shows you the error of this view?
- What does this book teach you about how Christians should respond to the reality of Satan's power?
- What examples do you see of Satan's work in the world? How should you respond to these situations?

TRUSTING GOD'S GOODNESS (1:20-22; 2:10; 3:1-26; 6:1-29; 7:1-21; 9:1–10:22; 12:1–14:22; 16:1–17:16; 19:1-28; 21:1-34; 23:1–24:25; 26:1–31:40; 40:3-5; 42:1-6)

God is all-wise and all-powerful. His will is perfect, yet he doesn't always act in ways we understand. Job's suffering didn't make sense, because everyone believed that good people were supposed to prosper. When Job was at the point of despair, God spoke, revealing his great power and wisdom.

Although God is present everywhere, at times he may seem far away. This may cause us to feel alone and to doubt his care for us.

We should serve God for who he is, not for what we feel. He is never insensitive to our suffering. Because God is sufficient, we must hold on to him. This fact is greater than any feeling we might have that he has abandoned us.

- What do you think it means to trust God with your circumstances? How did Job demonstrate this trust in God?
- How did God reveal to Job that he (God) was worthy of that trust?
- What circumstances or problems in the world cause people to question God's goodness?
- What can you do to build your trust in God even when it feels as though his goodness is not present (for example, during pain and suffering)?

PRIDE (33:1-33; 42:1-11)
Job's friends were sure that they were correct in their judgment of him. God rebuked them for their pride and arrogance. Human wisdom is always partial and temporary.

We must be careful not to judge others who are suffering because we may be demonstrating the sin of pride. Also, we should be cautious in declaring how sure we are about why God treats us the way he does. When we congratulate ourselves for being right, we become proud. We should always be willing to listen and to learn.

- How did each of Job's friends display pride?
- Why is pride so dangerous? Give an example of how a person's pride (someone you have known or read about) led to disaster.
- How does God view pride? Why does he see it that way?
- When did you struggle with pride in your attitude toward another person? How were you feeling about the person? About yourself?
- What specific actions can you take to keep from falling into this sin?

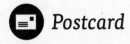 *Postcard*

Job's problem, like ours, wasn't that he asked why. Rather, it was that he began to assume that God owed him an answer. In all likelihood you will have experiences in your life that will cause you to ask why. Often you will discover an accurate and understandable cause for what happened. That answer may require repentance, confession, and efforts to make things right between you and God or you and someone else. But don't allow your failure to lead you to distrust God. At the end of this day, consider how well you are doing with trusting God despite the circumstances.

PSALMS

 Snapshot of Psalms

Emotions. We experience countless feelings every day, ranging from exuberant joy to deep grief. We feel pain when a loved one dies. We feel anger when things go wrong. We feel confusion when we don't understand. And we feel joy when something good happens. Emotions add spice and color to life.

The book of Psalms is about emotions. The pages are filled with them: anger, confusion, joy, pain, humility, bewilderment, contentment—all directed toward God. God created us with emotions, and he knows that emotions will be involved in our dealings with him.

Many people read the book of Psalms because of its honesty. Rather than ignoring their negative emotions or condemning those emotions as sinful, the writers faced their feelings and continued to talk with God.

Psalms also is loved because of the clear picture of God it presents. Our emotions change constantly, but God is unchanging. While we fret, worry, and shout about injustice, God remains calm. When we fall on our face before him because of our awful sin, he isn't surprised—he is gentle and ready to forgive. Psalms reminds us that God is exalted, that he is the Creator and Ruler of the world, and that he is worthy of worship. He alone is God.

How are you feeling today? Angry? Afraid? Frustrated? Or are you joyful, happy, and excited? Read Psalms and express yourself honestly to God.

PURPOSE:
To provide poetry for the expression of praise, worship, and confession to God

AUTHORS:

David wrote seventy-three psalms; Asaph wrote twelve; the descendants of Korah wrote nine; Solomon wrote two; Heman (with the descendants of Korah), Ethan, and Moses each wrote one; fifty-one psalms are anonymous, though the New Testament ascribes two of the anonymous psalms—2 and 95—to David (see Acts 4:25; Hebrews 4:7).

TO WHOM WRITTEN:

Israel, Judah, and God's people everywhere

DATE WRITTEN:

Between the time of Moses (around 1440 BC) and the Babylonian captivity (586 BC)

SETTING:

For the most part, the Psalms were not intended to be narrations of historical events. However, they often parallel events in history, such as David's flight from Saul and his sin with Bathsheba.

KEY PERSON:

David

KEY PLACE:

God's holy temple

SPECIAL FEATURES:

Psalms has a unified plan, but each psalm can be read and understood alone. Psalms is probably the most widely read book of the Bible because it is easy to relate to the writers' emotions.

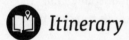 *Itinerary*

Psalms is the ancient hymnbook of the people of Israel. The individual psalms have been gathered in five loosely connected "books." While these books are not organized by topic, it is helpful to compare the dominant themes in each section of Psalms to the five books of Moses.

Book 1 (1:11–41:13)

In book 1 we find psalms written mainly by David. The themes of these psalms parallel the book of Genesis. Just as Genesis tells how humankind was created, fell into sin, and then was promised redemption, many of these psalms meditate on humans as blessed, fallen, and redeemed by God.

Book 2 (42:1–72:20)
Book 2 includes psalms written by David and the sons of Korah. Just as the book of Exodus describes the nation of Israel, many of these psalms describe the nation as ruined and then recovered. As God rescued the nation of Israel, he also rescues us. We do not have to work out solutions first, but we can go to God with our problems and ask him to help.

Book 3 (73:1–89:52)
The psalms in book 3 were mainly written by Asaph or Asaph's descendants. They share similarities of theme with the book of Leviticus. Just as Leviticus discusses the Tabernacle and God's holiness, many of these psalms discuss the Temple and God's enthronement. Because God is almighty, we can turn to him for deliverance. These psalms praise God because he is holy, and his perfect holiness deserves our worship and reverence.

Book 4 (90:1–106:48)
Book 4 contains psalms whose authors are unknown. The dominant themes echo the book of Numbers. Just as Numbers discusses the relationship of the nation of Israel to surrounding nations, these psalms often mention the relationship of God's overruling Kingdom to the nations of the world. Because we are citizens of the Kingdom of God, we can keep the events and troubles of earth in their proper perspective.

Book 5 (107:1–150:6)
Book 5 includes another collection of psalms mainly written by David. Like the book of Deuteronomy, these psalms focus on God and his Word. They are anthems of praise and thanksgiving for God and the Word. Most of these psalms were originally set to music and used in worship. We can still use these psalms today as they were used in the past, as a hymnbook of praise and worship. These ancient words can still make our heart sing!

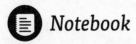 *Notebook*

PRAISE (9:1-20; 18:1-50; 22:23-31; 43:1-5; 48:1-14; 56:9-13; 63:1-11; 66:1-20; 67:1-7; 68:1-35; 71:1-24; 100:1-5; 103:1-22;

104:1-35; 106:1-48; 113:1-9; 119:7, 12, 108, 164, 171, 175;
135:1-21; 138:1-8; 145:1-21; 146:1-10; 148:1-14; 149:1-9; 150:1-6)
Psalms are songs of praise to God as Creator, Sustainer, and Redeemer.
Praise is recognizing, appreciating, and expressing God's greatness.

When we think about God, we want to praise him. The more
we know of him, the more we will appreciate what he has done. We
should focus on God's specific and unique attributes as we worship
him.

- Read Psalm 145. How do you think David was feeling
  toward God when he wrote these verses? How do you feel
  when you read them?
- What specific characteristics of God are praised?
- Does praise always begin with positive feelings toward God?
  Explain.
- How can praising God lead to a change of attitude,
  thoughts, and feelings?
- In what ways can you live a life of praise to God? In other
  words, how can you become a living psalm?

GOD'S POWER (14:1-7; 19:1-11; 21:1-13; 29:1-11; 40:1-17;
45:1-17; 68:1-35; 78:1-72; 89:1-52; 147:1-20; 150:2)
God is all-powerful, and he always acts at the right time. He is
in control of every situation. God's power is shown as he reveals
himself in creation, history, and the Bible.

When we feel powerless, God can help us. His strength can
overcome the despair of any pain or trial. We can always pray that
he will deliver, protect, and sustain us. And he will answer.

- How is God's power revealed in the following psalms: 19;
  21; 78?
- How have you seen God's power in your life?
- In what ways do you need God's power at the present time?
  How do you think you may need him in the future?
- What do you learn from Psalms about relying on God's
  power during these times of need?

FORGIVENESS (19:12-14; 24:3-6; 25:1-22; 26:1-12; 32:1-11;
51:1-19; 79:5-11; 86:1-17; 130:1-8)
Many psalms are intense prayers asking God for forgiveness. God
forgives us when we confess our sins and turn from them.

Because God forgives us, we can pray to him honestly and directly. When we receive God's forgiveness, we move from being separated from him to being close to him, from feeling guilty to feeling loved.

- Psalm 51 is David's prayer after his sin with Bathsheba. As you read this prayer, answer these questions: How was David feeling about himself? How was David feeling toward God?
- What are David's specific prayer requests?
- When you are facing a sin that you need to confess and repent of, how do you feel about yourself? About God?
- Take a few moments to seek God's forgiveness in areas in which you have sinned.

THANKFULNESS (7:17; 26:6-8; 30:11-12; 50:23; 75:1; 92:1-15; 95:1-7; 100:1-5; 106:1-48; 107:1-43; 118:1-29; 136:1-26; 138:1-8; 147:1-20)
We should be grateful to God for his personal concern, help, and mercy. God protects, guides, and forgives, and he provides everything we need.

When we realize how much we benefit from knowing God, we can fully express our thanks to him. By thanking God often, we will develop spontaneity in our prayer life.

- Why are Psalms 100 and 136 called "thanksgiving psalms"?
- Make your own thanksgiving list using the following statements: I thank God that he is _____. I thank God for showing me his love by _____ _____. I thank God for the people I love, including _____. I thank God for providing me with _____. I thank God for helping me _____. I thank God that I am _____.
- How can you pray to help you remember that God is your source of all that is good and eternal? Write out that prayer.

TRUST (4:1-8; 20:1-9; 22:1-31; 23:1-6; 25:1-22; 32:1-11; 37:1-40; 56:3-13; 112:1-10; 115:1-18; 125:1-5; 143:1-12)
God is faithful and just. When we put our trust in him, he calms us. Because he has been faithful throughout history, we can trust him now.

People can be unfair, and friends may desert us, but we can trust in God. Knowing God intimately drives away doubt, fear, and loneliness. We should remember that he is God, even when our feelings seem to be saying something else.

- Why is Psalm 23 seen as a psalm of trust in God? Complete this sentence: Psalm 23 shows that David trusts God because God _____.
- Psalm 91 also expresses trust in God. What do you learn from this psalm about the writer's relationship with God?
- What is the basis of your trust in God?
- In what area of your life do you find it the most difficult to trust God?
- What truths do you find in Psalms that can build your trust in God?

📧 Postcard

Give God the opportunity to work in your heart through Psalms. If you read a psalm a day, you will read the entire book more than twice each year. As you become familiar with these songs of faith, you will find yourself turning to them when you need to hear God speak to your deepest needs.

PROVERBS

 Snapshot of Proverbs

Thomas has a problem. He worked all summer to earn the money he now holds in his hands. It isn't a lot, a few hundred dollars, but it represents two months of long hours doing odd jobs. Thomas wonders what he should do with the money. Mom and Dad want him to put it into the bank. But his friends urge him to spend it. "After all," they say, "it's your money." Thomas isn't sure what to do. He wishes he were wiser about such things.

Most people would like to have more wisdom—the ability to make good (wise) decisions—in a lot of areas. Many people are smart, but only a few are wise.

Proverbs was written by Solomon, the wisest man who ever lived. In this book he shares his wisdom on such varied topics as money, marriage, family life, discipline, friends, laziness, speech, relationships, temptation, and leadership. Solomon's purpose was "to teach people wisdom and discipline, to help them understand the insights of the wise" (1:2).

Proverbs is a book of answers—answers to our questions about everyday life. As you read, ask God to make the wisdom of Solomon your wisdom too. And ask God to help you begin your steps toward wisdom by trusting him.

PURPOSE:
To teach people how to be understanding, just, and fair in everything they do; to make the simpleminded wise; to warn young people about problems

they will face; to help the wise become good leaders (see 1:2-6). In short, this book helps people apply divine wisdom to daily life and provides them with moral instruction.

AUTHORS:
Solomon wrote most of this book; Agur and Lemuel contributed some of the later sections.

TO WHOM WRITTEN:
Israel and all God's people

DATE WRITTEN:
King Solomon wrote and compiled most of these proverbs early in his reign.

SETTING:
This is a book of wise sayings, a textbook for teaching people how to live a godly life

SPECIAL FEATURE:
The book uses a wide variety of literary forms: poems, brief parables, pointed questions, couplets, antithesis, comparison, and personification.

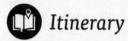 *Itinerary*

Wisdom for Young People (1:1–9:18)

The book of Proverbs is loosely organized into three general areas. The first of these includes lessons in wisdom for young people. Solomon instructs the young people of his day like a father giving advice to his child. The wisdom recorded in these proverbs applies to all of life and includes principles that are helpful to all believers, male and female, young and old. Why not begin the adventure of developing wisdom at the earliest possible time of life?

Wisdom for All People (10:1–24:34)

The second general area has wisdom for people of all ages. Solomon knew the value of wisdom throughout life. He collected wise sayings applicable regardless of age, sex, or position in society. These short, wise sayings give us practical wisdom for daily living. We should study them continually and integrate them into our life.

Wisdom for the Leaders (25:1–31:31)

The last general area features wisdom for leaders. In addition to Solomon's proverbs, Hezekiah's men collected many wise sayings from others. Most of these are widely applicable, but many are directed specifically to the king and those who deal with him. These are particularly useful for leaders or those who aspire to be leaders. They also give strong directions for followers.

 Notebook

WISDOM (1:1-7, 20-33; 2:1–4:27; 8:1–9:12; 10:8, 13, 17, 21, 23; 12:1, 15; 13:1, 18; 14:15, 18; 15:12, 14, 21, 31-32; 16:16, 22; 17:10, 24; 19:25; 21:11, 22; 22:5; 23:12; 24:5-6; 25:12; 28:26; 29:8, 11)
God wants his people to be wise. Two kinds of people portray two contrasting paths of life: the fool is the wicked, stubborn person who hates or ignores God; the wise person seeks to know and love God.

God grants wisdom to those who choose his way. God's Word, the Bible, teaches how to live right, have right relationships, and make right decisions.

- According to 1:7 and 9:10, what did Solomon teach as the key to being wise?
- What will be the results of wisdom in a person's life? (Check 3:13-26.)
- How has knowing God and learning about his Word made you a wiser person?
- In what areas of your life would you like to have more wisdom? Based on your study of Proverbs, how will you find that wisdom?

RELATIONSHIPS (1:8-19; 2:1-22; 3:1-4; 4:14-19; 5:3-23; 6:1-35; 7:6-27; almost every proverb in chapters 10–31 deals in some practical aspect of relationships)
Proverbs gives advice for developing personal relationships with others, including friends, family members, and coworkers. Every relationship should be characterized by love, dedication, and high moral standards.

In relating to others, we need consistency, sensitivity, and discipline to use our God-given wisdom. If we don't treat others according to that wisdom, our relationships will suffer.

- What types of relationships does Proverbs encourage? Discourage?

- Why does the writer devote so much attention to avoiding sexual immorality? What wisdom is given regarding sex outside of marriage?
- What qualities make relationships, including friendships and marriages, deeper and stronger? What ruins such relationships?
- List three important relationships in your life. From what you've read in Proverbs, what should you change in those relationships?

SPEECH (6:12-14; 8:13; 10:11, 19, 32; 11:9, 12-13; 12:6, 13-19, 25; 13:3; 15:1, 4, 23, 28; 16:23-24, 28; 17:9, 14; 18:8; 20:19; 21:23; 24:26; 25:15, 18, 23; 26:20-28; 27:9)
What people say reveals their true attitudes toward others. How they talk reveals what they're really like. A person's speech is a test of how wise that person has become.

To be wise in our speech, we need to use self-control. Our words should be honest and well chosen. We need to remember that what we say affects others.

- When is it most difficult for you to control what you say?
- What circumstances can cause you to lose control of your words? How do you feel after you blow it? How does this usually affect others?
- Proverbs encourages speaking honestly but with self-control. When have you been hurt by someone who did not speak with wisdom? How did it affect your relationship with that person?
- What specific actions can you take to develop honesty and self-control in your speech?

WORK (10:4-5, 26; 12:11, 14, 24, 27; 13:4; 14:23; 15:19; 18:9; 19:15, 24; 20:4, 13; 21:5, 17, 25-26; 22:13, 29; 24:30-34; 28:19)
God controls the final outcome of what people do. Still God expects his people to carry out their work with diligence and discipline, not laziness.

Because God evaluates how we live, we should work purposefully. We must never be lazy or self-satisfied. We don't always have to be the best in comparison to others, but we should always do our best with what God has given us.

- What does Proverbs teach about people who are lazy and unwilling to work?
- What does Proverbs teach about people who are diligent and self-disciplined?
- How does being disciplined help you as a student?
- How does being disciplined help you in your Christian life?
- In what one area do you need to develop this discipline? Write out a specific plan for this development. (Be diligent in carrying it out!)

SUCCESS (10:7; 12:3; 13:5; 16:3; 17:23-24; 19:8; 22:4; 25:27; 26:24-26; 27:2; 28:12-13)

Although people work very hard for money and fame, God considers a good reputation, moral character, and spiritual devotion to him to be the true measures of success.

A successful relationship with God counts for eternity. Everything else is only temporary. Because all our resources, time, and talents come from God, we should do our best to use them wisely.

- According to Proverbs, what is the value of riches? How important is wealth to most people who want to be successful?
- How do your friends measure success? How do you think they will measure success in ten years?
- Do you agree or disagree with your friends' values? Explain.
- How do you think God measures success?

 Postcard

The book of Proverbs is probably the hardest section in the Bible not to apply! Its thirty-one chapters offer a daily dose of wisdom you can spread out over a month. Keep track of proverbs that prove to be true in your life and in your observations.

ECCLESIASTES

 Snapshot of Ecclesiastes

"Party hearty! Do what feels good. Don't worry about tomorrow, because we're all going to die soon anyway."

You probably have heard expressions like that, or even know people who live that way. It's a very popular philosophy, and it's not a new one. In fact, essentially the same message appears in the Bible. Centuries ago King Solomon wrote, "People should eat and drink and enjoy the fruits of their labor, for these are gifts from God" (3:13). Solomon knew what he was talking about. As a very intelligent and wealthy king, he had spent a lifetime experiencing and analyzing everything the world had to offer. Wine, women, song . . . Solomon had done it all. His conclusion? Life is short, boring, and empty, so enjoy pleasure while you can!

"Wait a minute," you might interrupt. "You mean one of the Bible writers says that life is meaningless, so we should live it up?"

That's right. But there's a punch line. Solomon's last word is that to really enjoy life, we need to keep God right at the center of everything. Without God, people merely exist, moving quickly from the excitement of youth to the bitterness of old age. But with God, people can enjoy each moment, relationship, and experience along the way.

Read Ecclesiastes, Solomon's analysis of life . . . and then have a real party!

PURPOSE:

To spare future generations the bitterness of learning through their own experience that life is meaningless apart from God

AUTHOR:

Solomon, although no passages mention him by name

TO WHOM WRITTEN:

Solomon's subjects in particular and all people in general

DATE WRITTEN:

Probably around 935 BC, late in Solomon's life

SETTING:

Solomon looks back on his life, much of which was lived apart from God.

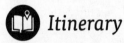 *Itinerary*

Solomon's Personal Experience (1:1–2:26)

Readers of Ecclesiastes accompany one man on a grand experiment with life. The book explains what the man does and what he has concluded about his experiences. The first part of the experiment summarizes Solomon's personal approach to life. He had practically unlimited choices, so he took them all! He has tried every goal and succeeded in every plan. He has gained the whole world but finds himself wondering where he has misplaced his soul.

Solomon's General Observations (3:1–5:20)

The second part of the experiment includes Solomon's general observations. He shows from his own choices that certain paths in life lead to emptiness. No achievement replaces the loss of one's soul.

Solomon's Practical Counsel (6:1–8:17)

In the third part of the experiment, Solomon offers practical counsel. He points toward true purpose in life. Such hard-earned wisdom can spare a person from the emptiness of living without God. Solomon demonstrates that people will not find meaning in life through knowledge, money, pleasure, work, or popularity. True satisfaction comes from knowing that what we are doing is part of God's purpose for our life.

Solomon's Final Conclusion (9:1–12:14)

The last part of Solomon's experiment includes his final conclusion. Few writers have ever written as clear and compelling a summary about the central purpose of life: "Fear God and obey his commands, for this is everyone's duty. God will judge us for everything we do, including every secret thing, whether good or bad" (12:13-14).

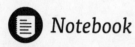 *Notebook*

SEARCHING (1:12–4:8; 6:7-8; 7:15-18; 8:9-15; 9:1-12)

Solomon searched for satisfaction almost as though it were a scientific experiment. In his search he discovered that life without God was meaningless. True happiness does not come from accumulating wealth or attaining honors—people always want more than they can have, and circumstances beyond one's control can snatch away all possessions and achievements.

People are still searching for meaning, enjoyment, fulfillment, and satisfaction. The more they try to get, however, the more they realize how little they really have. No lasting pleasure or happiness is possible without God. Above all else we should strive to know and love God, trusting him for true joy in life.

- How did Solomon search for happiness and satisfaction?
- How do people today search for happiness and satisfaction?
- How do most of your peers at school hope to find satisfaction right now? In the years to come?
- If you were to give a personal testimony of the satisfaction found in Christ, what would you say? To whom would you want to say this?
- How can you share this testimony by example and word with those at school and church who are searching for satisfaction and happiness?

EMPTINESS (1:1–2:25; 3:9–4:8, 13-16; 5:1–6:9; 7:15-18; 8:9-17)

Solomon wrote about how empty it is to pursue life's pleasures instead of a relationship with eternal God. The search for pleasure, wealth, and success ultimately is disappointing. Nothing in the world can satisfy the restless heart.

The cure for emptiness is to focus on God. Develop a fear or reverence for God, and fill your life with serving God and others rather than selfishly chasing after pleasures.

- What does it mean to be "empty" inside?
- What celebrities seem to have all they could want and yet live apparently empty lives (filled with drugs, broken relationships, sexual immorality, etc.)?
- According to the book of Ecclesiastes, what is the answer to the emptiness of life? How does this answer fill the emptiness?
- What choices are you making now to ensure that your life will continue to increase in fulfillment rather than becoming an empty shell? Why should you make these choices when you are young?

WORK (2:4-11, 17-26; 3:1-13; 4:4-8; 5:12-20)
Solomon tried to shake people's confidence in their own efforts, abilities, and wisdom. He did this to direct them to faith in God as the only sound basis for living. Without God, hard work has no lasting reward or benefit.

Work done with the wrong attitude leaves us empty. Work accepted as an assignment from God can be seen as a gift. Examine what you expect from your efforts at school and on the job. God gives you abilities and opportunities to work and to make a contribution with your life.

- What seems to be the attitude most people have toward working?
- How do you feel about the work you have to do, including schoolwork and responsibilities at home? What is your attitude?
- What does the book of Ecclesiastes present as the proper attitude toward work?
- What attitude will be most effective in enabling people to do their work for God? How can you develop this attitude, beginning with the work you have to do this week?

DEATH (2:16; 3:1–4:6; 6:1-12; 7:2-4; 8:7-8; 9:1-10; 11:7–12:8, 13-14)

The certainty of death makes all human achievements futile. God's plan for human destiny goes beyond life and death. The reality of aging and dying reminds us of the end to come, when God will judge each person's life.

Life seems to be long when a person is young, yet the years pass all too quickly. Because life is short, we need wisdom greater than this world can offer. We need the words of God. God's wisdom will spare us the bitterness of ending life without having fulfilled a worthwhile purpose.

- How can death be described to a person who does not know God through Christ?
- How can death be described to a person who is a Christian?
- How do you feel about your own death?
- How does your faith in Christ affect your thoughts and feelings regarding your death?
- How does the knowledge of life after death influence the way you live life before death?

WISDOM (1:12-18; 2:12-16, 26; 4:13-16; 7:1–8:1, 16-17; 9:1, 13-18; 10:2; 12:11-14)

Human wisdom doesn't have all the answers. Knowledge and education have limits. To understand life we need the wisdom that can be found only in God's Word, the Bible.

When we realize that God will evaluate all we do, we should learn to live wisely, remembering that God is with us at each moment. We can have God's wisdom only when we obey him.

- What limits of human wisdom frustrated Solomon?
- How can you tap into God's wisdom when human knowledge and understanding fail you?
- Because God has revealed himself, what can you do to get beyond the limits of human reasoning?

✉ *Postcard*

Notice that Ecclesiastes 3:1-8 talks about "a time" for certain actions. Life offers many opportunities that will be offered repeatedly. These verses, however, point to those special moments that may be unrepeatable. Solomon continually encourages us to live this day fully because tomorrow is not guaranteed. That's why it is so dangerous to put off serving and living for God until tomorrow. What important actions have you been avoiding that should be done today?

SONG OF SONGS

 Snapshot of Song of Songs

Check out the words to the Top 40 songs, and you'll probably find little more than a sensual mix of I've-got-to-have-you-now lyrics. Check out the supermarket tabloids, and you'll find stories of adultery, divorce, and affairs by an assortment of entertainment figures. The message comes through loud and clear: lust is in, love is out; independence is in, marriage is out. In fact, commitment seems to have become a dirty word.

That's not what God had in mind when he created sex and love or when he began marriage. Sex is meant to be an exciting, fulfilling physical union of a man and a woman who are protected by the commitment of marriage—not an act of self-gratification. Love is meant to be a self-giving action, not a self-centered emotion.

Nowhere are the true meanings of love and sex more beautifully portrayed than in the Song of Songs. Here we get an intimate glimpse into the personal relationship between the king (Solomon) and his bride. Love, sex, and marriage are celebrated in the context of living the way God designed us to live.

Don't fall for cultural lies and myths about love. Read Song of Songs and commit yourself to living God's way. The payoff is terrific!

PURPOSE:
To tell of the love between a bridegroom (King Solomon) and his bride, to affirm the sanctity of marriage, and to picture God's love for his people

AUTHOR:
Solomon

TO WHOM WRITTEN:
Israel and all God's people

DATE WRITTEN:
Probably early in Solomon's reign

SETTING:
Israel—the Shulammite woman's garden and the king's palace

KEY PEOPLE:
King Solomon, the Shulammite woman, and the daughters of Jerusalem

SPECIAL FEATURE:
This book has no direct reference to God, but the story has often been seen as an allegory of the relationship between God and his people.

 # Itinerary

Song of Songs reads like the script of a romantic play. The relationship between the leading actors supplies the subject of the drama. Sometimes the main actors are alone on the stage; sometimes they are together. A chorus, the "Young Women of Jerusalem," supplies comments and reactions to the central actors. The script breaks into seven scenes as follows:

The Wedding Day (1:1–2:7)
Scene 1 records the conversation between the bride and groom on their wedding day. They are delighted and overwhelmed to have found each other.

Memories of Courtship (2:8–3:5)
Scene 2 captures the memories, anxieties, and excitement of the couple's courtship.

Memories of Engagement (3:6–5:1)
Scene 3 recounts the couple's thoughts about each other during their engagement.

A Troubling Dream (5:2–6:3)
Scene 4 has the bride alone on the stage with the chorus. She tells about a troubling dream filled with the longing and waiting preceding the wedding.

Praising the Bride's Beauty (6:4–7:9)

Scene 5 places the groom on the stage with the chorus, trying to put into words the beauty of his beloved.

The Bride's Tender Appeal (7:10–8:4)

Scene 6 once again has the bride expressing her delighted impatience in looking forward to married life.

The Power of Love (8:5-14)

Scene 7 includes the thoughts of both the bride and the groom as they express wonder over love and their anticipated life together.

Although this book contains the most explicit statements on sex in the Bible, the writing is intended to honor marriage. The sensuous language in Song of Songs has been criticized through the centuries. Such criticisms usually say more about the critics than the book.

The purity, sacredness, and even playfulness of love represented here are greatly needed in this day of distorted and perverted views of love and marriage. God created sex and intimacy, both of which are holy and good when enjoyed within marriage. A husband and wife honor God when they love and enjoy each other.

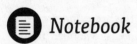 *Notebook*

LOVE (1:2; 2:4; 4:1-15; 8:6-7)

As the beauty and wonder of romance unfolded between Solomon and his bride, the intense power of love affected the two lovers' hearts, minds, and bodies.

Love is a powerful expression of feeling and commitment between two people; it is not to be regarded casually. We should not try to manipulate others into loving us, and love should not be forced.

- Song of Songs presents a very intense human love. How would you describe this love?
- In your marriage, what qualities do you want to be present in the love you will share with your spouse? What qualities do you want your spouse to have?

- What is God's role in the love between a man and a woman?
- What implications does this study have for dating?
- What impact does this study have on the way you view marriage? How could you apply this in the future?

SEX (1:2-4, 8-17; 2:3-6; 4:1-16; 5:2-6, 10-16; 6:4-12; 7:1-13; 8:8-10)

Sex is God's gift to his creatures. God endorses sex. Because sex is given as an ultimate gift for life, however, God says that its expression should be limited to those who are committed to each other in marriage.

God wants sex to be motivated by love and commitment, not lust. God is glorified by sex within a godly marriage—sex that is for mutual pleasure, not selfish enjoyment.

- What is different about Song of Songs' description of sex and sexual desire from the way sex is presented on TV and in the movies?
- How does Solomon feel about his bride? How does she feel about him?
- What is the primary attraction between the couple in this book?
- In reading the Song of Songs, what do you learn about God's design of sexuality for you?
- What biblical principles can serve as your guidelines for sexual decision making?

COMMITMENT (1:15-16; 2:16; 6:3; 8:6-7)

The power of love requires more than feelings to protect it. Sexual expression is such an integral part of a person's selfhood that we need the boundary of marriage to safeguard our love. Marriage is the celebration of a couple's daily commitment to each other.

Romance keeps a marriage interesting, and commitment keeps romance from dwindling away. The decision to commit yourself to your spouse alone begins at the marriage altar and must be maintained day by day. In a world filled with divorce and brokenness, God calls his people to learn to live according to commitment.

- What words in Song of Songs represent commitment?
- Would this commitment best be described as a onetime

commitment, a daily commitment, neither, or a combination of both? Explain.

- What impact does a marriage with strong commitment have on the children in that family? What impact does weak commitment have on them?
- What factors strengthen commitment in marriage? What factors weaken commitment?
- How can you make choices now, in friendship and dating, that will prepare you for a future marriage with a strong commitment? What role does God play in that preparation?

BEAUTY (1:8-10, 15-17; 4:1-7; 5:10-16; 6:4-10; 7:1-9)

The two lovers praised the beauty they saw in each other. The language they used shows the spontaneity and mystery of love. Our praise should not be limited to physical beauty—beautiful personality and moral purity also should be praised.

The love one feels for a husband or wife reveals that person's inner beauty, and those inner qualities keep love alive. Don't look for just physical attractiveness in a spouse. Look for the qualities that don't fade with time—spiritual commitment, integrity, sensitivity, and sincerity. Character lasts much longer than good looks.

- When you think of beauty, what comes to your mind first?
- What's the difference between a person's physical beauty and that person's inner beauty?
- What one person in your life exemplifies true inner beauty? What makes this person so beautiful?
- If you were looking for a husband or wife, what inner qualities would you most want him or her to have? Why are these important to you?
- What inner qualities do you want to bring to a marriage? In what ways can you deepen those qualities in your present relationships?

PROBLEMS (1:6-7; 3:1-4; 5:2-7; 8:1-3, 8-12)

Over time, feelings of loneliness, indifference, and isolation came between Solomon and his bride. During those times love grew cold, and barriers arose.

Through careful communication, lovers can be reconciled, commitment can be renewed, and romance can be refreshed. When conflict arises, it's best to take care of the problem while it is still small.

- Why do all human relationships include conflict?
- What principles do you find in Song of Songs that can be applied to working through difficult problems in relationships?
- Where are your areas of interpersonal conflict? What are you doing in response to the problems you are facing now?
- What can you do to apply the principles of Song of Songs to the conflicts you are facing in your relationships?

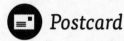 *Postcard*

As you read Song of Songs, remember that you have been designed by God and are loved by him. Commit yourself to seeing life, sex, and marriage from God's point of view.

ISAIAH

Snapshot of Isaiah

Slowly, on shaky legs, Matt walked to the front of the room, the fluttering in his stomach growing with every step. As he turned to face the class, he was sure everyone could hear the relentless pounding of his heart. Wiping his sweat-moistened palms on his pants, he pulled out his note cards and began to speak.

Stage fright. We know it all too well. According to many studies, the greatest fear most people have is doing what Matt did—giving a speech. You're in front of everyone, exposed and vulnerable—the pressure can be incredible.

If you think that's tough, imagine being a prophet. Not only would you have to speak in public, but usually the messages you gave would not be what people wanted to hear. As a prophet you would have to speak about sin, judgment, and necessary life changes. Often you would have to confront royalty, kings and queens who could pronounce the death sentence on a whim. Sometimes, to really make a point, you would have to act out your messages. That wouldn't be too enjoyable either. But true prophets spoke out for God regardless of how they felt.

Isaiah was one of the greatest prophets who ever lived, and the book of Isaiah contains his messages. This book shows Isaiah in action as he stays close to God and speaks to the people. That takes courage! As you read, listen to God's word for you, and determine to be a person of courage, too, faithfully taking God's message wherever he sends you.

PURPOSE:
To call the nation of Judah back to God and to tell of God's salvation through the Messiah

AUTHOR:
The prophet Isaiah, son of Amoz

TO WHOM WRITTEN:
Judah, Israel, the surrounding pagan nations, and God's people everywhere

DATE WRITTEN:
The events of chapters 1–39 occur during Isaiah's ministry, so they were probably written about 700 BC. Chapters 40–66, however, may have been written near the end of Isaiah's life, about 681 BC.

SETTING:
Isaiah is speaking and writing mainly in Jerusalem.

KEY PEOPLE:
Isaiah; his two sons, Shear-jashub and Maher-shalal-hash-baz

SPECIAL FEATURES:
The book of Isaiah contains both prose and poetry and uses personification (attributing personal qualities to divine beings or inanimate objects). Also, many of the prophecies foretell both a soon-to-occur event and a distant, future event at the same time.

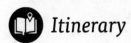 Itinerary

The book of Isaiah has two very distinct parts. So different in theme from each other are these two sections, some have suggested they must have been written by two people. But bad news and good news can be delivered by the same messenger. In fact, the two-author explanation for the contrasting themes in Isaiah creates more problems than it solves. It is a great tribute to the inspiration of the Holy Spirit and the importance of God's crucial two-part message for it to have been delivered through one well-equipped messenger.

Words of Judgment (1:1–39:8)
Part 1 of Isaiah presents the message of judgment for sin. Isaiah brings the message of judgment to Judah, Israel, and the surrounding pagan nations. The people of Judah have a form of godliness, but in their hearts they are corrupt. Isaiah's warnings are intended

to purify the people by helping them understand God's true nature and message. The people ignore the repeated warnings that Isaiah brings, however. Today we are just as capable of ignoring God's Word and repeating the same kinds of errors.

Words of Comfort (40:1–66:24)
Part 2 of Isaiah presents forgiveness, comfort, and hope. This message of hope looks forward to the coming of the Messiah. The book of Isaiah contains more about the Messiah than any other Old Testament book. It describes the Messiah as both a suffering servant and a sovereign Lord. This dual role of the Messiah would not be understood clearly until New Testament times. The prophet Isaiah foretells the eternal work of Jesus, the Messiah. Through him God freely offers forgiveness to all who turn to him in faith. This is God's message of comfort to us as well, because those who heed it find eternal peace and fellowship with him.

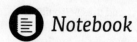 *Notebook*

HOLINESS (1:4; 5:16, 24; 6:1-8; 8:14; 10:17, 20; 12:6; 17:7; 29:23; 30:11-17; 31:1; 37:23; 41:14, 16, 20; 43:3, 14-28; 45:11; 47:4; 49:7; 55:5; 57:15; 60:9-14; 63:10-18)
God is highly exalted above all his creatures. His moral perfection contrasts with evil people and nations. Because God is perfect and sinless, he is in perfect control of his power, judgment, love, and mercy. His holy nature is the yardstick for morality.

Because God alone is without sin, he alone can help us with our sin. It is only right that we regard him as supreme in power and moral perfection. We must never treat God as common or ordinary. He—and only he—deserves our devotion.

- God's holiness reveals how much he is beyond human beings. How do you feel when you consider his holiness?
- How did Isaiah respond to God's holiness (6:1-8)?
- What did God do for Isaiah because of his reaction?
- What do you learn about God when you consider both his holiness and his personal love for you? How do you feel? How will you respond? (Check how Isaiah responded.)

PUNISHMENT (1:24-25; 3:1–4:1; 5:1-30; 7:17-25; 8:5-8; 10:5-34; 14:24-32; 18:1-7; 28:23-29; 29:1-8; 31:1-3; 32:9-14; 37:6-35; 40:2; 42:24; 51:17)

Because God is holy, he requires his people to treat others justly. He promised to punish Israel, Judah, and other nations for faithless immorality and idolatry. Their faith had degenerated into national pride and empty religious rituals.

We must trust in God alone and obey his commands. We cannot ignore his call to justice nor give in to selfishness. If we harden our heart against his message, we surely will be punished.

- Whom does God punish?
- If God forgives us, can we avoid all the consequences of our sins? Explain your answer, giving biblical support.
- How would you answer this question from a Christian friend: "What difference does it make whether or not I sin?"
- God does not want you to obey him just to avoid punishment. What is the heart motivation God wants you to have as you obey? Give yourself a heart checkup. How are you doing?

SALVATION/MESSIAH (1:16-20; 7:9; 28:16; 30:15; 40:2; 42:1-7, 10-12; 43:25; 44:22; 45:6, 22-24; 49:1-9; 50:4-11; 51:21-22; 52:13–53:12)

God promised to send a Savior—he knew that without one everyone would stand condemned. Christ's perfect sacrifice, his servant life, and his coming Kingdom were foretold by Isaiah. Through Christ the promises of redemption and restoration are fulfilled.

Christ died to save his people from sin. Salvation comes only through Christ. Those who trust him fully experience the forgiveness and the wholeness he brings as their Prince of Peace.

- What do 9:6 and chapter 53 reveal about Christ?
- The Messiah was sent by God to save those who trusted him for their deliverance. How did you come to know and trust Christ?
- What difference does it make in your daily life that Christ is your Savior?
- What areas of your life need recommitting to Christ? Open yourself up to him in trust. Christ came to deliver you and will not reject you if you seek him as Lord.

HOPE (8:11-22; 9:1-7; 10:20-27; 11:1–12:6; 25:1–26:21; 31:5-7; 37:21-38; 40:1, 31; 42:4; 49:23; 51:3, 7; 57:18; 61:2; 66:13)

God promises comfort, deliverance, and restoration in his future Kingdom. The Messiah will rule over his faithful followers in the age to come. Hope is possible because Christ is coming.

We can be hopeful because God has compassion for those who repent. No matter how bleak the current situation or how evil the world, we must continue to be God's faithful people who hope for his return.

- In the latter part of the book, Isaiah begins to focus on the future, when Christ will reign in his full glory. What seems to be Isaiah's attitude about this future? How did it affect his present?
- When in your life did you almost lose all hope? What enabled you not to give up?
- What can we expect God to provide in the future? How does this help you keep going even when everything feels hopeless?
- How would you live differently if there were no hope?

✉ Postcard

The Dead Sea Scrolls contain at least one complete copy of Isaiah that has been dated from earlier than the time of Jesus. The prophecies of that Old Testament prophet regarding Jesus were not invented by Christians; they were included by Isaiah, from God. What does it mean to you that Jesus is both your promised Lord and suffering Savior?

JEREMIAH

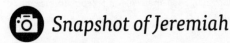 *Snapshot of Jeremiah*

"You big crybaby. Stop your blubbering!"

Tears can seem embarrassing and awkward—even a sign of weakness. For children tears come easily over a broken toy, a skinned knee, and other assorted real or imagined hurts. As the years pass, however, children learn to hide their feelings, especially sadness. Often they try to look tough or put on a happy face. That's a shame, really, because tears are important. In fact, tears can reveal a lot about people, letting others see what affects them deeply, what they care about . . . what breaks their hearts.

Jeremiah is called the weeping prophet. In his books (Jeremiah and Lamentations) it seems as though all he did was cry. But Jeremiah's tears did not stem from immaturity, self-centeredness, or weakness. Jeremiah wept because he loved deeply and because he knew the truth: that his beloved nation was in trouble and that God would punish it. Jeremiah tried to tell the people, but they wouldn't listen. So he cried.

What brings tears to your eyes? About what do you cry? We need to be more like Jeremiah, filled with compassion and concern. We need to cry out to God and minister to others with broken and loving hearts.

PURPOSE:
To urge God's people to turn from their sins and back to God

AUTHOR:
Jeremiah

TO WHOM WRITTEN:
Judah (the southern kingdom), specifically the capital city, Jerusalem, and God's people everywhere

DATE WRITTEN:
During Jeremiah's ministry, approximately 627–586 BC

SETTING:
Jeremiah ministers during the reigns of Judah's last five kings—Josiah, Jehoahaz, Jehoiakim, Jehoiachin (Coniah), and Zedekiah. The nation is sliding quickly toward destruction and is eventually conquered by Babylon in 586 BC (see 2 Kings 21–25). The prophet Zephaniah preceded Jeremiah; Habakkuk is Jeremiah's contemporary.

KEY PEOPLE:
Judah's kings (listed above), Baruch, Ebed-melech, King Nebuchadnezzar, the Recabites

KEY PLACES:
Anathoth, Jerusalem, Ramah, Egypt

SPECIAL FEATURES:
The book of Jeremiah is a combination of history, poetry, and biography. Jeremiah often used symbolism to communicate his message.

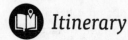 *Itinerary*

By human standards the book of Jeremiah tells the story of a failure. By God's standards Jeremiah was a shining success. Regardless of opposition and personal cost, this prophet courageously and faithfully proclaimed the word of God. He was obedient to his calling.

God's Judgment on Judah (1:1–45:5)
The book begins with God's call of Jeremiah (1:1-19). These verses capture the way in which God knows us, cares for us, and calls us into service in the world.

The next thirty-eight chapters are prophecies about Israel (God's people as a whole) and Judah (the southern kingdom). The basic theme of Jeremiah's message is simple: Repent and turn to God, or he will punish you. Because the people rejected this warning, Jeremiah then began predicting the destruction of Jerusalem. This terrible event and its immediate results are described in chapters 39:1–45:5.

God's Judgment on the Nations (46:1–52:34)
The book of Jeremiah concludes with prophecies concerning a variety of nations, similar to the prophecies against Judah, Jeremiah's own people. Jeremiah's words describe God's righteous anger and judgment against the nations. People as well as nations who refuse to confess and repent of their sins bring God's judgment upon themselves.

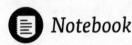 Notebook

SIN (2:1-13, 23-37; 5:1-6; 7:16-34; 11:1-17; 17:1-4; 18:1-17; 23:9-40)
King Josiah's reformation failed because the people's repentance was shallow. They continued in their sin. All the leaders rejected God's law and will for the people. Jeremiah listed all their sins, predicted God's judgment, and begged the people to repent.

Judah's deterioration and disaster came from the nation's callous disregard and disobedience of God. When we ignore our sin and refuse to listen to God's warnings, we invite disaster. Our heart must remain "tuned in" to his will for us.

- What were the people's sins during the reign of King Josiah (3:6-10)? You may want to read 2 Kings 22:1–23:30 in order to review Josiah's reign.
- How does God expect you to respond when you discover a sin in your life?
- What difference does it make whether or not you deal with your sin?
- In what areas of your life do you think God wants you to make changes to avoid sin or to stop sinning? Based on this study, what will you do to respond to his will in these areas?

PUNISHMENT (4:3-18; 9:3-26; 12:14-17; 15:1-9; 16:5-13; 19:1-15; 24:8-10; 25:1-38; 39:1-10; 44:1-30; 46:1–51:14)
Because of sin Jerusalem was destroyed, the Temple was ruined, and the people were carried off to Babylon. The people were responsible

for their destruction and captivity because they refused to listen to God's message.

Unconfessed sin brings God's full punishment. It is useless to blame anyone else for our sins. We must answer to God for how we live.

- How did God punish Israel and Judah?
- How do you feel about these punishments? Do they seem harsh or lenient to you? Explain.
- What provision does God supply so that you can be forgiven of your sins?
- What principles can you see in Jeremiah that you can use as reasons for why you should not sin against God?

LORD OF ALL (5:22, 24; 7:1-15; 10:12-16; 14:22; 17:5-10; 18:5-10; 25:15-38; 27:5-8; 31:1-3; 42:1-22; 51:15-19)

God is the righteous Creator. He is accountable to no one. He wisely and lovingly directs all creation to fulfill his plans, and he brings events to pass according to his timetable. He is Lord over all the world.

Because of God's majestic power and love, our only duty is to submit to his authority. By following his plans, we can enjoy a loving relationship with God and serve him with our whole heart.

- What evidence do you see in chapters 46–52 that God is indeed the Lord of all?
- What types of attitudes and actions in your life currently reflect God's lordship over you?
- What attitudes and actions do you need to change or adjust to comply with his lordship?
- During the next two weeks, in what two ways will you respond to God's lordship? Be specific, and hold yourself accountable for doing it.

NEW HEARTS (24:7; 29:4-14; 32:36-42)

Jeremiah predicted that after the destruction of the nation, God would send a new Shepherd, the Messiah. The Messiah would lead the Israelites into a new future, a new covenant, and a new day of hope. He would accomplish this by changing their sinful hearts into hearts that loved God.

God still restores his people by renewing their hearts. His love can transform the problems created by sin. We can have hope for a new heart by loving God, trusting Christ to save us, and repenting. Rejoice in the new heart that is God's gift in Christ.

- What does the text mean when it speaks of providing a new heart?
- How does a person receive a new heart when he or she becomes a disciple of Christ?
- How does becoming a Christian involve a change in behavior? In the motivation for behavior? In the person's view of God?
- In what ways are you living out your new heart? How can this be improved?

FAITHFUL SERVICE (1:1-10; 8:18–9:2; 10:23-25; 12:1-6; 14:11-22; 15:10-21; 16:19-21; 17:14-18; 20:7-18; 26:1-24; 37:11-21; 38:1-28; 40:1-6; 42:1-6; 43:1-7)

Jeremiah served God faithfully for forty years. During that time the people ignored, rejected, and persecuted him. Jeremiah's preaching was unsuccessful by human standards, yet he did not fail. He remained faithful to God.

People's acceptance or rejection of us is not the measure of our success. God's approval alone should be our standard for service. We must bring God's message to others even when we are rejected. We must do God's work even if it means suffering. As Jeremiah shows, being faithful is not always easy.

- What do you think Jeremiah must have felt as he brought these judgments to the people? (Begin with how he felt about God's calling him in chapter 1.)
- What do you think kept Jeremiah going through all of his difficult experiences and encounters with people who opposed him?
- When does it seem difficult for you to continue to serve God faithfully (for example, when others reject you, when it feels like God is distant, etc.)?
- How could 1:4-8 provide you with confidence that God can use you even when you feel useless? When you face rejection? When it seems too difficult to keep going?

- What can you do to be sure that you will not let go of this confidence? How can you help young Christian friends develop this same confidence?

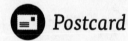 Postcard

Fortunately, Jeremiah only had to experience his trials one day at a time. His life reminds us that there will be suffering and difficulty for anyone who lives for God. God preserved Jeremiah; God can preserve you. To what degree do you live according to God's promise? "I will be with you and will protect you" (1:8).

LAMENTATIONS

 Snapshot of Lamentations

After Susan broke up with Brad, depression filled his sad eyes for weeks.

Tears streamed down Pam's face as she gave a last hug to her best friend. She stood waving good-bye as the moving van pulled out of the driveway.

The night Chris lost the election, he cried himself to sleep.

As the final seconds of the state tournament ticked away, the cheerleaders wept uncontrollably.

What breaks your heart? Losing? Saying good-bye? Being dumped or ignored? These are emotional experiences worthy of tears. But other situations should tug at our feelings too: injustice, poverty, war, and famine, to name just a few. And what about the fact that people who don't know Christ are lost and bound for destruction?

The things that make someone weep say a lot about that person. They show whether he or she is self-centered or God-centered. The book of Lamentations reveals what made Jeremiah sorrowful. As a prophet and one of God's choice servants, he stands alone in the depths of his emotions, his care for the people, his love for the nation, and his devotion to God.

Read Lamentations, and discover what it was that broke Jeremiah's (and God's) heart. As you do so, begin to see your world in a new light, through tears. Then determine to do something about it—for God.

PURPOSE:
To teach people that to disobey God is to invite disaster and to show that God suffers when his people suffer

AUTHOR:
Jeremiah

TO WHOM WRITTEN:
The nation of Judah and believers everywhere

DATE WRITTEN:
Soon after the fall of Jerusalem in 586 BC

SETTING:
Jerusalem has been destroyed by Babylon and its people killed, tortured, or taken captive.

KEY PEOPLE:
Jeremiah, the people of Jerusalem

KEY PLACE:
Jerusalem

SPECIAL FEATURES:
Three strands of Hebrew thought meet in Lamentations—prophecy, ritual, and wisdom. Lamentations is written in the rhythm and style of ancient Jewish funeral songs or chants. It contains five poems corresponding to the five chapters.

 Itinerary

With words filled with deep sadness, Jeremiah weeps over the ruins of the once great city of Jerusalem. Her shattered walls and empty streets represent the total desolation of the nation called "God's people." Each of the five sorrowful songs of Jeremiah that make up this book has a distinct theme.

Jeremiah Mourns for Jerusalem (1:1-22)
The first song expresses the depth of Jeremiah's grief over Jerusalem and her scattered population. The few people that are left have nothing. Past glories are only a faint memory.

God's Anger at Sin (2:1-22)
The second song reviews the reason for the disaster. God has poured out his long-overdue punishment on the people.

Hope in the Midst of Affliction (3:1-66)

The middle song of the book offers a distinct note of hope in the darkness. God's compassion is ever present. His faithfulness is great. Jeremiah realizes that only the Lord's mercy has prevented total annihilation.

God's Anger Is Satisfied (4:1-22)

The fourth song affirms the limits of God's punishment. God's anger has been satisfied. A day of restoration will come.

Jeremiah Pleads for Restoration (5:1-22)

The last song is Jeremiah's prayer for the renewal and forgiveness of the people.

The words and tone of this book show us the serious consequences of sin and how we can still have hope while experiencing great tragedy because God is able to turn even the worst situation into good. We see the timeless importance of prayer and confession of sin. We will face tragedy in life, but even then we can have hope in God.

 Notebook

DESTRUCTION OF JERUSALEM (1:1-2:22; 4:1-22)

Lamentations is a sad funeral song for Jerusalem, the great capital city of the Jews. The Temple had been destroyed, the king was gone, and the people were exiled. God had warned the nation that he would destroy it if the people abandoned him. After experiencing God's punishment, the people realized their condition and confessed their sin.

God's warnings will be fulfilled. He will do what he promises, and his punishment for sin is certain. Only if we confess and renounce our sin will he deliver us. How much better to do so before his warnings are fulfilled.

- What feelings does Jeremiah express over the devastation of Jerusalem and the Jews?
- Jeremiah had predicted this destruction and the Exile. So why would seeing his prophecy fulfilled be especially painful?

- What results of sin in your world cause you to feel sad?
- What can you do to help others see the destruction that comes from sin? How can you help them avoid these results?

SIN'S CONSEQUENCES (1:5, 8-11, 18-20; 2:1-8, 17; 4:1-22; 5:1-14)

God was angry at the prolonged rebellion of his people. Sin had caused their misery and had led to destruction. The destruction of the nation shows the emptiness of human glory and pride.

To continue to rebel against God invites disaster. We should never trust our own leadership, resources, intelligence, or power more than God. If we do, we will suffer painful consequences.

- What specific sins of the people led to their exile? What had they put in place of God as most important in their lives?
- What things or relationships might threaten to replace God as most important in your life?
- When you placed something or someone before the Lord, what were the consequences? What did you learn from that experience?
- What are you doing right now to make sure that God remains first in your life?

GOD'S MERCY (1:20; 3:21-33, 55-59; 4:22; 5:1-22)

God's loving compassion was at work even when the Israelites were suffering under their Babylonian conquerors. Although the people had been unfaithful to God, he was faithful to them. God used the people's suffering to bring them back to him.

God will always be faithful to his people. His mercy is evident even during suffering. At those times we must pray for forgiveness and then turn to God for deliverance. He always hears our cries of repentance.

- What evidence do you find that God had not abandoned the Jews, even in their slavery?
- What should be your attitude toward God when you suffer the consequences of a sinful choice?
- How have you needed God's mercy in your life? In what ways has he proven faithful?

- How does God want you to respond to his mercy?

HOPE (1:21; 3:21-33, 55-59; 4:22; 5:19-22)

God's mercy in sparing some of the people offered hope for better days. Eventually they would be restored to a close relationship with God.

Only God can deliver us from sin. Without him there is no comfort or hope for the future. Christ's death for us and his promise to return give us bright hope for tomorrow.

- God provided hope during punishment. What do you learn about God's character from his sparing the faithful group?
- How would you encourage a suffering friend to find hope in God?
- What could you tell a non-Christian friend regarding the need to place ultimate hope in Christ? What would it mean for that friend to do so?
- What difference does it make in your life that you can place your hope in God? How will that affect your future choices? The choices you make this week?

📧 *Postcard*

Lamentations provides an example of ruthless self-examination. It may be painful, but take time to lay open your life before God with a prayer for understanding your sins and errors and with a spirit of confession and repentance.

EZEKIEL

Snapshot of Ezekiel

"Don't worry," Danny chided his friends. "I can get away with anything. I'm my father's favorite." Danny's dad had gone out of town, leaving his new sports car in the garage. Danny was allowed to drive the family station wagon, but not the sports car. "Come on, you guys," he continued, "Dad will never even know."

The drive to the movie was great. Girls honked and guys stared. After the movie they headed to the car. It was late, and the parking lot was no longer full. "Danny! Danny!" one of his friends suddenly yelled when he reached the car. "It's gone!" Wires dangled where the stereo used to be.

"Your father will kill us!" another friend said.

Danny smiled weakly. "No sweat!"

Israel reacted like Danny. They thought they could get away with anything. The book of Ezekiel was written to Jews who were captives in Babylon. They were "God's favorites." Surely Jerusalem (their capital) would not be harmed, and they would return home very soon. Ezekiel corrected their thinking: they were captives in Babylon because they had disobeyed God. Though they were his chosen people, God could not overlook sin.

The message of Ezekiel reminds us that no one can sin without punishment. Just as God loves us, he also loves justice.

As you read Ezekiel, stand in awe of the God who judges all sin. Then thank him for providing a way (through Jesus) to escape the judgment that we all deserve for our sins.

PURPOSE:
To announce God's judgment and to foretell the eventual salvation of God's people

AUTHOR:
Ezekiel—the son of Buzi, a Zadokite priest

TO WHOM WRITTEN:
The Jews in captivity in Babylon and God's people everywhere

DATE WRITTEN:
Approximately 571 BC

SETTING:
While Jeremiah ministers to the people still in Judah, Ezekiel prophesies to those already exiled in Babylon after the defeat of Jehoiachin. He was among the captives taken there in 597 BC.

KEY PEOPLE:
Ezekiel, Israel's leaders, Ezekiel's wife, Nebuchadnezzar, "the prince"

KEY PLACES:
Jerusalem, Babylon, Egypt

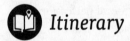 *Itinerary*

Messages of Doom (1:1–24:27)
The book of Ezekiel records the prophet Ezekiel's life and ministry. Following his call as a prophet and commissioning as a "watchman for Israel" (1:1–3:27), Ezekiel immediately begins to preach and demonstrate God's truth. Among his immediate audience are thousands of Jews who have already been deported to Babylon. They vainly hope that God will preserve their homeland.

Ezekiel's message focuses on bad news for the exiles. He predicts the approaching siege and destruction of Jerusalem (4:1–24:27). Ezekiel warns the Jews that punishment is certain because of their sins and that God is purifying his people. God will always punish sin, whether we believe it or not.

Messages against Foreign Nations (25:1–32:32)
In the next section, Ezekiel also condemns the sinful actions of seven surrounding nations. The people in these nations are wrongly concluding that God is obviously too weak to defend his people and the city of Jerusalem. God points out to them through Ezekiel

that the Promised Land was overrun because of sin, not because of God's weakness. These pagan nations would face a similar fate and learn that God is all-powerful. Those who dare to mock God today will also face a terrible fate.

Messages of Hope (33:1–48:35)
After the fall of Jerusalem, Ezekiel delivers messages of future restoration and hope for the people. God is holy, but Jerusalem and the Temple have become defiled. The nation of Israel has to be cleansed through seventy years of captivity. This book gives a vivid picture of the unchangeable holiness of God. We, too, must gain a vision of the glory of God, a fresh sense of his greatness, as we face the struggles of daily life.

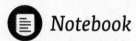 *Notebook*

GOD'S HOLINESS (1:4–3:15; 5:11-13; 8:1–10:22; 18:1-32; 22:17-22; 28:25-26; 38:17-23; 39:7, 21-29; 43:1-12; 44:1-23)
Ezekiel wrote of his vision revealing God's moral perfection. God was spiritually and morally superior to Israel's corrupt and compromising society. Ezekiel also wrote to let the people know that God was present with them in Babylon, not just in Jerusalem.

Because God is morally perfect, he can help us live above our tendency to compromise. He can give us the power to overcome sin and to reflect his holiness. Moral purity is an important part of Christian discipleship.

- What key visions did God give to Ezekiel? How did Ezekiel respond to these visions?
- What did these visions reveal about God?
- Why were the messages of these visions so important for the people during their captivity?
- Why is moral purity important for any person who wants to glorify God?

SIN (2:3-5; 4:1–7:27; 8:5–9:10; 11:1–18:32; 20:1–23:49; 36:22-32)
The people of Israel sinned, so God punished them. God used the fall of Jerusalem and the Babylonian exile to correct the rebels and

draw them back from their sinful way of life. Ezekiel warned that the nation was responsible for its sin, and each individual was also accountable to God.

We cannot excuse ourselves from our responsibilities before God. We are accountable to him. Rather than avoid God, we must recognize sin for what it is—rebellion against God—and choose to follow him instead.

- What sins had the people committed?
- What was God's purpose for punishing the people as he did?
- How did God want individuals to respond to his warnings and punishments? How did he want the nation to respond?
- How has God specifically dealt with sin in your life? How have you responded?

RESTORATION (16:53-63; 17:22-24; 29:8-16; 33:10-20; 36:1-38; 37:1-28)
Ezekiel consoled the people by telling them that a day would come when God would restore those who would turn away from sin. God would be their King and Shepherd. He would give his people a new heart to worship him and establish a new government and a new Temple.

Knowing that they will eventually be rescued and restored should encourage believers during difficult times. But we must be faithful to God because we love him, not for what he can do for us. Our faith must be in him, not in possible future benefits.

- What qualities of God do you see revealed in his promise of restoration?
- Suppose you had a friend who was a Christian yet had chosen to be deeply involved in a continuous habit of sin. What would you tell this friend about God's restoration as an encouragement to turn from sin and toward God?
- In what ways can you continue to seek and experience God's restoration on a daily basis?

LEADERS (9:1-11; 11:1-13; 13:1–14:11; 22:1-31; 34:1-31)
Ezekiel condemned the unfaithful priests and leaders ("shepherds") who were leading the people astray. By contrast, Ezekiel was a

caring shepherd and a watchful sentry as he warned the people about their sin.

Jesus is our perfect leader. If we truly want him to lead us, our devotion must involve more than talk. If we are given the responsibility of leading others, we must take care of them even if that means sacrificing personal pleasure, happiness, time, or money. We are responsible to God for witnessing to and teaching those we lead.

- Contrast Ezekiel as a man of God and leader of the people with the Hebrew priests and leaders who led them away from God.
- What qualities does Jesus have that make him the greatest of all leaders? Which of these qualities did Ezekiel have?
- Based on this study, what are the most important qualities of a godly leader? Why?
- Like Ezekiel, we are to reflect godly qualities. We have Jesus' perfect example as well as the example of people like Ezekiel. If someone were to examine your life, what would that person see that reflects the qualities of Jesus?
- Complete this sentence: In order to be the most effective I can be in leading others to God, I want to grow more like Jesus in the area of _____. Commit to God the choice you intend to make in order to develop in this area.

WORSHIP (1:4-28; 40:1–48:35)

An angel gave Ezekiel a detailed vision of the Temple. God's holy presence had left Israel and the Temple because of sin. This ideal Temple pictures the return of God's presence when God will cleanse his people and restore true worship.

All of God's promises will be fulfilled under the rule of the Messiah. Faithful followers will be brought back to perfect fellowship with God and with one another. To prepare for this, we must focus on God through regular worship, learning about God's holiness, and making needed changes in our life.

- What was the role of the Temple in Hebrew worship during Ezekiel's lifetime?
- How did you worship God during the past week (place, program, attitudes, thoughts, feelings, fellow worshipers, etc.)?

- How would you evaluate your worship of God in the past week (value, importance, strengths and weaknesses)? What do you think you should change?

 Postcard

God instructed Ezekiel to begin his work by letting God's words "sink deep into your own heart first" (3:10). Make sure that your own efforts to speak for God and about God to others are rooted in your experience of listening and obeying God yourself.

DANIEL

 Snapshot of Daniel

Courage is . . . risking injury to help a friend . . . doing what is right against all odds . . . standing for the truth despite the consequences . . . living for God no matter what.

Daniel had courage. Living in a foreign land, he stood for what he believed and did what was right despite incredible pressure from society, peers, and the government. And courage was Daniel's trademark throughout his life, through the reigns of four kings. He boldly interpreted dreams, rejected royal food and drink, and publicly lived his faith. Daniel was a man of great courage and faith in God.

God still wants men and women of courage and faith. What kinds of risks do you face? What kinds of pressures do you feel to conform or to turn away from God?

As you read the book of Daniel, marvel at the man who refused to give in or give up. Ask God to give you the courage to live out your faith, just as Daniel did, as you develop a stronger relationship with "the greatest of gods, the Lord over kings" (2:47).

PURPOSE:

To give a historical account of the faithful Jews who lived in captivity and to show how God is in control of heaven and earth, directing the forces of nature, the destiny of nations, and the care of his people

AUTHOR:

Daniel

TO WHOM WRITTEN:
The other captives in Babylon and God's people everywhere

DATE WRITTEN:
Approximately 535 BC, recording events that occurred from about 605 to 535 BC

SETTING:
Daniel was taken captive and deported to Babylon by Nebuchadnezzar in 605 BC. There he will serve in the government for about sixty years during the reigns of Nebuchadnezzar, Belshazzar, Darius, and Cyrus.

KEY PEOPLE:
Daniel, Nebuchadnezzar, Shadrach, Meshach, Abednego, Belshazzar, Darius

KEY PLACES:
Nebuchadnezzar's palace, the fiery furnace, Belshazzar's banquet, the den of lions

SPECIAL FEATURE:
Daniel's apocalyptic visions (chapters 7–12) give a glimpse of God's plan for the ages, including a direct prediction of the Messiah.

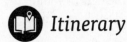 *Itinerary*

Daniel's Life (1:1-6:28)
The book of Daniel has two major sections. The first section emphasizes Daniel's life in a foreign land. Daniel and his three friends choose not to eat the king's food. Although they are faithful servants, they do not bow down to the king's image even under penalty of death. Daniel continues to pray even though he knows he might be noticed and sentenced to death. Daniel and his friends are inspiring examples of how to live a godly life in a sinful world. When we face trials, we can expect God to be with us through them. We can trust God to give us similar courage to remain faithful under pressure.

Daniel's Visions (7:1-12:13)
The second major section in Daniel records the prophetic visions that God gives to Daniel. These visions offer the Jewish captives added confidence that God is in control of history. They are to wait patiently in faith and not worship the gods of Babylon or accept that society's way of life. God still rules over human activities, and evil will be overcome. So we should wait patiently and

not give in to the temptations and pressures of the sinful ways of life around us.

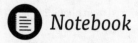 *Notebook*

GOD'S CONTROL (2:24–5:31; 6:16-28; 7:1-28; 12:1-13)
God is all-knowing, and he is in charge of world events. God overrules and removes rebellious leaders who defy him. God will overcome evil; no one will escape. He will, however, deliver the faithful who follow him.

Although nations compete for world control now, one day Christ will rule. Our future is sure if our faith is secure in him. We must have courage and put our faith in God, who controls everything. Our role is to be faithful to Christ.

- Compare the way Nebuchadnezzar responded to God's sovereign control and the way Daniel, Shadrach, Meshach, and Abednego responded.
- What differences can you see between the lives of young people who submit to God's control and the lives of those who refuse to acknowledge him?
- What will be the final results in the lives of those who refuse to submit to God's control?
- Why do you think so many people choose not to submit to God?
- In what one specific area do you need to submit to God's control? What can you do to submit this area to him daily?

PURPOSE IN LIFE (1:1–2:28; 3:1-30; 6:1-28)
Daniel and his three friends are examples of dedication and commitment. These three young men, still in their teens at the time of captivity, determined to serve God regardless of the consequences. They did not give in to pressures from an ungodly society, because they had a clear purpose in life: to glorify God.

Trusting and obeying God should be the focus of our life. This will give us direction and peace in any situation. And we should disobey anyone who asks us to disobey God. Young people who make this type of commitment can make a tremendous impact on their world.

- If you could interview Daniel, how do you think he would respond to this question: "What is your purpose in life?"
- How do you think most of the kids in your school would answer that same question?
- If someone were to spend a week with you, following you around, listening to your conversations, and observing your behavior, what would that person identify as your priorities in life? Your purpose?
- Considering your response to the last question, what adjustments should you make based on the purpose that you want to have for your life?
- Write a short statement of your life's purpose. Keep this in a place where it will remind you as you make your daily choices.

PERSEVERANCE (1:8-21; 2:24-28; 3:1-30; 6:1-28; 9:3-19; 12:1-13)

Daniel served for seventy years in a foreign land that was hostile to God, yet he did not compromise his faith in God. He was truthful, persistent in prayer, and humble.

In order to fulfill your life's purpose, you need staying power. Don't let your Christian values and commitments slip away just because you are surrounded by others who are not Christ's followers. Be relentless in your prayers, stay firm in your integrity, and be content to serve God wherever he puts you.

- What do you think Daniel might have been feeling in each of these situations: when he chose not to eat the king's food; when he interpreted the king's dreams; when he was thrown into the lions' den?
- What kept Daniel from giving in or giving up?
- When do you find it most difficult to obey God and keep your commitment to Christ strong?
- What keeps you from giving up?

GOD'S FAITHFULNESS (1:17-21; 2:24-28; 3:19-30; 6:16-28; 9:3-19; 12:1-13)

God was faithful in Daniel's life, delivering him from prison, from a den of lions, and from enemies. God cares for his people and deals patiently with them.

We can trust God to take us through any trial because he promises to be with us. God has been faithful to us, so we should remain faithful to him.

- At what important time in your life did you experience God's faithfulness? How did this affect your relationship with God?
- In what ways can thinking about God's faithfulness to you strengthen your faith?
- Complete this sentence with as many statements as you can from your understanding of God in Scripture, especially in Daniel: I can be confident of God's faithfulness in my life because _____.

 ## Postcard

Daniel provides an excellent model of godly living. God wasn't merely a part of Daniel's routine; God was the center of Daniel's life. Every habit, decision, and opportunity was weighed with God's will and Word in mind. To what extent are you living this day to please God?

HOSEA

 Snapshot of Hosea

"Oh," she whispered, "I love you, too!" Together the reunited lovers rode off into the sunset.

Isn't love wonderful? We've grown up believing love is a cure-all; someday we'll meet "Mr. Right" or "Miss Perfect." He will be gorgeous (big muscles and beautiful eyes); she will be lovely (long hair and a stunning smile). The rest of the world will then lose its meaning as the two of you enter your own private paradise, a totally honest relationship where neither of you ever hurts the other. Now that would be wonderful.

Hosea is a book about love, but with an unusual twist. Hosea was a prophet, and he married Gomer (believe it or not, that was her name). But far from being "Miss Perfect," Gomer was a prostitute. In fact, after they were married, she remained a prostitute. But God told Hosea to marry her anyway.

The book of Hosea is a love story—but it's not just about Hosea and Gomer—it's about God's love for his people, who, incidentally, acted a lot like Gomer.

As you read this story, you'll learn a lot about God and what he expects of his followers. But look for yourself in the story too. Are you like Hosea? Gomer? Israel? Then decide to have a true love relationship with God.

PURPOSE:
To illustrate God's love for his sinful people

AUTHOR:
Hosea son of Beeri (Hosea means "salvation")

TO WHOM WRITTEN:
Israel (the northern kingdom) and God's people everywhere

DATE WRITTEN:
Approximately 715 BC, recording events from about 753 to 715 BC

SETTING:
Hosea begins his ministry during the end of the prosperous but morally declining reign of Jeroboam II of Israel (the upper classes are doing well, but they are oppressing the poor). He prophesies until shortly after the fall of Samaria in 722 BC.

KEY PEOPLE:
Hosea, Gomer, their children

KEY PLACES:
The northern kingdom (Israel), Samaria, Ephraim

SPECIAL FEATURE:
Hosea employs many images from daily life—God is depicted as husband, father, lion, leopard, bear, dew, rain, moth, and others; Israel is pictured as wife, sick person, grapevine, grapes, early fig, olive tree, woman in labor, oven, morning mist, chaff, and smoke, to name a few.

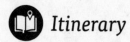 *Itinerary*

Hosea's Wayward Wife (1:1–3:5)
The book of Hosea begins with God's marriage instructions to Hosea (1:1-3). After the marriage of Hosea and Gomer, children are born, and each is given a name signifying a divine message. Then, as predicted, Gomer leaves Hosea to pursue her lusts (2:1-13). But Hosea (whose name means "salvation") finds her, redeems her (buys her from slavery), and brings her home again, fully reconciled (3:1-5). Images of God's love, judgment, grace, and mercy are woven into the story of Hosea and Gomer's marriage.

God's Wayward People (4:1–14:9)
Next God outlines his case against the people of Israel. Their sins will ultimately reap terrible consequences (4:1–5:15). Even while continuing to describe their punishment, God calls his people to repentance (6:1–10:15). The book closes with tough-love descriptions of God's compassion for his people, the depth of

their offenses, and God's promise of healing for those who repent (11:1–14:9).

In the book of Hosea, we discover a shocking and shameless portrait of God's love—even God's love for us. How can we not be humbled into bowing before such an awesome God?

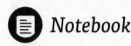 *Notebook*

THE NATION'S SIN (1:2-11; 4:1-19; 5:1-7; 6:7-10; 7:1-16; 11:1; 12:1, 7-8, 11-13)

Just as Hosea's wife, Gomer, was unfaithful to him, so the nation of Israel had been unfaithful to God. Israel's idolatry was like adultery. It had sought "illicit" relationships with Assyria and Egypt to give itself military might, and it was mixing Baal worship with the worship of God.

Like Gomer, we can chase after other loves—power, popularity, pleasure, money. The temptations in this world can be very seductive. Are you loyal to God, remaining completely faithful, or do you have other loves taking God's rightful place?

- In what ways did Gomer represent the nation of Israel?
- In today's world, what sins tempt God's people to stray from him?
- How can you, as a Christian, live close to God in a world filled with opportunities to be unfaithful to him?

GOD'S JUDGMENT (2:1-13; 5:8-15; 6:1-6, 11; 8:1-14; 9:1-17; 10:1-15; 12:2-6, 9-10, 14; 13:1-16)

Hosea was solemnly warning Judah not to follow Israel's example. Because Judah broke the covenant, turned away from God, and forgot her Maker, she experienced a devastating invasion and exile. Sin has terrible consequences.

Disaster follows rebellion and ingratitude toward God. The Lord is our only true refuge. We will find no safety or security anywhere else. No one who rebels against God will escape his judgment.

- What happened to Israel as a result of her disobedience?
- Describe the qualities of God you see revealed both in his promise to judge and in his warning not to fall into judgment.

- When you consider the reality of God's judgment, how do you feel about him? How does that affect the way you relate to God? The way you live your life daily?

GOD'S LOVE (2:14-23; 11:1-11; 14:1-6)

Just as Hosea went after his unfaithful wife to bring her back, so the Lord pursues his people with his love. His love is tender, loyal, unchanging, and undying. No matter what, God still loves his people.

Have you forgotten God and become disloyal to him? Don't let prosperity diminish your love for God or success blind you to your need for his love.

- God used Hosea's relationship with Gomer to illustrate God's relationship with his people. What do you learn about God from this illustration?
- In what ways did Gomer's failure to remain faithful to Hosea lead her to miss out on love?
- Gomer's life was sad and empty. How is this like people who know God but fail to respond to his love?
- What in your life threatens to keep you from fully experiencing God's love for you? Remove this obstacle before it robs you of the best love you will ever know.

RESTORATION (3:1-5; 14:7-9)

God promised to discipline his people for sin, but he encouraged and restored those who repented. True repentance opens the way to a new beginning. God forgives and restores those who return to his love.

There is hope for all who turn back to God. Nothing compares to loving him. Turn to the Lord while the offer is still good. No matter how far you have strayed, God is willing to bring you back, because his love never fails.

- After surveying chapters 11 and 14, describe what you discover about God.
- Through Hosea we see that God wants to rebuild the relationship with the person who has sinned. What does he expect from the sinner for this to happen?
- Think of an area in your life that has been or is being affected by sin. How did God bring you back to himself?

- What about this study of restoration can be used to bring hope to those who feel guilty and think God could never love them? What about your experience with God could you share with a person who was feeling and thinking that way?

 Postcard

As you read this book, ask yourself about the limits of your obedience to God. How do you respond when God's Word instructs you to do something difficult? When you ask God for directions, would you say that your attitude is more like someone who wants to know in order to decide whether or not to obey, or are you wanting to know so that you can obey?

JOEL

 Snapshot of Joel

"Okay, students, your final papers are due. Students who do not hand in a paper will receive a zero for 25 percent of this quarter's grade. Don't look startled—we discussed the penalty for late papers when I gave you this assignment." Mr. Donley was a good teacher, but he was tough. Tina expected to get an A or a B in his class, but her paper wasn't ready. She had meant to write it last weekend but hadn't gotten around to it. Maybe if she talked to him . . .

Tina walked up to Mr. Donley's desk. "Mr. Donley," she began, "I know what you said about the paper being due, but I've been really busy. Can I hand it in next week?"

Mr. Donley frowned and answered, "Tina, you are one of my better students, but two months ago I told the class there would be only a few acceptable reasons for a late paper. Not having time isn't good enough. I can't extend the deadline for you. I'm sorry."

Tina left the room sadly.

Deadlines and penalties are a part of life. The book of Joel also is about a deadline . . . for Judah to turn back to God. Joel called this deadline "the day of the Lord," when God would judge people for their actions. The people of Judah had forgotten about God and were living evil, rebellious lives. Joel reminded them that those who ignored God would one day face God's wrath.

Joel forces us to remember that God judges sin. As you read this book, ask God to make you aware of the areas in your life where you need to repent. Remember, there is a deadline.

PURPOSE:
To warn Judah of God's impending judgment because of its sins and to urge the people to turn back to God

AUTHOR:
Joel son of Pethuel

TO WHOM WRITTEN:
The people of Judah, the southern kingdom, and God's people everywhere

DATE WRITTEN:
Probably during the time Joel prophesied, from about 835 to 796 BC

SETTING:
The people of Judah have become prosperous and complacent. Taking God for granted, they have turned to self-centeredness, idolatry, and sin. Joel warns that this kind of lifestyle will inevitably bring God's judgment.

KEY PEOPLE:
Joel, the people of Judah

KEY PLACE:
Jerusalem

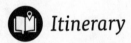 *Itinerary*

The Day of the Locusts (1:1–2:27)
Joel begins by describing a terrible plague of locusts that covers the land and devours the crops. The devastation caused by these creatures is but a foretaste of the coming judgment of God, the "day of the Lord." Joel, therefore, urges the people to turn from their sin and turn back to God. This is God's timeless call to repentance with the promise of blessing.

The Day of the Lord (2:28–3:21)
As Joel continues, the "day of the Lord" gets further attention. The consequences of God's judgment affect the world. God will have the last word, and it will be a good word for his people. God's gracious invitation remains: "Everyone who calls on the name of the LORD will be saved" (2:32).

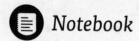 Notebook

PUNISHMENT (2:1-11; 3:1-16)

Like a destroying army of locusts, God's punishment for sin is overwhelming, dreadful, and unavoidable. When it comes, there will be no food, no water, no protection, and no escape. The day for settling accounts with God for how we have lived is fast approaching.

Every person is accountable to God—not to nature, the economy, rulers of nations, or an invading army. We can't ignore or offend God forever. We must pay attention to his message now or face the consequences of his anger later.

- In what ways were the locusts an accurate illustration of God's judgment and punishment?
- God's holiness leads him to punish sin severely. What does this teach about the holiness of God? The danger of sin?
- Our need for salvation is often illustrated by a large gap between us and God. This gap is caused by our sin. Why does sin cause such a gap?
- Based on this study of sin and punishment, what do you learn about the importance of the sinless Christ bridging that gap?

FORGIVENESS (2:12-32; 3:17-21)

God was ready to forgive and restore all those who would come to him and turn away from sin. God wanted to shower his people with his love and restore them to a proper relationship with him.

We receive forgiveness when we turn from sin and turn toward God. As long as we are alive, it is not too late to receive God's forgiveness. God's greatest desire is for you to enjoy his love and forgiveness.

- What promise is found in 2:32? How is that promise available to sinners today?
- The sinless Christ bridged the gap caused by our sin. What specifically has Christ done for you in relationship to God's holiness?
- In what specific ways could you and your Christian friends

communicate this message of forgiveness and restoration to non-Christians in your school and community?
- Develop a plan for sharing this hope of forgiveness with a non-Christian.

PROMISE OF THE HOLY SPIRIT (2:28-29)

Joel predicted the time when God would pour out his Holy Spirit on all people. It would be the beginning of new and fresh worship of God by those who believed in him but also the beginning of punishment for those who rejected him.

God is in control. Justice and restoration are in his hands. The Holy Spirit confirms God's love for us just as he did for the first Christians (Acts 2). We must be faithful to God and place our life under the guidance and power of his Holy Spirit.

- What does Joel teach about the work of the Holy Spirit?
- Why is the Holy Spirit a significant part of God's provision for his people?
- John 14, Acts 2, and Ephesians 1 give insight on the role of the Holy Spirit. Look at these passages with the following question in mind: As a Christian, how should I respond to the presence of the Holy Spirit in my life?

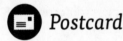 *Postcard*

Use Joel's picture of an army of consuming locusts to help you develop a reaction to sin. Imagine how sin, which often seems appealing and harmless, actually eats away at everything in life. Ask God to keep you responsive to his Spirit and ready to turn from sin.

AMOS

Snapshot of Amos

"Sit down right here!" Mr. Evans, the principal, demanded of the four boys he marched into his office. On the couch were Bobby Thomas, Eric Hardin, and Sheldon Milroy: the most feared trio in school. Near Mr. Evans's desk sat Robert Bledsoe—the bullies' skinny, smart, pimply-faced target.

"You boys," began Mr. Evans, pointing at the terrible trio, "had better quit. I won't stand for your harassment of Robert. Such behavior is totally unacceptable."

Mr. Evans's face was turning red, and his volume was increasing. "If I ever catch you three bothering anyone in the schoolyard again, I will make sure you are expelled. Understand?" All three nodded.

"And you, Mr. Bledsoe." Mr. Evans turned to a startled Robert. "You are not without blame. These boys were wrong, but . . . I might have done the same thing if you had treated me like you treated them. You teased these boys, saying they are stupid and probably headed for lives as bums." Mr. Evans was yelling again. "Mr. Bledsoe, you have been the victim here, but you are just as guilty. Now, all of you, get out."

Amos wasn't a professional prophet, but as God's spokesman he gave a similar message to the "bullying" nations and to Israel, the victim. And Amos has lessons for us today. He reminds us to be careful in pointing fingers at others, since they could end up pointed back at us. If God asked to have a talk with you, in what areas would he find you lacking?

PURPOSE:
To show God's judgment on Israel, the northern kingdom, for their idolatry and oppression of the poor

AUTHOR:
Amos

TO WHOM WRITTEN:
Israel, the northern kingdom, and God's people everywhere

DATE WRITTEN:
Probably during the reigns of Jeroboam II of Israel and Uzziah of Judah (about 760 to 750 BC)

SETTING:
The wealthy people of Israel are happy, but at the cost of the poor! Soon, however, Israel will be conquered by Assyria, and the rich will themselves be made slaves.

KEY PEOPLE:
Amos, Amaziah, Jeroboam II

KEY PLACES:
Bethel, Samaria

 *Itinerary*

Announcement of Judgment (1:1–2:16)
The book opens with Amos, a humble shepherd, watching his sheep. Yet God chooses Amos to be his spokesperson, sends him to the north, to Israel, and fills his life with disturbing visions (1:1-2). Through Amos God pronounces condemnation on all the nations who have sinned against him and harmed his people (1:3–2:3). Beginning with Aram, God's message of judgment moves quickly through Philistia, Tyre, Edom, Ammon, and Moab. All are condemned, and with each statement the people of Israel can almost be heard shouting "Amen!" Then Judah, Amos's homeland, is included in God's scathing denunciation. How Amos's listeners must have enjoyed hearing those words about their "relatives" and rivals to the south. Suddenly, however, Amos turns to the people of Israel and pronounces God's judgment on them.

Reasons for Judgment (3:1–6:14)
The next four chapters list and describe Israel's sins. Amos's words are frank and brutal in denouncing sin and calling for repentance.

Visions of Judgment (7:1–9:15)
Having pronounced God's judgment, Amos adds an account of the five visions God has given him. No wonder Amaziah the priest intervenes and tries to stop the prophet's preaching. But Amos will not be silenced or intimidated. He continues to deliver his message, which includes God's promise of eventual restoration.

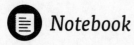 *Notebook*

EVERYONE ANSWERS TO GOD (1:1–2:16; 4:6-13)
Amos pronounced God's judgment on all the surrounding nations. Then he included his own people, Judah and Israel. God is in supreme control of the nations. Everyone is accountable to him.

All people will have to account for their sins. When those who reject God seem to be living the good life, don't be jealous of their prosperity or feel sorry for yourself. Remember, every person must answer to God.

- At times it seems that terrorists and evil leaders are able to avoid punishment for their violent and terrible actions. What does Amos say that contradicts this apparent injustice?
- How does this truth apply in general to men and women who feel they don't have to be responsible for the way they behave?
- How would you respond to the following statement from a non-Christian? Everybody has to decide what is right for himself or herself as an individual. Nobody can say what is and is not a sin.
- How does the fact that you must answer to God affect your relationship with Christ? How you live?

COMPLACENCY (3:10-11; 6:1-8)
Everyone was optimistic, business was booming, and people were happy in Israel (except for the poor and oppressed). With all the

comfort and luxury came self-sufficiency and a false sense of security. But prosperity brought corruption and destruction.

A complacent present can lead to a disastrous future. Don't congratulate yourself for the blessings and benefits you enjoy. They are from God. If you are more satisfied with yourself than with God, remember that everything is meaningless without him. A self-sufficient attitude may be your downfall.

- What factors often cause Christians to become complacent about God or take him for granted?
- When did you take God's relationship with you for granted? How did you feel about God during this time? About yourself? What shook you out of it?
- What have you learned about being complacent in your relationship with God from the book of Amos?
- What can you do to avoid becoming complacent in your relationship with Christ?

OPPRESSION (2:6-8; 4:1-3; 5:10-13)

The wealthy and powerful people of Samaria, the capital of Israel, had become prosperous, greedy, and unfair. Illegal and immoral slavery had come as the result of overtaxation and land-grabbing. There also was cruelty and indifference toward the poor. God grows weary and angry with greed and will not tolerate injustice.

Every person is a unique and invaluable creation of God, so ignoring the poor means ignoring those whom God loves and whom Christ came to save. We must go beyond feeling bad for the poor and oppressed. We must act compassionately to stop injustice and to help care for those in need.

- In what ways were the wealthy taking advantage of the poor? What seems to have been their attitude about the poor?
- How does God view the poor? The rich who oppress the poor?
- Who are the poor in your community? In what ways could they be described as oppressed?
- Who are the outcasts in your school? In what ways could they be described as oppressed?

- How might you be able to stand against oppression in your school and community?

SUPERFICIAL RELIGION (4:4-5; 5:18-27)

Although many people had abandoned real faith in God, they still pretended to be religious. They performed as religious people, just going through the motions instead of having spiritual integrity and practicing heartfelt obedience toward God.

Merely participating in ceremony or ritual falls short of true faith. This leads to religion without relationship. God wants trust in him, not a show. Don't settle for impressing others when God wants sincere obedience and commitment.

- What are some examples of what would qualify as superficial religion?
- When in your own life were you just going through the motions? How do you feel about this type of living?
- Many people identify a "good Christian" as a person who goes to church and behaves morally. Based on Scripture, what does it mean to be a true disciple of Christ? How is this different from going through the motions?
- What will you do in the coming week to deepen your relationship with God? What will you do to avoid becoming involved in superficial religion?

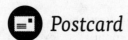 ## Postcard

Amos demonstrates the truth that a person's relationship with God, while deeply personal, must not be private. How we treat others and how we respond to the mistreatment of others will often indicate the depth of our faith in God. What have you done for poor people out of obedience to God?

OBADIAH

Snapshot of Obadiah

"Let me tell you a joke!" Five-year-old Alice bubbled with excitement as she spoke. "Which do you want first, the bad news or the bad news?"

"You dummy," her brother Al retorted, "don't you know anything? Those jokes are supposed to have good news and bad news, not just bad news."

"Not this one," answered Alice.

Like those jokes, most of life includes both good news and bad news.

The books of Isaiah through Malachi are like that. The bad news was that Israel was going to be punished for their sins by becoming prisoners to their enemies. The good news was that God would someday bring his people back from captivity and restore Israel's glory.

But one prophetic book is unique: it has no good news. That book is Obadiah. Writing about Edom (a nearby nation), the prophet graphically described the utter ruin that was about to come. Why? Because Edom had rejoiced when Israel was taken captive and had taken advantage of Israel's plight.

God loves his children. He will protect them and deal harshly with those who attempt to hurt them.

If you are God's child, God loves you just as he loved Israel. He will guard and protect you and react angrily against any who might attempt to harm you.

As you read Obadiah, ask God to help you be more aware that he indeed is watching over you.

PURPOSE:
To show that God judges those who have harmed his people

AUTHOR:
Obadiah. Little is known about him. His name means "servant of the Lord" or "worshiper of Jehovah."

TO WHOM WRITTEN:
The Edomites, the Jews in Judah, and God's people everywhere

DATE WRITTEN:
Possibly during the reign of Jehoram in Judah, 853–841 BC

SETTING:
Historically, Edom has constantly harassed Israel. Prior to the time this book was written, they participated in attacks against Judah. Given the dates above, this prophecy comes after the division of Israel into the northern and southern kingdoms and before the conquering of Judah by Nebuchadnezzar in 586 BC.

KEY PEOPLE:
The Edomites

KEY PLACES:
Edom, Jerusalem

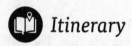 *Itinerary*

Edom's Destruction (1:1-16)

Obadiah, the shortest book in the Old Testament, is a dramatic example of God's response to anyone who would harm his children. The book begins with the announcement that disaster is coming to Edom (1:1-9). Despite their rocky fortress in the mountains (modern-day Petra), they will not be able to escape God's judgment.

Next Obadiah summarizes the reasons for Edom's destruction (1:10-16). These boil down to their blatant arrogance toward God and their persecution of God's children.

Israel's Restoration (1:17-21)
Last Obadiah echoes the prophetic theme of the "day of the Lord" when Israel will be restored and judgment would fall on all who have harmed God's people.

 Notebook

JUSTICE (1:15-18)
Obadiah predicted that God would destroy Edom as punishment for helping Babylon invade Judah. Because of their treachery, Edom's land would be given to Judah in the day when God righted the wrongs against his people.

God will judge and fiercely punish all who harm his people. We can be confident in God's final victory. He is our champion, and we can trust him to bring about true justice.

- What sin of the Edomites violated God's holy will?
- What have you learned in the book of Obadiah about God's qualities as a father to his people?
- What is meant by the statement "God is a just God"?
- What hope does this provide for the person who is being persecuted for being a believer?

PRIDE (1:2-4, 12-14)
Because of their seemingly invincible rock fortress, the Edomites were proud and self-confident. But God humbled them, and their nation disappeared from the face of the earth.

All those who defy God will meet their doom, as Edom did. Any nation that trusts in power, wealth, technology, or wisdom more than in God will be brought down. All who are proud will one day be shocked to discover that no one can escape God's justice.

- Edom had an attitude of self-reliance and pride. How did their pride lead to their destruction?
- How does knowing, experiencing, and responding to God as Lord eliminate the roots of pride?
- In what situations do you tend to be self-reliant and prideful?
- What knowledge and experience of God leads you to depend on him? What can you do to depend more on God?

Postcard

Obadiah offers a striking reminder that success and security ought to be cause for humility rather than pride. Are you grateful to God for your successes? Ask God to give you opportunities to serve him.

JONAH

 Snapshot of Jonah

"Don't get mad, get even." That's a common phrase, repeated often. Movies reflect the "get even" idea as well. Patrons watch, cheering and yelling as the victim evens the score, and the bad guys get what they deserve. We often live that way too, sometimes without even knowing it. We do or say things to get back at those we think have offended us.

Jonah was like that. He's famous for being swallowed by a "great fish," but he ended up in that fish because of his "get even" attitude.

God told Jonah to go to Assyria (Israel's greatest enemy) and warn the people of Nineveh (the capital) to repent from their evil lifestyle to stop God from destroying them. But Jonah thought Assyria should be destroyed, so he went as fast as he could in the opposite direction—straight into the fish. Finally, when Jonah cried out to God and was rescued, he obeyed and preached in Nineveh.

Fortunately, God doesn't operate on the "Don't get mad, get even" philosophy. Instead, he is "a merciful and compassionate God, slow to get angry and filled with unfailing love" (4:2). That's what our attitude should be too. As you read Jonah, give your attitude to God, and ask him to replace it with his attitude.

PURPOSE:

To show the extent of God's grace—the message of salvation is for all people

AUTHOR:
Jonah son of Amittai

TO WHOM WRITTEN:
Israel and God's people everywhere

DATE WRITTEN:
Approximately 785–760 BC

SETTING:
Jonah precedes Amos and ministers under Jeroboam II, Israel's most powerful king (793–753 BC, see 2 Kings 14:23-25). Assyria is Israel's greatest enemy, and they conquer Israel in 722 BC; evidently Nineveh's repentance is short lived.

KEY PEOPLE:
Jonah, the ship's captain and crew

KEY PLACES:
Joppa, Nineveh

SPECIAL FEATURES:
This book is different from the other prophetic books because it centers on the prophet, not his prophecies. Only one verse summarizes Jonah's message to Nineveh (3:4). Jonah is a historical narrative. It also is mentioned by Jesus as a picture of his death and resurrection (Matthew 12:38-42).

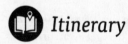 *Itinerary*

Jonah Forsakes His Mission (1:1–2:10)

Jonah's true-life adventure reads like the summary of a great novel. When the story begins, Jonah is already a prophet. God comes to him with a special mission (1:1-2). Jonah runs from God's command and gets himself—and others—into deep and troubled waters (1:3-17).

Alive but captive within a large fish, Jonah realizes his error and surrenders himself to God (2:1-10).

Jonah Fulfills His Mission (3:1–4:11)

Much to Jonah's surprise, the fish spits him up, and God sends him on his mission again—to deliver a last warning to the great city of Nineveh (3:1-10). The city-kingdom's people repent after hearing Jonah's message, and God spares them.

The closing chapter reveals Jonah's hatred for the people to whom God has sent him. So God teaches the prophet a loving lesson about the value of life and God's deep compassion for people (4:1-11).

 ## Notebook

GOD'S SOVEREIGNTY (1:1-4, 9, 14-17; 2:9-10; 3:10; 4:6-11)
Although the prophet Jonah tried to run away from God, God was in control. By controlling the stormy seas and a great fish, God displayed his absolute yet loving guidance.

Rather than running from God, trust him with your past, present, and future. Saying no to God quickly leads to disaster. Saying yes brings new understanding of God and his purpose in the world. Just say yes to God and his will for you.

- What do you think Jonah was thinking and feeling in these situations: when he ran from God's command to go to Nineveh; when he was on the ship in the storm; when he was in the belly of the great fish?
- What did Jonah learn about God's sovereignty through these experiences?
- When have you felt the way Jonah did when he ran from God? What made it difficult for you to obey God at that time?
- In what ways has God revealed his control in your life even when you were not aware of it or were in rebellion against his will? What does this teach you about God's sovereignty?

MISSIONARY MESSAGE (1:1-2; 3:1-10; 4:10-11)
God had given Jonah a purpose—to preach to the great Assyrian city of Nineveh. Jonah hated Nineveh, so he responded with anger and indifference. Jonah had yet to learn that God loves all people. Through Jonah God reminded Israel of its missionary purpose.

God wants his people to proclaim his love in words and actions to the whole world. He wants us to be his missionaries wherever we are and wherever he sends us.

- Why was Jonah so opposed to preaching to Nineveh?
- Jonah seemed to understand and accept part of God's

message, yet he missed a key ingredient. What was it that he failed to understand or accept? Why do you think this happened?

- Put God's message for the Ninevites into your own words.
- What message do you think God might want to send to your school? How do you think most of the students would respond to that message?
- What opportunities do you have to communicate God's message through your own life?

REPENTANCE (2:1-9; 3:5-9)

When the reluctant preacher went to Nineveh, there was a great response. People turned from their sins and turned to God. This was a powerful rebuke to Israel, who thought it was better than nations like Nineveh and yet refused to respond to God's message of repentance and forgiveness.

God doesn't honor those who fake it. He wants the sincere devotion of each person. It is not enough to share the privileges of Christianity; we must ask God to forgive us and to remove our sin. Refusing to repent is the same as loving our sin—it keeps us from God.

- What were the people of Nineveh like before Jonah's message? Afterward?
- Why was repentance (turning away from sin) so necessary for the Ninevites?
- Why is repentance necessary for those who do not know God today? For those who already are believers?
- In what areas of your life do you need to repent in order to be living fully in God's will?

GOD'S COMPASSION (3:10; 4:2, 10-11)

God's message of love and forgiveness was not just for the Jews. God loves people from all the nations of the world. The Assyrians didn't deserve it, but God spared them when they repented. In his mercy God did not reject Jonah for aborting his mission. God demonstrated his great love, patience, and forgiveness.

God loves us even when we fail him. He also loves people outside our social group, cultural background, race, and church denomination. When we accept his love, we must also learn to accept all those he loves. We will find it much easier to love others when we receive and return God's love.

- How did God's view of the Ninevites compare with Jonah's view?
- What does it mean to have a godly attitude toward people who are not Christians? Toward those who are racially or culturally different?
- Who are the people in your world who need to experience God's love through you? How will you demonstrate love and compassion to them?

Postcard

God's love and plan of salvation have always included the world. God wants us to see people from other cultures and races as also embraced by his love. Does your list of interests and relationships include people from other cultures?

MICAH

 Snapshot of Micah

Yesterday, at 2:00 a.m., our country officially surrendered. Realizing our situation was hopeless, generals from both sides agreed to end the bloodshed, provided we hand over all guns and ammunition. Morale is low. The most perplexing question yet unanswered is, How could we have been overrun?

Imagine reading that in your newspaper. What a terrible thought! Yet history proves that it is possible. This happened to both Israel (the northern ten tribes) and Judah (the southern two tribes). They couldn't understand how they could have been defeated because, after all, they were God's chosen people. God had a special love for them; he had rescued them out of slavery in Egypt; he had destroyed mighty forces to give them their homeland; he had protected them.

God had been faithful—but neither Israel nor Judah had. Micah wrote, "Why is this happening? Because of the rebellion of Israel" (1:5). Israel and Judah were being judged for their sins. Instead of worshiping the true God, the people were worshiping idols they had made. Many were using the religious ceremonies God had prescribed to make money. Those who were rich and influential were harassing the poor. God would punish them all because all were guilty.

There are lessons in Micah we need to learn. God punishes sin—even in those to whom he has shown special favor—by sometimes humbling whole nations.

As you read Micah, remember that individuals and the whole nation are responsible before God to serve him.

PURPOSE:
To warn God's people that judgment is coming and to offer pardon to all who repent

AUTHOR:
Micah, a native of Moresheth, near Gath, about twenty miles southwest of Jerusalem

TO WHOM WRITTEN:
The people of Israel (the northern kingdom) and of Judah (the southern kingdom)

DATE WRITTEN:
Possibly during the reigns of Jotham, Ahaz, and Hezekiah (742–687 BC)

SETTING:
The political situation is described in 2 Kings 15–20 and 2 Chronicles 26–30. Micah was a contemporary of Isaiah and Hosea.

KEY PLACES:
Samaria, Jerusalem, Bethlehem

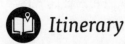 *Itinerary*

The Trial of the Capitals (1:1–2:13)
In seven short chapters, Micah presents this true picture of God—the almighty Lord hates sin and loves the sinner. Much of the book is devoted to spelling out God's judgments on Israel, Judah, and all the earth. First, God mourns and judges the capital cities, Jerusalem and Samaria. They represent rotten cores of the divided nation God has chosen for his own.

The Trial of the Leaders (3:1–5:15)
Second, God finds fault with the leaders of his people. They are deeply corrupted. But this section also includes some of the clearest prophecies about the coming and eventual rule of Jesus (4:1-5; 5:2).

The Trial of the People (6:1–7:20)
Third, Micah presents God's case against the people. Yet even as God thunders hatred of unkindness, idolatry, injustice, and empty ritual, he continues to pour out his love. God hasn't changed his

view of sin today, and he continues to love sinners and offer them the opportunity to repent and receive forgiveness.

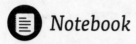 *Notebook*

PERVERTING FAITH (2:6-11; 3:5-12)

God said that he would judge the false prophets, dishonest leaders, and selfish priests in Israel and Judah. While they publicly carried out religious ceremonies, they privately were seeking to gain money and influence. Mixing selfish motives with an empty display of religion perverts faith.

Don't mix selfish desires with true faith in God. One day God will reveal how foolish it is to substitute anything for loyalty to him. Designing your own private blend of religion will pervert your faith.

- What were the specific sins of the religious leaders? Why were those sins so offensive to God?
- What does it mean for someone to pervert the faith today?
- What can you do to keep your faith pure rather than ruining it by making self-centered choices?

OPPRESSION (2:1-5; 3:1-4; 6:9-16)

Micah predicted ruin for all nations and leaders who were oppressing others. The upper classes were oppressing and exploiting the poor. Yet no one was speaking against them or doing anything to stop them. God will not put up with such injustice.

We dare not ask God to help us while we ignore those who are needy and oppressed, or silently condone the actions of those who oppress them. Sharing God's love includes meeting the needs of those who are rejected and neglected by society.

- What types of oppression were present in Micah's day?
- What types of oppression are found in today's world?
- What are Christians doing to bring about God's justice for the poor and oppressed people in your community?
- What could you do to help people become more aware of the poor in your community and God's concern for them?
- What can you do to help those who are poor or oppressed?

PLEASING GOD (4:1-8; 6:6-8; 7:14-20)

Micah preached that God's greatest desire was not the offering of sacrifices at the Temple. Instead, God delights in faith that produces fairness, love to others, and obedience to him.

True faith in God generates kindness, compassion, justice, mercy, and humility. We can please God by seeking these results in our school, family, church, and neighborhood.

- In Micah, what false ideas did the people have about pleasing God?
- What false ideas do you see in the world about what it means to please God?
- What individuals have you seen who are truly pleasing God?
- What ways in your own life do you find to please God?
- Commit yourself to specific ways that you can be pleasing to God in the next week at school, home, church, and work.

Postcard

If you ever wondered what exactly God expects from your life, Micah offers you three big areas to consider: (1) do what is right; (2) love mercy; (3) walk humbly with your God (see 6:8). Keep reading Micah—and the rest of God's Word—for the details.

NAHUM

 Snapshot of Nahum

"Oh no," thought Bobby, "we're going to lose again. 'Supe' is on their side." "Supe" was Jeff Owens, the best athlete in the school. Whichever team got Supe always won. Bobby's phys ed class was beginning to play football, and he loved it—except when Supe was on the other team. Bobby was good, but Supe was great. He could outrun, outthrow, outcatch, out-everything anyone.

Nineveh, the Assyrian capital, was like Supe. No one had been able to stand against the Assyrians. They had overthrown Israel, and their sights were on Judah. The people of Judah were afraid; how could they withstand such a terrible enemy?

Through Nahum, God brought words of comfort to Judah and words of doom to Assyria. He said, "The LORD is a jealous God. . . . He takes revenge on all who oppose him and continues to rage against his enemies!" (1:2). To Judah God declared, "Now I will break the yoke of bondage from your neck and tear off the chains of Assyrian oppression" (1:13). To Assyria God announced, "I am your enemy! . . . Your chariots will soon go up in smoke. . . . The voices of your proud messengers will be heard no more" (2:13).

Such will be the end of those who oppose the Lord and hurt his people. God loves his children and will protect them at all costs.

Let Nahum remind you of the futility of fighting against God; let his words encourage you. God protects those whom he loves.

PURPOSE:
To pronounce God's judgment on Assyria and to comfort Judah with this truth

AUTHOR:
Nahum

TO WHOM WRITTEN:
The people of Nineveh and Judah and God's people everywhere

DATE WRITTEN:
Sometime during Nahum's prophetic ministry (probably between 663 and 612 BC)

SETTING:
This particular prophecy took place after the fall of Thebes in 663 BC (see 3:8-10).

KEY PLACE:
Nineveh, the capital of Assyria

 Itinerary

Like the book of Jonah, Nahum focuses on the city of Nineveh, capital of Assyria. Jonah's visit took place a hundred years earlier. But the repentance that saved the city was short-lived. Evil is reigning again, and Nahum delivers God's judgment on this city-kingdom.

Nineveh's Judge (1:1-15)
Nahum begins with a description of the divine judge. The awesome God sits in judgment. Nahum declares God's character and God's righteous offense over sin. In the defendant's chair sits Nineveh—full of pride and ripe for judgment. Among the victims hoping for justice sits Judah, God's chosen people.

Nineveh's Judgment (2:1–3:19)
The judge speaks. Nineveh's fate is sealed. The city has been found guilty and liable for capital punishment. After God passes judgment, the book ends. For Nineveh the end comes without hope. God's judgments are just and final. A much better life and future awaits those who decide to live under God's guidance and within his rules, commands, and guidelines for life.

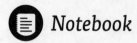
Notebook

GOD JUDGES (1:2-3, 5-6, 8-15; 2:13; 3:5-19)

God would judge the city of Nineveh for its idolatry, arrogance, and oppression. Although Assyria was the leading military power in the world, God would completely destroy this supposedly invincible nation. God allows no person or power to assume superiority or scoff at his authority.

Anyone who remains arrogant and resists God's authority will face his anger. No ruler or nation will get away with rejecting him. No individual will be able to hide from his judgment. But those who keep trusting God will be kept safe forever.

- What sins were leading to Nineveh's punishment?
- In your world what things do you see that God will certainly judge in the future?
- What would you say to a person living an ungodly lifestyle with the attitude "I can do what I please"?
- What is your hope in light of the holiness of God's judgment?

GOD RULES (1:3-15)

God rules over all the earth, even over those who don't acknowledge him. God is all-powerful, and no one can thwart his plans. God will overcome any who attempt to defy him. Human power is futile against God.

If you are impressed by or afraid of any weapons, armies, or powerful people, remember that God alone can truly rescue you from fear or oppression. We must place our confidence in God because he alone is all-powerful.

- What powerful forces exist in the world today?
- Which of the forces are the most feared? Why?
- What does Nahum teach about God's ability and power to control the awesome forces that so many people fear?
- How does knowing about God's power make you feel? What difference does it make in how you live?

 *Postcard*

Cities can certainly act like people! In his judgment of Nineveh, God is judging a sinful world. The message is clear: Disobedience, rebellion, and injustice will not prevail but will be punished severely by a righteous and holy God who rules over all the earth. We can't afford to treat God lightly!

HABAKKUK

 Snapshot of Habakkuk

It was Sunday, and Julie had some questions she wanted answered. She sat in Sunday school listening intently. Each week they had discussed questions that seemed to have no easy answers: Is there a God? If God is so good, why is there suffering in the world? How do we know that people can't get to heaven except by Jesus?

But Julie had her own question to ask. Finally, as the room settled down, Julie awkwardly raised her hand. She began, "Why does it seem like those who are trying to live the way Jesus would want them to are so often abused by those who don't care how they live? Doesn't God care? It doesn't seem fair!"

Many centuries ago Habakkuk posed a similar question. He looked over his own country, Judah, and saw that wherever he looked there was "destruction and violence. . . . The wicked far outnumber the righteous" (1:3-4). He questioned God's care for those trying to live righteous lives; it seemed the wicked always got the upper hand.

God answered Habakkuk. He answered him well enough that Habakkuk replied, "I have heard all about you, LORD. I am filled with awe by your amazing works. In this time of our deep need, help us again as you did in years gone by. And in your anger, remember your mercy" (3:2).

As you read this book, take note of God's answer. It may surprise you. And then, like Habakkuk, resolve to trust God to care for you.

PURPOSE:
To show that God is still in control of the world despite the apparent triumph of evil

AUTHOR:
Habakkuk

TO WHOM WRITTEN:
Judah (the southern kingdom) and God's people everywhere

DATE WRITTEN:
Between 612 and 588 BC

SETTING:
Babylon is becoming the dominant world power, and Judah will soon feel Babylon's destructive force.

KEY PEOPLE:
Habakkuk, the Chaldeans (Babylonians)

KEY PLACE:
Judah

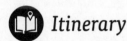 *Itinerary*

Habakkuk's Complaints (1:1–2:20)
Habakkuk and God have an extended conversation. The first two exchanges have to do with the prophet's complaints and God's answers. Habakkuk is troubled, but he brings his concerns to God. His questions are urgent, but he is also willing to wait and trust in God's answers.

Habakkuk's Prayer (3:1-19)
After God gives his answer, Habakkuk pours out his heart in prayer. In fact, he sings his prayer. Again Habakkuk states his basis for hopeful living—not based on circumstances, but on the faithfulness and power of God.

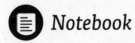 *Notebook*

STRUGGLE AND DOUBT (1:1-4, 12-17)
Habakkuk asked God why the people of Judah were not being punished for their sin. He couldn't understand why a just God would

allow such evil to exist. God promised to use the Babylonians to punish Judah. When Habakkuk cried out for answers in his time of struggle, God answered him with words of hope.

God wants us to come to him with our struggles and doubts, but his answers may not be what we expect. God sustains us by revealing himself to us. Trusting in God leads to quiet hope, not bitterness because we do not see the immediate results we want.

- In chapter 1 how did Habakkuk feel about God?
- When have you felt that way? How did you deal with your emotions and thoughts during that time?
- What did Habakkuk do with his emotions and thoughts? How did God respond?
- Describe Habakkuk's feelings toward God in chapter 3. What had made the difference?
- When in doubt a Christian must rely on God's revealed truth, even if it temporarily does not feel true. How can you build your confidence for those times of doubt and struggle?

GOD'S SOVEREIGNTY (1:5-11; 2:2-20; 3:1-19)
Habakkuk asked God why he would use the wicked Babylonians to punish his people. God said that he would also punish the Babylonians after they had fulfilled his purpose.

God is still in control of this world, despite the apparent triumph of evil; God doesn't overlook sin. One day he will rule the whole earth with perfect justice.

- How did God use Babylon? What made this so difficult for Habakkuk to accept?
- When is it most difficult for you to understand God's sovereignty?
- What confuses you about God and his control? What questions would you ask if you could have a direct conversation with God?
- For now, how does knowing that God is sovereign help you deal with your questions?

HOPE (1:12–2:1; 3:1-19)
God, the Creator, is all-powerful. God has a plan that he will carry out, and he will punish sin. God is our strength and our place of

safety. We can have confidence that he will love us and guard our relationship with him forever.

Hope means going beyond our unpleasant daily experiences to the job of knowing God. We live by trusting in him, not in the benefits, happiness, or success we may experience in this life.

- What can you learn from Habakkuk about hope?
- How can you build your confidence in God and his love and control in your life?
- How can you get to really know God?
- On what do you base your hope? Do you need to redirect the focus of your hope to God? How can you do that?

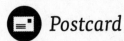 Postcard

Habakkuk didn't hesitate to ask God his deepest questions. You can do the same. How often do you ask God questions? How long are you willing to wait for answers? Do you ask because you want to hold God accountable, or do you ask because you want to understand and live obediently before God?

ZEPHANIAH

 Snapshot of Zephaniah

It was the day for report cards and parent-teacher meetings—probably the most dreaded day on the school calendar. No classes were held, but appointments were set between student, parents, homeroom teacher, and the most recent report card. What a deadly mix!

Most students hated the idea of such a grand gathering, especially those who were not doing well in school. It was one thing to get bad grades but quite another to sit in a room with three adults and talk about those grades. Parents were known to scream or cry or both. One never knew. At times the teachers would get emotional too. Even students who were doing well in school sometimes got reprimanded—they could be doing better. Few students slept well the night before meeting day.

When the school paper wrote an article about this day (affectionately termed "death day"), the reactions were varied—but most of the student body agreed with one student who was quoted as saying, "I don't think Judgment Day could be any worse!"

Well, that student was wrong. Judgment Day will be much worse! God's prophet Zephaniah tells us about it in his book. Like "death day" it will be a day of reckoning. Judgment Day will be a time of terrible wrath and punishment—it also will be a time of mercy.

As you read Zephaniah, tremble at the awesomeness of God on

the Day of Judgment—and be thankful that he is merciful to those who are faithful to him.

PURPOSE:
To shake the people of Judah out of their complacency and urge them to return to God

AUTHOR:
Zephaniah

TO WHOM WRITTEN:
Judah and all nations

DATE WRITTEN:
Probably near the end of Zephaniah's ministry (640–621 BC), when King Josiah began his great reforms

SETTING:
King Josiah of Judah is attempting to reverse the evil trends set by the two previous kings, Manasseh and Amon. Josiah extends his influence because there isn't a strong superpower dominating the world at this time (Assyria is declining rapidly). Zephaniah's prophecy may have been the motivating factor in Josiah's reform. Zephaniah is a contemporary of Jeremiah.

KEY PEOPLE:
Zephaniah, the people of Judah

KEY PLACE:
Jerusalem

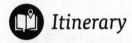 *Itinerary*

The Day of Judgment (1:1–3:8)
From the first words of Zephaniah, the fate of Judah is sealed (1:1-18). All that remains of hope will depend on those who repent. Only God will be able to keep them safe in the disaster to come (2:1–3).

God has also reached a point of irrevocable judgment on other nations (2:4-15). Out of their destruction will come a global awareness of God.

Particular judgment will be poured out on the city of Jerusalem (3:1-8). It has received countless opportunities to experience and to observe God's justice, power, and mercy. As a whole, however, Jerusalem has remained unmoved. God remains in the city (3:5), but he is ignored.

The Day of Hope (3:9-20)

Suddenly, Zephaniah begins to explain God's final work with the world. It won't be a work of judgment but of mercy and hope. The invitation to worship will be universal. God gives his unbreakable pledge to preserve a people for himself.

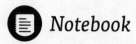 *Notebook*

DAY OF JUDGMENT (1:2-18; 2:4–3:8)

Destruction was coming because Judah had forsaken the Lord. The people were worshiping Baal, Molech, and nature. Even the priests were mixing heathen practices with faith in God. God's punishment for sin was on the way.

To escape God's judgment, we must listen to him, accept his correction, trust him, and seek his guidance. If we accept God as our Lord, we will escape his condemnation.

- What is God's attitude toward worshiping idols? Why do you think he has such an intense response to this false worship?
- In what ways do people worship false idols today?
- Based upon this book, how can worshipers of false idols expect God to respond?
- What are the consequences for Christians who replace God with contemporary idols? What can you do to prevent this from happening in your life?

INDIFFERENCE TO GOD (1:5-6, 12-13; 3:1-8)

Although there had been occasional attempts at renewal, Judah had no sorrow for her sins. The people were prosperous and no longer cared about God. God's demands for righteous living seemed irrelevant to the people of Judah, whose security and wealth made them complacent.

Don't let material comfort be a barrier to your commitment to God. Prosperity can produce an attitude of proud self-sufficiency. The only answer is to admit that money won't save us and that we cannot save ourselves. Only God can save us and cure our indifference to spiritual matters.

- How did prosperity hinder the people's repentance?
- Do you agree or disagree with this statement? Prosperity is a false sense of security. Explain.
- What tempts you to become indifferent to God?
- Do you need to sell all your possessions and give up everything you enjoy in order to avoid becoming indifferent to God? Explain.

DAY OF JOY (3:9-20)

The Day of Judgment will also be a day of joy. God will judge all those who mistreat his people. He will purify his people, purging all sin and evil. God will restore his people and give them hope.

When people are purged of sin, there is great relief and hope. No matter how difficult our experience now, we can look forward to the day of celebration when God will completely restore us.

- Condemnation is not inevitable, because of God's gift of Jesus. How does Jesus provide hope for a day of great joy?
- When you think about the hope you have in Jesus and the destiny that would be yours without Jesus, how do you feel about God?
- What difference does this hope make in your daily life as a Christian?

 Postcard

As you read Zephaniah, listen carefully to the words of judgment. God does not take sin lightly, and he will punish it. But be encouraged by the words of hope—our God reigns, and he will rescue his own. Decide to be part of that faithful group who worships and obeys the living God.

HAGGAI

 Snapshot of Haggai

Hal and Jimmy were camping. Actually, they were in Jimmy's backyard, but it was a big backyard. You could barely see the lights in the house from their tent. On "camping nights," Hal and Jimmy would talk. Their conversations sometimes went on and on. Of course, the topic often was girls, but sometimes they discussed other things.

"Jimmy," Hal asked, "if you had to give up everything but one thing in your life, what would you keep?" Hal was not very serious most of the time, but he was that night.

"I'd have to give up everything?" Jimmy responded.

"All but one thing. What's the most important thing to you?" Hal really was being serious.

Jimmy thought and answered, "I can narrow it down to three. I would keep my family, Becky (the girl he had just started liking), and my TV."

"What about God?" Hal questioned. "You would give him up for Becky?"

"Oh," laughed Jimmy, "I didn't even think about God."

The Jews, who had returned from captivity, were like Jimmy—they had forgotten about God. They had let God slip from their lives. So God sent Haggai, a prophet, to remind them of what was really important in life.

God refuses to be forgotten. He demanded priority in the Jews' lives, and he demands top priority with us as well. As you read the book of Haggai, notice how God blesses those who make him number one. Then ask God to help you live with him in first place.

PURPOSE:
To call the people to complete the rebuilding of the Temple

AUTHOR:
Haggai

TO WHOM WRITTEN:
The people living in Jerusalem, those who had returned from exile, and all believers everywhere

DATE WRITTEN:
520 BC

SETTING:
The Temple in Jerusalem was destroyed in 586 BC Cyrus allows the Jews to return to their homeland and rebuild their Temple in 538 BC They begin the work but are unable to complete it. During the ministry of Haggai and Zechariah, the Temple is completed (520–515 BC).

KEY PEOPLE:
Haggai, Zerubbabel, Jeshua, the people of Judah

KEY PLACE:
Jerusalem

SPECIAL FEATURES:
Haggai is the first of the postexilic prophets. The other two are Zechariah and Malachi. The literary style of this book is simple and direct.

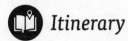 *Itinerary*

The Call to Rebuild the Temple (1:1-15)
God gives four motivating messages to the prophet Haggai to deliver to his people. God has already allowed them to return to the Promised Land. One of their objectives was to rebuild the Temple, but the work has bogged down.

In the first message (1:1-11), Haggai confronts the people's misplaced priorities. It is followed by a renewed willingness to work, led by Zerubbabel.

The second message (1:13-15) confirms God's pleasure with the people's efforts to rebuild. God pledges himself to help.

Encouragement to Complete the Temple (2:1-23)

The third message (2:1-9) is directed to Zerubbabel himself. The leader is assured of God's blessing and help. God also promises to use the rebuilt Temple in a glorious way. In the last of the messages (2:10-23), Haggai again confronts the people. This time it is their spiritual commitment rather than their building effort that receives God's examination. God expects the rebuilding of the Temple to be accompanied by a renewed commitment to internal obedience on the part of the people. God also adds further words of encouragement and counsel for Zerubbabel.

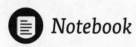 *Notebook*

RIGHT PRIORITIES (1:2-11; 2:10-19)

God had given the Jews the assignment to finish the Temple in Jerusalem when they returned from captivity. But after fifteen years, they still had not completed it. They were more concerned about building their own homes than about finishing God's work. Haggai told them to get their priorities straight.

It is easy to make other activities more important than doing God's work. But God wants us to build his Kingdom. Don't stop, and don't make excuses. Set your heart on what is right, and do it. Get your priorities straight by centering them on Christ.

- How had the people begun to live (their lifestyle) in Jerusalem? Contrast this lifestyle with the way they lived when they first returned from captivity.
- What had happened in the past fifteen years that changed their priorities?
- What are your priorities?
- How have your priorities changed in the past five years? The past year?
- As you think about the next five years, what do you think will be God's challenge to you about right priorities?

GOD'S ENCOURAGEMENT (1:7-8, 13-14; 2:4-9, 19-23)

Haggai encouraged the people as they worked, assuring them of the presence of the Holy Spirit, final victory, and the future reign of the Messiah.

If God gives you a task, don't be afraid to get started. His resources are infinite. God will help you complete it by giving you encouragement from others along the way.

- What do you find in 2:14-19 that served as an encouragement to the people?
- How would you expect such words of encouragement to affect them?
- Think of two instances in which someone's encouragement made a real difference in your life. What did he or she do or say? Why was this so important to you at the time?
- Think of two people who could use encouragement, especially in their relationship with God. Develop a plan for being God's encourager to them.

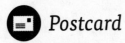 ## Postcard

Some tasks can be accomplished in moments; others take a lifetime. Personal fulfillment and God's pleasure are not the result of starting tasks but of finishing them. What unfinished tasks in your life, particularly efforts you know God wants you to undertake, need to be carried on or finished?

ZECHARIAH

 Snapshot of Zechariah

Almost everyone wants to know the future. Some people fear the future, wondering what evils lurk around the corner; others consult psychic hotlines, palm readers, astrologers, and other future-telling charlatans who make a living providing personal prophecies.

But tomorrow's story is known only by God and by those special messengers, the prophets, to whom he has revealed a chapter or two. A prophet's job was to proclaim the word of the Lord, point out sin, explain its consequences, and point men and women to God.

Nestled here, among what are known as the Minor Prophets, lies the book of Zechariah. As one of God's spokesmen, the prophet Zechariah ministered to the small group of Jews who had returned to Judah to rebuild the Temple and the nation. Zechariah encouraged them, but his message went far beyond that as he gave a spectacular and graphic description of the Messiah, the one whom God would send to rescue his people and reign over the earth.

Zechariah is an important prophetic book because it gives detailed messianic references that were clearly fulfilled in Jesus. Jesus is the Messiah, the promised Great Deliverer of Israel, and the only hope for humankind.

God knows and controls the future. We may never see a moment ahead, but we can be secure if we trust in him. Read Zechariah, and strengthen your faith in God—he alone is your hope and security.

PURPOSE:
To give hope to God's people by revealing God's future deliverance through the Messiah

AUTHOR:
Zechariah

TO WHOM WRITTEN:
Jews in Jerusalem who had returned from their captivity in Babylon and God's people everywhere

DATE WRITTEN:
Chapters 1–8 were written approximately 520–518 BC. Chapters 9–14 were written around 480 BC.

KEY PEOPLE:
Zechariah, Zerubbabel, Jeshua, the Jews rebuilding the Temple

KEY PLACE:
Jerusalem

SPECIAL FEATURE:
This book is the most apocalyptic and messianic of all the Minor Prophets.

 Itinerary

Messages while Rebuilding the Temple (1:1–8:23)
As prophets went, Zechariah had a long, effective career, speaking for God for about forty years. The book that bears his name covers two distinct periods during which Zechariah worked. The first period parallels the time in which Haggai also ministered. The Temple remains in partial reconstruction, and the people need God's encouragement to persevere to the completion of their task. Zechariah receives seven visions in which God displays proof that he remains in control of world events.

Messages after Completing the Temple (9:1–14:21)
The second period, after the completion of the Temple, includes God's word through Zechariah that God's rule in the world will not get to full power in the Messiah right away. Although the Savior will come, God's people will still face many difficulties and struggles. But God's guarantee of future blessings ought to fill with hope all those waiting on his plan.

📄 *Notebook*

GOD'S JEALOUSY (1:2-6; 7:8-14; 10:1-5)

God was angry at his people for neglecting his prophets through the years, and he was concerned that they not follow the careless and false leaders who were exploiting them. Disobedience was the root of their problems and the cause of their misery. God was jealous (zealous) for his people's devotion.

God wants our devotion. To avoid Israel's ruin, don't walk in their steps. Don't reject God, follow false teachers, or lead others astray. Turn to God, faithfully obey his Word, and make sure to lead others correctly. God calls you to complete loyalty to his lordship.

- Jealousy is usually considered a negative quality. How is God's jealousy a positive characteristic of his love?
- What is it that God seems to desire so jealously from his people? Why do you think this is so important?
- How are you remaining faithful to God's perfect love? In what areas may you be lacking in faithfulness?
- What is your motivation for remaining faithful to God?
- How do you plan to maintain that faithfulness throughout your life?

REBUILDING THE TEMPLE (4:1-14; 8:9-13)

The Jews were discouraged. They were free from exile, but the Temple was not completed. Zechariah encouraged them to continue rebuilding it. God would both protect his workmen and also empower them by his Holy Spirit to carry out and complete his work.

More than the rebuilding of the Temple was at stake—the people were staging the first act in God's wonderful drama of the end times. Those who believe in God must complete his work. To do so we must have the Holy Spirit's help. God will empower us to carry out his will in our relationships and daily tasks.

- What did the men of Israel supply for the rebuilding of the Temple? What did God supply?
- How were the people responding to God's partnership with them in their task?

- How does God want you to live for him? What is he supplying? What must you supply?
- How are you responding to God's partnership in your life? What could you do to increase your productivity in the tasks God has called you to accomplish?

THE COMING KING (9:9-17; 12:10-11; 14:1-21)

The Messiah will come both to rescue people from sin and to reign as King. He will establish his Kingdom, conquer all his enemies, and rule over all the earth. Everything will one day be under his loving and powerful control.

The Messiah came as a servant to die for his people. He will return to earth as a victorious King. At that time he will usher in peace throughout the world. Submit to the King's leadership now to be ready for his triumphant return.

- According to Zechariah, what will the King be like?
- In what ways is Christ's rule evident in people's lives today? How does that evidence compare with how things will be when he returns in glory?
- What evidence could someone find that Christ is King of your life?

GOD'S PROTECTION (1:14-17; 2:1-13; 7:4-10; 8:2-23; 9:9-17; 10:3-12; 12:2-9; 13:7-9; 14:3-21)

There was opposition to God's plan in Zechariah's day, and Zechariah said there would be future times of trouble. Regardless of the circumstances, God's Word endures. God remembers his agreements with his people. God cares for his people and will deliver them from all who oppress them.

Evil is still present, but God's infinite love and personal care have been demonstrated through the centuries. God keeps his promises. Although our body may be destroyed, we need never fear our future and final destiny if we love and obey him.

- What evidence is there in Zechariah that God's protection was present during times of trouble?
- What potential trouble do you face in living a godly life in your school or community?
- How would you describe the protection God has promised to you? How do you feel about this protection?

- Complete this statement with appropriate phrases: I need you, Lord, to provide me with your loving care and protection in the areas of: _____.

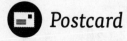 ## Postcard

If you are trusting in God, you have a priceless opportunity to face the future with confidence. Remember, it's not as important to know what the future holds as it is to know who holds the future! Live today for the one who knows about tomorrow.

MALACHI

 Snapshot of Malachi

"Mom, she did it again!" Tina's angry voice echoed throughout the house. "Mom!"

Tina's little sister, Mary, was really cute. Except she never learned. Mary was four, old enough to know better. She did know better, but she kept doing it. Because their house was small, Tina and Mary shared a room . . . and a closet. Mary had been told to keep out of Tina's clothes—but as often as she was told, Tina or her mother often found Mary in the bedroom, sitting on the floor, surrounded by Tina's clothes. Lectures hadn't helped; neither had spankings. Nothing seemed to be able to stop Mary from playing in Tina's clothes. Tina wondered if Mary would ever learn.

God must have thought the same thing about his people. He had warned them repeatedly that he would punish them if they did not stop sinning—but they didn't repent, so God punished them. Israel was taken into captivity, and some years later so was Judah. All because they hadn't learned their lesson.

Then God brought his people back, forgiving them of their sin and offering them a fresh start. Certainly they must have learned.

But they hadn't. God's people, rather than learning from the mistakes of their ancestors, chose to repeat their actions. Because they hadn't learned, Malachi came to warn them that God was watching—and he cared.

As you read, ask God to help you be aware of areas where you need to learn.

PURPOSE:
To confront the people with their sins and to restore their relationship with God

AUTHOR:
Malachi

TO WHOM WRITTEN:
The Jews in Jerusalem and God's people everywhere

DATE WRITTEN:
About 430 BC

SETTING:
Malachi, Haggai, and Zechariah are postexilic prophets to Judah (the southern kingdom). Haggai and Zechariah rebuke the people for their failure to rebuild the Temple. Malachi confronts them with their neglect of the Temple and their false and profane worship.

KEY PEOPLE:
Malachi, the priests, the people of Judah

KEY PLACES:
Jerusalem, the Temple

SPECIAL FEATURE:
Malachi's literary style displays a continual use of questions asked by God and his people (for example, see 3:7-8).

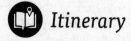 *Itinerary*

The Sinful Priests (1:1–2:9)

The book of Malachi consists of three messages to three different groups. In the first message, Malachi delivers God's word of love and judgment to sinful priests. God accuses the priests of failing to honor, respect, or keep their duties. Their work as priests is only superficial.

The Sinful People (2:10–3:15)

In the second message, God widens his judgment to include the people as a whole. God particularly denounces the growing habit of divorce among them. They are choosing to marry pagans. As a result their children are growing up without much opportunity to really learn about God.

The Faithful Few (3:16–4:6)

Malachi's final message is reserved for the faithful few. Their trust in God will be richly rewarded with freedom and joy. In contrast to pagan families, the homes of the faithful will be united and loving.

 Notebook

GOD'S LOVE (1:2; 3:6-12, 16-18)

God loves his people even when they neglect or disobey him. He has great blessings for those who are faithful to him. God's love never ends.

Because God loves us so much, he hates hypocrisy and careless living. This kind of living denies God the relationship he wants to have with us. What we give and how we live reflect the sincerity of our love for God. Live a life of love for God!

- What do you learn about God's love in the book of Malachi?
- Contrast the love of God experienced by those who are obedient with the love of God experienced by those who are disobedient.
- What areas of your life are hindering you from completely enjoying God's love for you?
- What is it about God's love that you want to know and experience more deeply? Commit yourself to remove hindrances and to actively seek more of God's love.

THE PRIESTS' SINS (1:6–2:9; 3:3-5)

Malachi singled out the priests for condemnation. They knew what God required, yet their sacrifices were unworthy, their service was insincere, and they were lazy, arrogant, and insensitive. They had a casual attitude toward worshiping God and meeting his standards.

If religious leaders go wrong, how will the people be led? We all are leaders in some capacity. Don't neglect your responsibilities or be ruled by what is convenient. Neglect and insensitivity are acts of disobedience. God wants leaders who are faithful and sincere. You can make a difference in how others understand and respond to God.

- What were the specific sins of the priests (see 1:6–2:9)?
- What attitudes toward God are apparent in these sinful choices?
- Why were the priests' sins especially harmful to the people?
- What attitudes and actions enable leaders to have a positive impact on the church and community?
- Which of these attitudes are areas of strength for you? Which ones are weak? How can you strengthen the weak areas?

THE PEOPLE'S SINS (2:10-17; 3:3-15)

The people had not learned from their exile, nor had they listened to the prophets. Men were callously divorcing their faithful wives to marry younger, heathen women. This disobeyed God's commands about marriage and threatened the religious training of the children—but pride had hardened the people's hearts.

God deserves our total honor, respect, and faithfulness—but sin hardens us to our true condition. Don't let pride keep you from giving God your devotion, money, future marriage, and family.

- How do you feel toward people when you hear about their sins?
- How does God see their sins?
- Based on this study, how do you feel about the sins you have committed?
- Explain your response to this statement: little sins are not that big of a deal.
- What can you do to prepare yourself to live in a way that brings God pleasure rather than grief?

THE LORD'S COMING (4:1-6)

God's love for his faithful people is demonstrated by the Messiah's coming to earth. The Messiah's purpose was, and is, to lead the people to the realization of all their fondest hopes. The day of his final coming will be a day of comfort and healing for a faithful few and a Day of Judgment for those who reject him.

Christ's first coming brought purification to all those who believe in him. His second coming will expose and condemn those who are proud, insensitive, or unprepared. Yet God can heal and mend. Forgiveness is available now to all who come to Christ.

- What did God accomplish through Jesus' first coming?
- What differences has Jesus' coming made in the last two thousand years?
- What changes will take place in humanity when Christ returns?
- As Christians we know that Jesus will return. How should this knowledge affect our life in the present?

 Postcard

When you turn the page between Malachi and the next book, you will jump over four hundred years of history. The opening chapters of Matthew are the fulfillment of Malachi's prophecies. God's future promises are sure. You can depend on them. Do you? In what ways has your life been affected by the promises you have read in God's Word?

NEW
TESTAMENT

MATTHEW

 Snapshot of Matthew

Who would you put on a list of the most influential people of all time? Think beyond stars and athletes. We're talking about the real heavyweights of history. People who took civilization by the scruff of the neck and shook it. Folks about whom we say, "Because of his (or her) presence, the world will never be the same."

Using that criteria your list might include Karl Marx, Martin Luther King Jr., William Shakespeare, Abraham Lincoln, Genghis Khan, Muhammad, Buddha, Mohandas Gandhi, or Henry Ford.

Those people and many others deserve to be on such a list. But if you're looking for one person who changed the world more than anyone, look at Jesus Christ. Of course, naming a first-century carpenter and itinerant preacher "the most influential person of all time" probably won't sit well with some people. They may prefer to put Jesus on a list of influential "religious" figures. But here's why the founder of Christianity cannot be ignored: two thousand years ago, Jesus of Nazareth launched a spiritual revolution that is still going strong. He has been the motivation behind more songs and sermons, the inspiration underlying more works of charity, and the object of more affection than all the other great figures of history combined. And don't forget the millions of lives that have been transformed by his timeless touch.

Dive into the Gospel of Matthew. See for yourself how Jesus succeeded in turning ancient Israel on its ear. You'll see why he still rocks the planet.

PURPOSE:

To prove that Jesus is the promised Messiah, the eternal King

AUTHOR:

Matthew (Levi)

TO WHOM WRITTEN:

All people, everywhere, especially the Jews

DATE WRITTEN:

Probably between AD 60 and 65

SETTING:

Matthew is a Jewish tax collector who becomes one of Jesus' disciples. This Gospel forms the connecting link between the Old and New Testaments because of its emphasis on the fulfillment of prophecy.

KEY PEOPLE:

Jesus, Mary, Joseph, John the Baptist, the disciples, religious leaders, Caiaphas, Pilate, Mary Magdalene

KEY PLACES:

Bethlehem, Jerusalem, Capernaum, Galilee, Judea

SPECIAL FEATURES:

Matthew includes several unique events and miracles from Jesus' life that add to the particular flavor and tone of this Gospel: Joseph's dream (1:20-24); the visit by the wise men (2:1-12); the escape to Egypt (2:13-15); the slaughter of the children of Bethlehem (2:16-18); the healing of two blind men (9:27-31); casting the demon out of the mute man (9:32-33); paying tax with money found in a fish (17:24-27); the death of Judas (27:3-10); the dream of Pilate's wife (27:19); the other resurrections (27:52); the bribery of the guards (28:11-15); the baptism emphasis in the great commission (28:19). Matthew's Gospel is also filled with messianic language. The title "Son of David" is used repeatedly. There are fifty-three direct quotes and seventy-six references from the Old Testament.

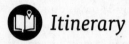 Itinerary

Matthew's account of Jesus' biography has a noticeable Jewish perspective. He often notes the way in which an event fulfills prophecy. In fact, ancient tradition holds that Matthew's purpose is to point out for Jewish believers just how clearly Jesus proved to be the Messiah, the eternal King promised throughout the Old Testament.

Birth and Preparation of Jesus, the King (1:1–4:11)

Jesus' earthly story begins in the town of Bethlehem in the Roman province of Judea. His birth and personal training are quickly reviewed. As a final act of preparation, he submits to baptism by John the Baptist, thereby identifying with the sinful race he has come to save.

Message and Ministry of Jesus, the King (4:12–25:46)

The bulk of Matthew's Gospel takes up the second section, which records the ministry and message of Jesus. Of particular note among these chapters are 5–7, which summarize Jesus' Sermon on the Mount. The flow of Matthew's narrative goes from the words Jesus says to the actions he takes, from the stories Jesus tells to the reactions he creates.

Death and Resurrection of Jesus, the King (26:1–28:20)

The last section of Matthew details Jesus' final week: from his triumphal entry into Jerusalem to his even more triumphal resurrection from the dead. Matthew's Gospel closes with the great commission (28:19-20)—Jesus' sending those who had witnessed his return from the grave, into the world to spread the Good News everywhere.

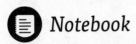 *Notebook*

JESUS IN CHARGE (1:1–2:12; 8:1–10:42; 11:20–12:13; 14:13-36; 15:21-28, 32-39; 17:1-13; 21:12-17, 23-27; 27:37; 28:16-20)

Jesus is revealed as the King of kings. His miraculous birth, his life and teaching, and his triumph over death show his true identity.

Jesus cannot be compared with any other person or power. He is the supreme ruler of time and eternity, heaven and earth, people and angels. We should give him his rightful place as King and Lord in our life.

- In what ways is Jesus revealed as King in the book of Matthew?
- In what ways did Jesus, though the King of kings, display humility as recorded in Matthew?
- What do you learn about the personal qualities of Jesus from these two lists? Why did so many people reject Jesus as King?

- How does Jesus reign in the world today? What does it mean in terms of daily living for Jesus to be "Lord" of your life?

HE FINALLY CAME (2:14-15, 21-23; 3:1–4:11; 4:13-16; 12:15-21; 13:13-15; 16:1-4, 13-20; 20:29–21:11; 22:41-46; 24:1-35; 26:1–27:66)

Jesus is the Messiah, the one for whom the Jews had waited to deliver them from Roman oppression. Tragically, they didn't recognize him when he came. They were not ready to accept his kingship, because it was not what they expected. They didn't understand that God's anointed deliverer was to die to free his people from their sins.

Because Jesus was sent by God, we can trust him with our life. It is worth everything we have to accept Christ and give ourselves to him because he came to be our Messiah, our Savior.

- In what ways did Jesus fulfill the prophecy of a coming Savior who would rescue the people?
- How was Jesus' plan of deliverance different from what the people had anticipated? How was Jesus' deliverance actually greater than they could have imagined?
- In what ways has Jesus delivered you?
- Based on the fact that Jesus, the Messiah, has rescued you, what will you do to live for him?

LIFELINES AND GUIDELINES (4:17, 23-25; 5:17-20; 9:35; 11:1-19; 12:22-37; 13:10-52; 16:24-27; 18:1-6; 19:13–20:16; 20:20-28; 21:28–22:14; 24:36–25:46)

Jesus came to earth to begin his Kingdom. His full Kingdom will be realized at his return and will be made up of all those who have faithfully followed him.

The way to enter God's Kingdom is by faith, believing in Christ to save us from sin and to change our life. Then we must do the work of his Kingdom, helping prepare the world for his return.

- Chapters 5–7, known as the Sermon on the Mount, introduce the values of Christ's Kingdom. In accordance with these chapters, make a list of at least ten guidelines that Jesus gave showing how he wants those who belong to the Kingdom to live.

- What would it mean for a person in your school to live by these Kingdom guidelines?
- Chapter 13 is filled with parables that Jesus used when teaching to help describe his Kingdom. What do you learn about the Kingdom of God from these parables? What is the importance of the Kingdom of God?
- In what ways are you living out the Kingdom guidelines or values? In what areas do you need to become more obedient to Christ's call to Kingdom values?

WHAT DID HE SAY? (5:1-12; 12:38-50; 15:1-20, 29-31; 16:5-12; 17:14-21, 24-27; 18:7-20; 21:18-22; 22:15-22, 34-40; 23:1-39; 28:19-20)

Jesus taught the people using sermons, illustrations, and parables. He showed the true ingredients of faith and how to guard against being ineffective and hypocritical.

Jesus' teachings explain how to prepare for life in his Kingdom by living properly right now. His life was an example of his teachings, as our life should be.

- What were the main purposes of Jesus' teachings?
- How did different individuals and groups of people react to Jesus' teachings?
- In what ways, positive and negative, do people today respond to Jesus' teachings?
- Why do some people accept Jesus' teachings and others reject the same teachings?
- How are Jesus' teachings to be your authority in life? In what ways does this authority influence your decisions?

DEATH: NO FEAR (16:21-23; 17:22-23; 20:17-19; 22:23-33; 28:1-10)

When Jesus rose from the dead, he rose in power as the true King. In his victory over death, he established his credentials as King and his power and authority over evil.

The Resurrection shows that Jesus is all-powerful and that not even death can stop his plan of offering eternal life. People who believe in Jesus can hope for a resurrection like his. Our role is to live in that victory and share the message of his victory with those who do not yet know that Jesus is alive.

- What difference does it make whether or not Jesus was raised from the dead?
- What impact did Jesus' resurrection have on his disciples?
- What impact has Jesus' resurrection made on humankind as a whole? On you specifically?

 *Postcard*

The fact that Jesus is King of kings ought to affect your attitude toward him and your attitude toward his commands. How do your worship habits, your use of Jesus' name, your practice of prayer, and other aspects of your life show that you are a subject of the King of kings?

MARK

 Snapshot of Mark

Has this ever happened to you? Friends invite you to a just-released, critically acclaimed movie. "It's supposed to be great," they insist. "You'll like it. Trust us."

So you go—with high expectations. Only the movie isn't great. It drags on and on. As far as excitement goes, this particular film ranks right up there with reading the phone book as a mystery novel.

You keep thinking, "This has got to get better. Surely there's a car chase or a joke or some sort of surprise plot twist in the next scene!" But nothing happens—nothing at all. The most adventurous moment of the film comes at the end when two of the actors go to a fancy French restaurant and eat snails. It's gross, but at least they're finally doing something. When the final credits roll, you leave the theater, vowing, "Never again!"

Guess what? You don't have to spend your time with stale stories, boring characters, or tedious plots! Instead, you can read one of the most exciting books in existence! And it's right here, on the next few pages.

You name it, and the Gospel of Mark has it—demons, death, and outrageous special effects (also called miracles), all served up in a swirling atmosphere of intrigue, jealousy, controversy, and murder. In short this book is an action-packed biography of the most influential person in the history of the world.

Go for it! And when you're done, you will vow, "Never again . . . never again will I think of the Bible as a boring book!"

PURPOSE:
To present Jesus' person, work, and teachings from a Roman perspective

AUTHOR:
John Mark. He accompanied Paul on his first missionary journey (Acts 13:13).

TO WHOM WRITTEN:
The Christians in Rome, where Mark probably wrote the Gospel, and all believers everywhere

DATE WRITTEN:
Between AD 55 and 65

SETTING:
The Palestinian area of the Roman Empire. The empire, with its common language and excellent transportation and communication systems, is ripe to hear Jesus' message.

KEY PEOPLE:
Jesus, the twelve disciples, Pilate, the Jewish religious leaders

KEY PLACES:
Capernaum, Nazareth, Caesarea Philippi, Jericho, Bethany, Mount of Olives, Jerusalem, Golgotha

SPECIAL FEATURES:
Mark was the first Gospel written. The other Gospels quote all but thirty-one verses of Mark. Mark records more miracles than does any other Gospel.

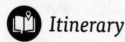 *Itinerary*

Preparation of Jesus, the Servant (1:1-13)
Mark can be called the "action-adventure" Gospel. The opening chapter quickly introduces John the Baptist and moves immediately into the adult life and ministry of Jesus. The reader catches a brief look at Jesus' baptism, temptation in the desert, and call of the disciples. Mark focuses his attention on Jesus' public ministry, with glimpses of his inner life (1:35-37). He is interested in Christ's works, not just his words. In fact, Mark records eighteen of Jesus' miracles and only four of his parables.

Message and Ministry of Jesus, the Servant (1:14–13:37)

Although Mark presents events in chronological order, he gives little or no historical linkage between the events. And to keep things moving and to heighten the sense of action, Mark continually uses words like "immediately." Readers feel, "Jesus is on the move; we'd better stay alert, or we'll miss something!" Mark sustains this tone of fast-paced action throughout the main section of the Gospel. Jesus' impact is felt first in Galilee, then beyond.

Death and Resurrection of Jesus, the Servant (14:1–16:20)

Finally, Jesus arrives in Jerusalem for the climax of Mark's account. The closing section in Mark focuses on the death and resurrection of Jesus.

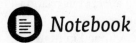 *Notebook*

JESUS CHRIST (1:1, 9-11, 21-34; 2:1-12, 23-28; 3:7-12; 4:35-41; 5:1-20; 8:27-31; 9:1-13; 10:46-52; 11:1-19; 13:24-37; 14:32-42, 60-65; 16:1-8)

Jesus Christ alone is the Son of God. In Mark's Gospel Jesus demonstrates his divinity by overcoming disease, demons, and death. Although he has the power to be King of the earth, Jesus chooses to obey the Father and die for us. Thus we see him in Mark as both Son of God and servant.

When Jesus rises from the dead, he proves that he is God, that he can forgive sin, and that he has the power to change our life. By trusting in Christ for forgiveness, we can begin a new life with him. As our guide, Jesus calls us to follow his example of obedience and service.

- Which of Jesus' character qualities do you see demonstrated most clearly in the Gospel of Mark?
- Which of these qualities have you seen demonstrated in your church? Your youth group?
- Which of these qualities have you experienced personally?
- Which of Jesus' qualities do your non-Christian friends find it most difficult to understand or accept?
- In what specific ways have you tried to model or explain Jesus' unique character to your friends?

SERVANT (1:40-45; 3:1-12; 7:31-37; 8:22-26, 34-38; 9:33-50; 10:13-45; 12:38-44; 14:17-26, 32-50; 15:1-5, 12-47)

As the Messiah (Savior), Jesus fulfilled the prophecies of the Old Testament by the way he came to earth and lived while here. He did not come as a conquering King; he came as a servant. Jesus helped humankind by telling about God, showing compassion, and healing. But his ultimate act of service was giving his life as a sacrifice for sin.

Because of Jesus' example, we should be willing to serve God and others. Because he gave us strict orders, we are under command to serve. Because he offers us his guidance and strength, we have the power to serve.

- Read the incident that Mark records in 10:35-45. In what ways does Jesus' description of himself affect your relationship to him and your relationship to others?
- In what ways did Jesus display his servanthood in Mark? What have you learned about being a servant from Jesus' example?
- What examples of servanthood (received or practiced) can you describe from your life? How do you feel about being a servant to others? How do you think a person should deal with negative feelings they may have about being a servant?
- In what specific ways do you think your service could improve toward the following people: family members, friends at school, people who don't like you, someone in the community who gets overlooked, a non-Christian who may not have been shown Jesus' love? Hint: identify special needs they may have.
- What specific action can you take to move you in the direction of greater servanthood . . . on purpose?

MIRACLES (1:29-34, 40-45; 2:1-12; 3:1-12; 4:35-41; 5:1-43; 6:30-56; 7:24-37; 8:1-10, 22-26; 9:17-29; 10:46-52; 16:1-8)

Mark records more of Jesus' miracles than his sermons. Jesus was clearly a man of power and action, not just words. Jesus did miracles to confirm his message to the people and to teach the disciples his true identity as God. His miracles of forgiveness bring healing, wholeness, and changed lives to those who trust him.

- Why were the miracles such an important part of Jesus' ministry?
- What do you learn about Jesus from Mark's record of his miracles?
- What displays of Jesus' power do you see today?
- How would you describe Jesus' ability to change lives through his miraculous power?
- In what situations in your life, or in the lives of your friends and family, do you see the need for Jesus' healing power? Speak to God in prayer about those situations, and ask for eyes to notice how God answers.

DISCIPLESHIP (1:16-20; 3:13-19; 6:7-13; 8:27–10:52; 13:1–14:52; 15:42–16:8)

Mark records in painful detail the disciples' difficulty in understanding Jesus' true identity. Mark's source was Peter, one of Jesus' closest followers. The disciples didn't understand Jesus' parables (4:13, 34), his miracles (4:35-41), his teaching on divorce (10:10-12), or his predictions of his approaching death and resurrection (8:32-33). Their failure to understand lasted until the shattering truth of the Resurrection itself changed their lives.

We who live many centuries after Christ have the benefit of reading about his life, death, and resurrection. We see the whole picture. But do we understand what it means to know this God and man as Savior and Lord? Do we realize the cost of being his disciple? Following Jesus means dying to self, obeying him, and serving others (8:34-35). His directions for disciples remain as true today as when those first disciples heard them.

- With which of Jesus' disciples do you most closely identify (check the list in 3:13-19)? Why? Now that you have the list in mind, try to note at least one significant fact about each original disciple.
- What makes the biggest impression on you about the way Jesus chose and treated his disciples?
- At what point in your life did you most clearly sense Jesus' calling you to follow him?
- What have been your most challenging lessons in discipleship?

- People follow ideas, systems, and all kinds of earthly leaders. What difference does it make to follow Jesus Christ?

SPREADING THE GOSPEL (1:2-8, 14-20, 38-39; 2:13-17; 3:13-19, 31-35; 4:1-34; 5:1-20; 6:1-13; 7:24-37; 9:33-41; 10:13-31; 12:28-34; 13:1-23, 32-37; 14:9)
Jesus directed his public ministry to the Jews first. When the Jewish leaders opposed him, Jesus also went to the non-Jewish world, healing and preaching.

Jesus' message of faith and forgiveness is for the whole world and not just for our church, neighborhood, or nation. We must reach out beyond our own people and needs to fulfill the world-wide vision of Jesus Christ so that people everywhere might hear this great message and be saved from sin and death.

- How did Jesus show that God's love and grace are available to all types of people?
- The book of Mark literally pivots on verse 8:29. Read the context (8:27-30). What would people today say if they were asked to describe Jesus?
- How would you answer Jesus' question, "Who do you say I am?" What does your life say about who Jesus is?
- What is the central truth people need to know about Jesus? Which of your friends need to know this truth?
- What could you do and say to give them the Good News? In what specific ways could you communicate the Good News in the near future to those friends?

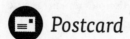 *Postcard*

Mark's Gospel is a personal, intimate, and fast-moving account of Jesus' impact. How does your gospel of Jesus Christ sound? If you haven't thought through what you would say if someone asked you what you believed, take some time to do that. In fact, ask a Christian friend to listen while you tell him or her your story.

LUKE

 Snapshot of Luke

They were two kids in love. In fact, they were engaged. And M. and J. had big plans, and even bigger dreams. Then the roof caved in. Our bride-to-be found out she was pregnant. The groom-to-be was hurt, confused, and angry—he knew he wasn't the father. From his perspective there was only one thing to do: call off the wedding.

But weird things started happening. M. claimed she'd been visited by a real-life angel, and that she'd been made pregnant by the Spirit of God! J. had heard some wild stories before, but angels? Divine fertilization? Come on!

Then J. started seeing angels! Surely it was all a dream . . . until the angel said (in a serious tone and with a straight face), "Hey, J., don't break off the engagement! The child inside M. really is the Savior of the world."

J. gulped and mumbled, "Um, yeah. . . . whatever you say."

Soon M. could no longer hide her pregnancy. People stared. Rumors flew. M. and J. purposely kept a low profile. Together they wondered what it would be like to be parents—especially of such a special child.

Did J. know that the child would one day speak such profound words or perform astounding miracles? Did M. realize her precious boy would die in a brutal manner?

Even if they were able to grasp any of these events, could they have ever anticipated that their murdered son would come back to life?

Read about M. and J. and their son—mainly about their son—in the following pages. The story is the Gospel of Luke. It's one you won't forget.

PURPOSE:

To present an accurate account of the life of Christ and to present Christ as the perfect man and Savior

AUTHOR:

Luke—a doctor (Colossians 4:14), a Greek, and a Gentile Christian. He is the only known Gentile author in the New Testament. He was a close friend and companion of Paul. He also wrote Acts, and the two books go together.

TO WHOM WRITTEN:

Theophilus ("one who loves God"), Gentiles, and people everywhere

DATE WRITTEN:

About AD 60

SETTING:

Luke writes from Caesarea or from Rome.

KEY PEOPLE:

Jesus, Elizabeth, Zechariah, John the Baptist, Mary, the disciples, Herod the Great, Pilate, Mary Magdalene

KEY PLACES:

Bethlehem, Galilee, Judea, Jerusalem

SPECIAL FEATURE:

About a third of Luke's material is found only in his Gospel. Most of this can be found in the details surrounding Jesus' birth and the parables Jesus tells. The following parables are unique to Luke: The Two Debtors (7:41-43); The Good Samaritan (10:25-37); The Persistent Friend (11:5-10); The Rich Fool (12:13-21); The Barren Tree (13:6-9); The Foolish Builder (14:28-30); The Foolish King (14:31-33); The Lost Sheep (15:1-7); The Lost Coin (15:8-10); The Lost Son (15:11-32); The Shrewd Manager (16:1-8); The Rich Man and Lazarus (16:19-31); The Humble Servant (17:7-10); The Persistent Widow (18:1-8); The Pharisee and the Tax Collector (18:9-14).

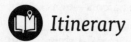 **Itinerary**

Birth and Preparation of Jesus, the Savior (1:1–4:13)

Luke begins his account in the Temple in Jerusalem, giving us the background of the birth of John the Baptist. The setting shifts to the city of Nazareth and the story of Mary, chosen to be Jesus' mother. As a result of Caesar's call for a census of all the populations under Roman domination, Mary and Joseph have to travel to their ancestral home in Bethlehem. There Jesus is born in fulfillment of prophecy. Jesus grows up in Nazareth and begins his earthly ministry by being baptized by John and tempted by Satan.

Message and Ministry of Jesus, the Savior (4:14–21:38)

Much of Jesus' ministry focuses on Galilee. He uses Capernaum as his "home base" from where he travels and teaches throughout the region. Later he visits the Gentile area of Gadara, where he heals a demon-possessed man. On another occasion Jesus feeds more than five thousand people with one lunch on the shores of the Sea of Galilee near Bethsaida. Jesus regularly travels to Jerusalem for the major feasts and enjoys visiting friends in nearby Bethany. On one such journey, he heals ten lepers on the border between Galilee and Samaria and helps a dishonest tax collector in Jericho turn his life around.

Death and Resurrection of Jesus, the Savior (22:1–24:53)

The small villages of Bethphage and Bethany on the Mount of Olives are Jesus' resting places during his final days on earth. He is crucified outside Jerusalem's walls, but he rises triumphantly from the grave. Luke closes his Gospel with the only account of one unique encounter between disciples and the risen Lord, the two with whom Jesus walks to Emmaus on Resurrection Sunday.

 Notebook

JESUS CHRIST, THE SAVIOR (1:26-38; 2:1-52; 3:21-22; 4:1–6:11, 46-49; 7:1-50; 8:22-56; 9:18-45, 57-62; 10:16, 21-24; 11:14-32; 12:8-12, 35-59; 13:31-35; 14:15-35; 17:20-37; 18:18-34; 19:28–20:47; 21:25-36; 22:14–24:53)

Luke describes how God's Son entered human history. Jesus lived as the perfect man. He understood who he was and what his life would mean. He continuously chose to do his Father's will. After a perfect, sinless ministry, he provided a flawless sacrifice for our sins so we could be saved.

Jesus is our perfect leader and Savior. He offers forgiveness to all who believe that what he says is true and accept him as Lord of their lives.

- How do you think Luke would answer this question: "What was Jesus like?"
- What insights into the character of Jesus the child do you get from 2:41-52?
- Why is it so important that Jesus shared our human experiences, including all types of temptations? (Check Hebrews 2:17-18.)
- Based on your responses to the above questions, how would you describe Jesus to someone who had never heard of him?
- In what specific ways have you acknowledged that Jesus Christ is your Lord and Savior? What difference has that made in your life and relationships?

HISTORY (1:1-4; 2:1-3; 3:1-2, 23-38; 13:1-4; 23:6-7)
Luke was a medical doctor and historian. He put great emphasis on dates, connecting Jesus to events and people in history. He also had a doctor's ear for important details that add insight to the biography he wrote.

Luke's devotion to accuracy gives us confidence in the reliability of the history of Jesus' life. Even more important, we can believe with certainty that Jesus is God.

- What difference does it make whether or not Luke was historically accurate?
- Why is it so important that Jesus actually lived, died, and rose again as opposed to his life's just being an allegory (symbolic story) that someone created to describe how much God loves us?
- What historical facts clearly reveal that Jesus was both man and God?
- How does the fact that Jesus was both man and God affect your relationship with him? How does it affect your life?

CARING FOR PEOPLE (4:42-44; 5:5-11, 27-32; 6:13-16, 27-42; 7:18-28, 36-50; 8:1-3, 19-21; 9:10-17, 47-48; 10:38-42; 12:1, 22-34; 18:15-17; 19:1-10; 21:5-24, 37-38; 23:42-43; 24:13-52)
Jesus was deeply interested in people and relationships. He showed warm concern for his followers and friends—men, women, and

children. Unlike many figures of his day, Jesus treated women with genuine respect.

Jesus' love for people is good news for everyone. His message is for all people in every nation. Each person has an opportunity to respond to him in faith.

- Jesus built his earthly ministry through relationships. To what degree have you let Jesus' approach shape the way you think about serving others?
- What does it take for you to feel loved by someone? To trust that the person truly cares for you?
- How would a person have to act to touch the people in your school with Christ's love?
- What can you do to show Christ's love to students at your school?

SOCIAL ACTION (4:31-41; 5:12-26; 6:6-10, 17-19; 7:1-17; 8:26-39, 41-56; 9:1-2; 10:25-37; 13:10-17; 14:1-6; 16:19-31; 17:11-19; 18:35-43; 22:50-51)
As a perfect human, Jesus showed tender mercy to the poor, the despised, the hurt, and the sinful. No one was rejected or ignored by him. Jesus healed the sick, the diseased, and the crippled. His compassion reached across racial lines and broke with convention (for example, healing on the Sabbath, 6:6-10).

Anyone seriously seeking to follow Jesus will have to check their lives for evidence of selfishness. Materialism and love of money make it almost impossible to care for others. Instead, those obeying Christ will reach out to the hurting and overlooked in society, offering loving care, emotional support, and material assistance. Jesus set the example.

- What commands of Christ clearly indicate his desire that his followers be active in helping others?
- To what degree is financial security the central focus of your life?
- How do you balance in your own life the challenge to depend on God, give to others generously, and make reasonable preparations for tomorrow?
- What people do you know who are experiencing sickness or poverty? In what ways could you extend them help?

- How much of what is yours is available to God for use any way he sees fit?

HOLY SPIRIT (1:15, 35, 41, 67-69; 2:25-32; 3:16, 22; 4:1, 14; 10:21; 11:13)

The Holy Spirit was present at Jesus' birth, baptism, ministry, and resurrection. As a perfect example for us, Jesus lived in dependence on the Holy Spirit.

The Holy Spirit was sent by God as confirmation of Jesus' authority. The Holy Spirit is given to enable people to live for Christ. By faith we can have the Holy Spirit's presence and power as we witness and serve.

- In 4:1-15, what role did the Holy Spirit play in Jesus' life?
- From what you know of God's Word, how do you explain the phrase *full of the Spirit*?
- In what ways does the Spirit work in you during times of temptation or weariness and during opportunities to do his ministry?
- How can you keep yourself filled with the Holy Spirit?
- In what areas of your life would you like to see the Holy Spirit make a greater difference? What steps do you need to take in order to keep yourself reliant on God's Spirit so that this will be accomplished?

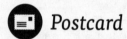 *Postcard*

Some Christians emphasize the internal changes that occur in a person when he or she experiences salvation through Christ; others emphasize the external changes in behavior that happen as a person lives in Christ. How has your life been an example of both these kinds of changes? Where is growth needed? (Check out the story of Zacchaeus in 19:1-10.)

JOHN

 Snapshot of John

Questions. Life is jam-packed with them.

Dumb questions: "If the plural of goose is geese, shouldn't the plural of moose be meese?" "If God can do anything, can he make a rock so big that even he couldn't lift it?"

Mysterious questions: "Since buttered bread usually falls butter-side-down and cats generally land feetfirst, what would happen if you dropped a cat with a piece of buttered bread strapped to its back off a two-story building?"

Serious questions: "What will bring me long-lasting fulfillment?" "How can I have a rich and satisfying life?" Even people who don't (or won't) openly discuss serious issues have ideas about where to find happiness. Ray's formula for fulfillment includes partying and an active sex life. Anne thinks she'll find it in a 4.0 grade point average and a college scholarship. Kevin is banking on his athletic ability to do the trick. Sherry's relying on beauty and bucks.

Nagging questions: "If happiness really is found in the things mentioned above, why are there people with awesome sex lives, staggering IQs, truckloads of trophies, drop-dead good looks, or bulging bank accounts who are unhappy?" "Why don't more people consider what Jesus had to say about happiness and fulfillment?"

Personal questions: "Have you ever really looked at and pondered Jesus' teachings in the Gospel of John?" "What are you waiting for?"

PURPOSE:
To prove conclusively that Jesus is the Son of God and that all who believe in him will have eternal life

AUTHOR:
John the apostle, son of Zebedee, brother of James, called a "Son of Thunder"

TO WHOM WRITTEN:
New Christians and searching non-Christians of the first century and all people everywhere

DATE WRITTEN:
Probably between AD 85 and 90

SETTING:
Written after the destruction of Jerusalem in AD 70 and before John's exile to the island of Patmos

KEY PEOPLE:
Jesus, John the Baptist, the disciples, Mary, Martha, Lazarus, Jesus' mother, Pilate, Mary Magdalene

KEY PLACES:
Judean countryside, Samaria, Galilee, Bethany, Jerusalem

SPECIAL FEATURES:
John records six miracles not found in the other Gospels. Over 90 percent of John is unique to his Gospel. He writes with the intimacy, confidence, and detail of an eyewitness. He leaves out matters like Jesus' birth, genealogy, and temptation, as well as several events from Jesus' life, because they have already been recorded by the earlier Gospels and because they are not crucial to his central purpose—to demonstrate that Jesus was and is the Son of God.

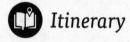 *Itinerary*

Preparation of Jesus, the Son of God (1:1–2:12)
Somewhat like Mark, John stresses Jesus' adult life in his Gospel. The descriptions of Jesus' origin present him as the Son of God rather than commenting on his earthly arrival. This section ends with the first of eight signs or miracles (turning water to wine) that John records to convince the world that Jesus is the Son of God.

Message and Ministry of Jesus, the Son of God (2:13–12:50)
John turns immediately to the message and ministry of Jesus. Example after example illustrates Jesus' identity as the Son of God.

Among them are six signs and miracles done by Jesus: healing the official's son (4:46-54); healing the lame man at the pool of Bethesda (5:1-9); feeding the five thousand with just a few loaves and fish (6:1-14); walking on the water (6:16-21); giving sight to the blind man (9:1-12); and raising Lazarus from the dead (11:1-44). The distinct responses of belief or unbelief by people are also recorded.

Death and Resurrection of Jesus, the Son of God (13:1–21:25)
The final section of John centers on the Resurrection—the miracle that defines all others. Here also we read about the eighth sign or miracle (giving the disciples an overwhelming catch of fish (21:1-14). Five chapters in this section describe Jesus' words and actions during the Last Supper with his disciples (13–17).

 Notebook

JESUS CHRIST, SON OF GOD (1:1-18; 2:1-11; 4:46–5:15; 6:5-14; 6:16-21; 9:1-12; 11:1-44; 19:1–20:31)
John shows us that Jesus is unique as God's special Son, yet he is fully God. Because Jesus is fully God, he is able to reveal God to us clearly and accurately. Because Jesus is God's Son, we can perfectly trust what he says. By trusting him we can gain an open mind to understand God's message and fulfill his purpose in our life.

- What key points does John emphasize in John 1:1-18?
- What do you learn about God by looking at Jesus?
- In what ways has knowing Christ made a difference in your life?
- Based on John's Gospel and your life, what would you say this statement means? Jesus Christ is God's perfect revelation of himself.

ETERNAL LIFE (3:15-16, 36; 4:14, 36; 5:24, 39-40; 6:27, 40, 47, 54, 58; 8:51; 10:10, 27-30; 11:25-26; 12:25, 49-50; 20:30-31)
Because Jesus is God, he lives forever. Before the world began, Jesus lived with God, and he will reign forever with God. In John we see Jesus revealed in power and magnificence even before his resurrection.

Jesus offers eternal life to us. We are invited to live in a personal, eternal relationship with him that begins now. Although we must eventually age and die, by trusting Christ we can have a new life that lasts forever.

- How does the idea of eternal life affect the way you view your earthly life?
- What effect should the promise of eternal life in Jesus Christ have on the way you relate to non-Christians?
- How can you be more faithful to the reality of eternal life in how you live your life now on earth?

FAITH (1:12, 50; 2:11, 23; 3:15-18; 4:39-42, 48-53; 5:24, 47; 6:30, 47, 64; 8:24, 31; 9:38; 10:25-42; 11:25-27; 12:37-46; 14:11-14; 16:9; 17:8, 20; 20:25-30)
The book of John contains eight specific signs or miracles that reveal the nature of Jesus' power and love. We see Christ's power over everything created, and we see his love for all people. These signs encourage us to believe in him.

Believing is active, living, and continuous trust in Jesus as God. When we believe in Jesus' life, words, death, and resurrection, and when we commit our life to him, he cleanses us from sin and empowers us to follow him. Jesus provides the cleansing and empowering; it is our role to respond in true belief.

- What did John want to communicate about Jesus through the eight miracles he included in his book?
- What did John want to communicate through the names or descriptions of Jesus?
- What is the difference between knowing about Jesus and believing in him?
- How did you come to believe in Jesus? What does it mean to you to be a believer?
- What would you want to communicate about Jesus to your non-Christian friends? What could you do to begin to clearly communicate that message?

HOLY SPIRIT (1:32-34; 3:5; 6:63; 7:39; 14:16-26; 15:26; 16:7, 15)
Jesus taught his disciples that after he went back to heaven, the Holy Spirit would come. Then the Holy Spirit would indwell,

guide, counsel, and comfort all those who would follow Jesus. Through the Holy Spirit, Christ's presence and power are multiplied in all who believe.

Through God's Holy Spirit, we are drawn to him in faith. We must know the Holy Spirit in order to understand all that Jesus taught. We can experience Jesus' love and guidance as we allow the Holy Spirit to do his work in us.

- In 14:15-31 and 16:5-15 Jesus teaches specifically about the Holy Spirit. What are the key points of his teaching?
- What resources does the Holy Spirit provide?
- Why does God give his Holy Spirit to believers?
- What can you do to develop a daily reliance on the Spirit so that you are able to enjoy his presence and blessings?

RESURRECTION (20:1–21:23)

On the third day after Jesus died, he rose from the dead. This was verified by his disciples and many eyewitnesses. This reality changed the disciples from frightened deserters to dynamic leaders in the new church. This fact is the foundation of the Christian faith.

We can be changed, as the disciples were, and have confidence that our body will one day be raised to live with Christ forever. The same power that raised Christ to life can give us the ability to follow Christ each day. God wants us to live in victory, not in fear or despair.

- What makes the Resurrection so essential to the Christian faith?
- How would you have felt if you had been one of the disciples who thought Jesus was dead and then saw him alive? What impact would this experience have had on your life?
- What does it mean to live as a Christian who takes the Resurrection seriously?

 *Postcard*

John himself provides the central application for his Gospel—he wrote it so that you could be sure you believed in Jesus (20:31). How do you know that you have reached a place of trust in Christ as Lord and Savior?

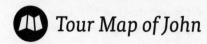

Tour Map of John

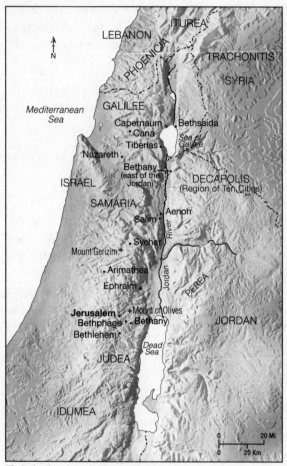

The broken lines (·–·–) indicate modern boundaries.

ACTS

 Snapshot of Acts

Assemble nine very different people:

1. The class cutup who makes everything funny;
2. The preppie rich kid with her very own BMW;
3. The minority student from the "bad" part of town;
4. The human computer who would rather do calculus problems than anything else;
5. The mammoth football jock who loves to bash things, especially quarterbacks;
6. The student whose recent "achievements" read like a sleazy novel;
7. The school airhead who is not exactly headed for a career as a genetic scientist;
8. The campus philosopher/political activist who loves to argue and hates "shallow" people;
9. The quiet classmate who never fits in.

Now give them a simple task to do . . . together.

Even if you could get them all in the same room, they'd never complete the assignment. What they'd most likely produce is non-stop arguing, bickering, and chaos! If they functioned as a team at all, it would be bumpy and very brief.

So how do we explain the first-century church? How did several hundred radically different people accomplish the complicated and time-consuming project of taking Jesus' story all over the world? How did they handle conflicts?

PURPOSE:
To give an accurate account of the birth and growth of the Christian church

AUTHOR:
Luke

TO WHOM WRITTEN:
Theophilus ("one who loves God") and people everywhere

DATE WRITTEN:
Between AD 63 and 70

SETTING:
Acts is the link between Christ's life and the life of the church, between the Gospels and the Epistles.

KEY PEOPLE:
Peter, John, James, Stephen, Philip, Paul, Barnabas, Cornelius, James (Jesus' brother), Timothy, Lydia, Silas, Titus, Apollos, Agabus, Ananias, Felix, Festus, Agrippa, Luke

KEY PLACES:
Jerusalem, Samaria, Lydda, Joppa, Antioch in Syria, Cyprus, Antioch in Pisidia, Iconium, Lystra, Derbe, Philippi, Thessalonica, Berea, Athens, Corinth, Ephesus, Caesarea, Malta, Rome

SPECIAL FEATURES:
Acts is a sequel to the Gospel of Luke. It provides the background and location for many of the letters that make up the rest of the New Testament. It is our earliest and clearest record of the spread of the gospel after Jesus' departure. Acts ends so abruptly that many scholars have thought that Luke must have planned to write a third book in the series.

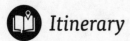 *Itinerary*

The book of Acts begins with the outpouring of the promised Holy Spirit and the commencement of the proclamation of the gospel of Jesus Christ. This Spirit-inspired evangelism begins in Jerusalem and eventually spreads to Rome, covering most of the Roman Empire. This is according to Jesus' plan: the gospel is to go from Jerusalem, to Judea, to Samaria, and to the ends of the earth (1:8). This, in fact, is the pattern that the Acts narrative follows. The glorious proclamation begins in Jerusalem (1–7) and continues into Judea and Samaria and the immediately neighboring countries (8–28).

Peter's Ministry (1:1–12:25)
The most prominent figure in these chapters is Peter, the leader of the early church. He boldly preaches the gospel and performs many miracles in Jesus' name. He is beaten and imprisoned for his faithfulness to Christ, but he stands firm in his faith and continues to lead the early church. During this time of intense expansion and resistance, a fierce enemy of Christians becomes a passionate spokesman for Christ (Saul the persecutor becomes Paul the persuader).

Paul's Ministry (13:1–28:31)
The remainder of Acts describes the ebb and flow of the gospel tide that floods the world. In this section Paul's ministry takes center stage. He and his companions take the gospel first to the Jews and then to the Gentiles. Some of the Jews believe, and many of the Gentiles receive the Good News with joy. New churches are started, and new believers begin to grow in the Christian life. As the book closes, Paul remains in prison, but his sights are still set on further horizons for the gospel.

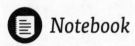 *Notebook*

CHURCH BEGINNINGS (1:4-8, 12-26; 2:1–8:40)
Acts is the history of how Christianity was founded and organized and how the church solved its problems. The community of believers began by faith in the risen Christ and in the power of the Holy Spirit, who enabled them to witness, love, and serve, and so reach their world for Christ.

New churches are continually being founded. By faith in Jesus Christ and in the power of the Holy Spirit, the church can be a vibrant agent for change. Acts gives important remedies for solving new problems we may face. God wants us to work together to bring his Good News to the world.

• What relationships do you see in the first gatherings of believers (see 2:42-47 and 4:32-37)?

- What is similar and what is different between your church and these early gatherings?
- What do you learn from 6:1-7 about how to deal with conflict in the church? What do you learn about the importance of servants in the church?
- What can you do to help resolve a conflict or to serve in your church?

HOLY SPIRIT (1:5, 8; 2:1-13, 17-18, 38-39; 4:8, 25, 31; 5:3, 9, 32; 6:3, 8; 7:51, 55; 8:15-24, 29; 9:17, 31; 10:19, 38, 44-47; 11:12-18, 24, 28; 13:2-12, 52; 15:8, 27-29; 16:6-7; 19:2-6, 21; 20:22-28; 21:4, 10-12; 28:25)

The church did not start or grow by its own power or enthusiasm. The disciples were empowered by God's Holy Spirit, the promised Counselor sent by Jesus when he went to heaven.

The Holy Spirit's work demonstrated that Christianity is supernatural. Thus the church became more Holy Spirit-conscious than problem-conscious. By faith any believer can experience the Holy Spirit's power to do Christ's work.

- What acts did God perform through the Holy Spirit as recorded in chapters 2–5? What was God's purpose in acting so dramatically?
- What were the key results of the Holy Spirit's work in the early church?
- When do you need to rely upon the Holy Spirit?

CHURCH GROWTH (2:37-47; 4:1-4, 32-37; 5:12-16, 42; 6:1-7; 8:12, 40; 9:31-35, 39-42; 10:44-48; 11:19-21, 24; 12:24; 13:42-49; 14:1, 21-28; 16:4-5, 13-15, 29-34; 17:1-4, 10-12, 32-34; 18:7-8; 19:17-20; 28:23-31)

Acts presents the history of a dynamic, growing community of believers, from Jerusalem to Syria, Africa, Asia, and Europe. In the first century, the faith spread from believing Jews to non-Jews in thirty-nine cities and thirty countries or provinces.

When the Holy Spirit works, there is movement, excitement, and growth. He gives us the motivation and ability to get the gospel to the whole world. You can be an important part of this great world movement. Begin in your neighborhood and school to live for Christ and share the gospel with others.

- How did the growth of the church in Acts accomplish Jesus' words in 1:8?
- Look again at 1:8. What would be your Jerusalem? Judea? Samaria?
- In what specific ways can you be used by God in each of the areas you listed above?

WITNESSING (1:8; 2:4-40; 3:12-26; 4:8-15; 5:29-32, 42; 6:7; 7:1-56; 8:4-40; 9:20-22, 28-29; 10:34-43; 11:4-17, 20-21; 13:4-6, 16-47; 14:1, 6-7, 14-17, 21; 16:9-15, 25-34; 17:2-4, 22-34; 18:4-11, 19-20, 24-28; 19:8-10; 20:7, 20-27; 22:1-21; 23:1, 6; 24:10-21, 24-26; 26:1-23, 28-29; 28:17-31)

Peter, John, Philip, Paul, Barnabas, and thousands more told others about their new faith in Christ. By personal testimony, preaching, or defense before authorities, they shared the story with boldness and courage.

We are God's people, chosen to be part of his plan to reach the world. In love and by faith, we can have the Holy Spirit's help as we share the gospel. Witnessing also strengthens our faith.

- In what ways did the early witnesses for Jesus share their message?
- Looking back at your responses under church growth, what are some of the opportunities you have for being a witness for Christ?
- What are you doing now to be a witness for Christ? What could you do to be more effective?

OPPOSITION (4:1-22, 29-30; 5:17-42; 6:8-14; 7:54-60; 8:1-3; 9:1-2, 22-30; 12:1-19; 13:50-52; 14:1-7, 19-20; 16:16-39; 17:5-9; 13; 18:12-17; 19:9, 23-41; 21:26-36; 22:22-29; 23:2, 7-10, 12-21; 24:1-9; 25:2-7)

Through imprisonment, beatings, plots, and riots, Christians were persecuted by both Jews and Gentiles. But the opposition became a catalyst, an energizer for the spread of Christianity. In the face of opposition, it soon became evident that Christianity was not the work of humans but of God.

God can work through any opposition. When you are treated harshly through ridicule, lies, or physical abuse from hostile un-believers, realize that it is happening because of your faithful witness. Take every opportunity, even those that opposition brings, for communicating the Good News of Jesus Christ.

- How did the various followers of Jesus respond to opposition and persecution?
- How do you think these individuals felt when they were being threatened, ridiculed, beaten, even stoned? What motivated them to continue?
- What potential opposition awaits you in your efforts to be a witness for Christ?
- What are some possible responses that you might have when faced with this opposition?
- How might God use the opposition you face to bring glory to himself and further his Kingdom?

 Postcard

If you are a believer in Jesus, Acts will introduce you to your ancient heritage. Remember that the commands and opportunities to bear witness about your faith to others remain constant. How will people know that you are one of the Christians today?

Tour Map of Paul's Missionary Journeys

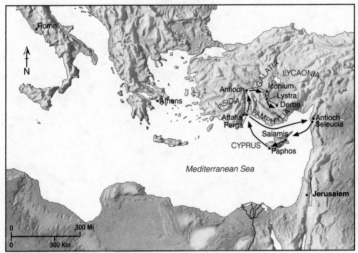

PAUL'S FIRST MISSIONARY JOURNEY (ACTS 13:1–14:28)

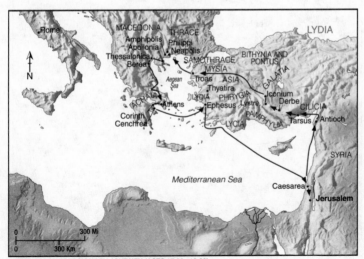

PAUL'S SECOND MISSIONARY JOURNEY (ACTS 15:36–18:22)

Paul's Missionary Journeys continued

PAUL'S THIRD MISSIONARY JOURNEY (ACTS 18:23–21:16)

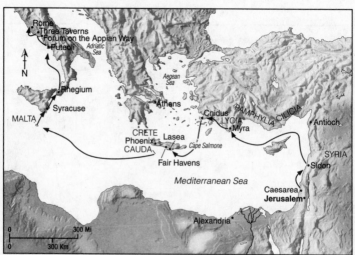

PAUL'S JOURNEY TO ROME (ACTS 21:17–28:31)

ROMANS

 Snapshot of Romans

Imagine you're out on an evening run when you happen upon your dream car. As you admire its beauty, you notice a key in the ignition . . . and unlocked doors. The car seems to say "Take me out for a quick spin." You glance around. The street is deserted.

"But that would be stealing!" your conscience protests. "No way!" another voice blurts in. "You're not going to keep it." The inner voices battle, and adventure wins out. You slide into the driver's seat, and the engine hums to life.

You intend to make one slow trip around the block—but the speedometer goes up to 160 mph, and when will you ever get another chance like this? You head for the open road.

What happens next is a blur. You remember the exhilaration of 143 mph, then flashing blue lights, cold steel handcuffs, being in court, and the judge's gavel pounding out a guilty verdict. The sentence: ten thousand dollars and six months' incarceration. You deserve punishment, but that's a severe penalty!

Then the judge does something curious. He removes his robe, whips out his checkbook, and pays your fine! Next he announces that he will serve your jail sentence. Then he looks you in the eyes and says, "I love you."

This analogy isn't perfect, but it does help explain how God deals with sinful humanity. The very penalty he demands (death for sin), he provided (the death of Christ on the cross). If you would like an even better explanation of God's perfect justice and his intense love for you, read the book of Romans.

PURPOSE:
To introduce Paul to the Romans and to give a sample of his message prior to his arrival in Rome

AUTHOR:
Paul

TO WHOM WRITTEN:
The Christians in Rome and believers everywhere

DATE WRITTEN:
About AD 57, from Corinth, as Paul was preparing for his visit to Jerusalem

SETTING:
Apparently Paul has finished his work in the east, and he plans to visit Rome on his way to Spain after first bringing a collection to Jerusalem for the poor Christians there (15:23-28). The Roman church is mostly Jewish but also contains many Gentiles.

KEY PEOPLE:
Paul, Phoebe

KEY PLACE:
Rome

SPECIAL FEATURE:
Stands out among Paul's letters as the most detailed, organized, and carefully presented statement of faith

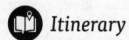 *Itinerary*

Paul had a standard plan for writing letters. He usually emphasized the points he wanted to make to his readers; then he showed how those points would affect their lives. Teaching was backed up with application. He followed this plan in Romans.

What to Believe (1:1–11:36)
The first major section covers the basics of what Christians believe. These chapters contain explanations of the core message that God wants each person to know and believe: sin, salvation, spiritual growth, and God's sovereignty. Each of these themes provides an important part of the puzzle of faith.

How to Behave (12:1–16:27)

The second major section of Romans spells out how Christians should behave. Paul doesn't hesitate to tell Christians that the glorious gift of the gospel comes with challenging responsibilities. He calls Christians to be individually and corporately faithful to God in practical ways in the world.

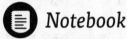 *Notebook*

SIN (1:18–3:20)

Sin means refusing to do God's will and failing to do all that God wants. Since Adam rebelled against God, it has become our nature to disobey God. Our sin cuts us off from God, and sin causes us to want to live our own way rather than God's way. Because God is morally perfect, just, and fair, he is right to condemn sin.

Each person has sinned, either by rebelling against God or by ignoring his will. No matter what our background or how hard we try to live a good and moral life, we cannot earn salvation or remove our sin. Only Christ can save us.

- Through Paul's writings to Rome, God reveals to us how destructive sin is in our world, how widespread it is in humankind, and how fatal it is to individuals. In chapters 1, 3, and 5, what key teachings do you find on the topic of sin?
- What are some of the consequences of humankind's choice to rebel against God's will?
- How does sin enslave a person?
- Now read 7:14-25 to catch a glimpse of Paul's personal battle with sin. How does Paul overcome his weaknesses?
- Check out your life in light of this study. What are the consequences of your sinful choices? At what points has sin enslaved you? Where can you identify with the feelings and thoughts of Paul?
- How does an awareness of your sin lead you to a deeper reliance upon Jesus Christ?

SALVATION (3:21–5:21)

Our sin points out our need to be forgiven and cleansed. Although we don't deserve it, God in his kindness reaches out to love and forgive us. He provides the way for us to be saved. Christ's death paid the penalty for our sin.

It is good news that God saves us from our sin. But we must believe in Jesus Christ and accept his forgiveness to enter into a wonderful new relationship with God.

- Read Romans 3:23; 5:8; 6:23; and 10:9-10. How would you use these verses to explain what it means to receive salvation through Jesus Christ?
- Describe your own personal response to the message of salvation. When did you first hear it? When did you first believe?
- What difference has your Christ-given salvation made in your daily life?
- How does knowing that God has forgiven your sins affect the way you live?

GROWTH (6:1–8:17; 12:1-2)

By God's power believers are made holy. This is known as sanctification. It means we are set apart from sin, enabled to obey and to become more like Christ. When we are growing in our relationship with Christ, the Holy Spirit frees us from the demands of the law and from the fear of God's judgment.

Because we are free from sin's control, the law's demands, and fear of God's punishment, we can grow in our relationship with Christ. By trusting in the Holy Spirit and allowing him to help us, we can overcome sin and temptation. Without the Holy Spirit, we would be unable to conquer sin's power.

- Rewrite 12:1-2 in your own words.
- How has God transformed you?
- In what areas of your life have you struggled—or are now struggling—with conformity to the world?
- What should you do to submit more fully to God?

SOVEREIGNTY (8:18–11:36)

God oversees and cares about his people—past, present, and future. God's ways of dealing with people are always fair. Because God is in charge of all creation, he can save whomever he wills.

Because of God's mercy, both Jews and Gentiles can be saved— we all need to respond to God's mercy and accept his gracious offer of forgiveness. God is sovereign, so let him reign in your heart.

- In what ways does the life of the person who seeks to accept and live under God's rule contrast with the person who ignores or rejects Christ as Lord?
- Describe Jesus' lordship in your life. What does it mean to let him be Lord over your life?
- What confidence do you have because of the sovereignty of God?

SERVICE (12:1–15:13)

When our purpose is to give credit to God for his love, power, and perfection in all we do, we can serve him properly. Serving God unifies all believers and enables them to be loving and sensitive to others.

No individual can be fully Christlike by himself or herself—it takes the entire body of Christ to fully express Christ. By actively and vigorously building up other believers, Christians can be a symphony of service to God.

- Chapters 12–15 include various teachings on how to live with fellow believers as members of Christ's body. In what ways are we to relate to each other to show that we are unified?
- Who are the Christians with whom you are the closest? Why do you feel close to these people?
- What Christians do you find difficult to love? What could you do to get along better with them?
- What acts of service could you do for those you listed in the previous two questions?

▣ *Postcard*

Since Romans provides a detailed, concise, and authoritative summary of Christianity, those who are determined to live a full and whole Christian life must sooner or later enter Paul's classroom and take his course. Make the decision that your faith will grow not only in obedience and feeling but also in knowledge. See Romans as a primary source.

1 CORINTHIANS

📷 Snapshot of 1 Corinthians

Fifteen-year-old Rick just recently accepted Christ. Yesterday he watched in total disbelief as two of the "leaders" of his church got into a shouting (and shoving!) match after Sunday services. Rick quietly asks you why supposedly "mature" Christians act that way. What do you say?

Kim has discovered that a man and woman who are active in the church aren't really married but are living together. "How can they do that? Why doesn't the preacher talk to them? Isn't that a sin?" Kim says, puzzled. What would you tell her?

Twelve-year-old Abby knows, as a Christian, that certain activities are wrong—drunkenness, premarital sex, lying, stealing, etc. But what about all those "gray areas" that God's Word doesn't address? Is it okay to dance, go to certain parties, or buy expensive clothes? What about her favorite videos on MTV and songs on the radio? And how does God feel about the movies she's watched recently? "I want to do what's right," she tells you, "but sometimes it's hard to know. Aren't there some guidelines from the Bible that can help?" How do you answer?

These questions are far from new. Christians (and churches) have struggled with immaturity, division, and immorality since the first hymn was sung. Fortunately, 1 Corinthians has some real and practical answers. If you are committed to living a godly life in a godless culture or you want to help someone else do so, keep reading.

PURPOSE:

To identify problems in the Corinthian church, to offer solutions, and to teach the believers how to live for Christ in a corrupt society

AUTHOR:

Paul

TO WHOM WRITTEN:

The church in Corinth and Christians everywhere

DATE WRITTEN:

About AD 55, near the end of Paul's three-year ministry in Ephesus during his third missionary journey

SETTING:

Corinth is a major cosmopolitan city, a seaport, and a major trade center—the most important city in Achaia. It is also filled with idolatry and immorality. The church is largely made up of Gentiles. Paul established this church on his second missionary journey.

KEY PEOPLE:

Paul, Timothy, members of Chloe's household

KEY PLACES:

Worship meetings in Corinth

SPECIAL FEATURES:

Probably best known for chapter 13, the great description of godly love. Also includes the most extensive teaching on the nature and functions of the church as well as the central importance of the resurrection of Jesus Christ

 # Itinerary

While on an extended stay in Ephesus, Paul receives disturbing news about the young church in Corinth. He also gets a letter filled with questions from that church. This first letter to Corinth tries to address those issues.

Paul Addresses Church Problems (1:1–6:20)

First Paul tackles the major problems of the church. The Corinthians are exhibiting a shocking lack of unity. Christians are taking each other to court over matters they should be able to settle alone. There are also scandalous examples of sexual immorality in the church. Paul calls them all to be faithful and consistent in obedience to God's Word.

Paul Answers Church Questions (7:1–16:24)

Next Paul responds to a list of questions he has received from the church. These questions concern issues like Christian marriage, eating meat offered to idols, worship, spiritual gifts, and the Lord's Supper. This section also includes the great chapters on love (13) and the Resurrection (15).

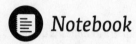 *Notebook*

LOYALTIES (1:10-31; 2:1-5; 3:1-15; 4:1-21; 9:1-27)

The Corinthians were rallying around various church leaders and teachers—Peter, Paul, and Apollos. These loyalties led to intellectual pride and divided the church.

Our loyalty to human leaders or human wisdom must never divide us into exclusive groups. We must care for our fellow Christians, not fight with them. Your allegiance must be to Christ. Let him lead you.

- How did Paul feel about the various groups who were giving their allegiance to him or Peter or Apollos?
- What did Paul want to change about their attitude? Why?
- Based on this passage, at what point does loyalty become a problem in the church?
- Who are the key Christian leaders you respect? What should be your attitude toward them?

IMMORALITY (1:8; 5:1-13; 6:9-20; 7:1-40; 9:24-27; 10:1-13; 16:13)

Paul received a report of uncorrected sexual sin in the church at Corinth. The people had grown indifferent to immorality. Others had misconceptions about marriage. The believer should live morally because he or she should be ready to serve God.

Christians must never compromise with sinful ideas and practices. You should not become just like those around you, even if everyone seems to disagree with your moral beliefs. You must live up to God's standard of morality and not go along with immoral behavior.

- What specific immorality does Paul condemn in chapter 5?

- Why is this type of immorality such an offense to God?
- Why do you think the Corinthians were tolerating this behavior?
- How did Paul indicate that they should deal with this ongoing sin?
- How is this different from the way they should have responded to someone who was sinning but was not claiming to be a Christian? (See 5:9-11.)
- How can you make an impact on your world without allowing the world to influence you?

FREEDOM (8:1-13; 9:19-27; 10:23-33; 11:1)

Paul taught freedom of choice on practices not expressly forbidden in Scripture. Some believers thought that certain actions—like buying the meat of animals used in heathen rituals—were wrong. Others believed they could do such things without sinning because they were free from the law.

We are free in Christ, yet we must not abuse our Christian freedom by being inconsiderate and insensitive to others. We must never encourage others to do wrong by anything we do. Love should guide our behavior.

- In chapter 8 Paul instructs the Corinthians on their freedom in Christ. What key principles do you find in this passage for dealing with areas of conduct that are "grays," not black or white?
- What are some of the gray areas about which Christians have different opinions?
- How could you as a Christian misuse your freedom in Christ and hurt someone else in these gray areas?
- In what specific ways could you apply the principles of chapter 8 to your freedom in Christ?

WORSHIP (11:2-34; 14:1-40)

Paul addressed disorder in worship. People were taking the Lord's Supper without first confessing sin. There was misuse of spiritual gifts and confusion over the role of women in the church.

Worship must be carried out properly and in an orderly manner. Everything we do to worship God should be done in a manner worthy of his high honor.

- What concerns did Paul have concerning worship in the Corinthian church? What does this teach you about Paul's view of worship?
- What actions or attitudes sometimes disrupt true worship in your church?
- What actions and attitudes encourage true worship in your church?
- What can you do in your church to help people's worship remain true?

RESURRECTION (15:1-58)

Some people denied that Christ rose from the dead. Others believed that people would not be physically resurrected. Christ's resurrection assures us that we will have a new, living body after we die. The fact of the Resurrection is the secret of Christian hope.

Because we will be raised again to life after we die, our life is not in vain. We must stay faithful to God in how we live and serve. And we should live today knowing that we will spend eternity with Christ. Eternal life has already begun!

- Read chapter 15. According to Paul, what is the importance of the Resurrection?
- What misconceptions did some of the Corinthians have regarding the resurrection of the dead? How did Paul correct those wrong ideas?
- What would be different about life if Jesus had not risen from the dead?
- How would you respond if asked to describe the difference Christ's resurrection has made in your own life?

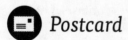 *Postcard*

The specific problems may change from time to time, but certain challenges remain constant for believers in Jesus. Because we live in a sinful world, we will face temptations in our relationships with each other. We will be tempted to make Jesus more acceptable to the world. We will be lured into following human leaders rather than Jesus. As you read through 1 Corinthians, recommit yourself to being faithful to God's Word in the specifics of daily life.

2 CORINTHIANS

 Snapshot of 2 Corinthians

Ministry . . . or Madness? A quiz just for you:

At Bible club it rains, a kid throws up on you, and one obnoxious six-year-old complains for ninety minutes about watery punch. Do you: (a) dump the watery punch on the obnoxious kid? (b) wipe up the vomit and dump the punch on the obnoxious kid? (c) retire from your Bible club career? (d) pray (really hard!) for patience and kindness?

Your youth group gives four hundred hard-earned dollars to a family whose house just burned down. The family never even acknowledges the gift! Do you: (a) break out your lecture on the importance of gratitude? (b) think of all the ways you could have used the cash? (c) ask for the money back? (d) trust that God is in control?

During a church missions trip, some older teens surround you and call you names, shove you, and make fun of the Christian message on your T-shirt. Do you: (a) "do a Samson" (beat them up in the name of Jesus)? (b) change your shirt? (c) vow never to stand up for Christ again? (d) consider it an honor to suffer for Christ?

Second Corinthians discusses: (a) living for the Lord when nothing seems to go right; (b) why it is worth it (no matter what happens) to serve God and others; (c) the amazing truth that we can't outgive God; (d) the importance of telling others about Jesus Christ; (e) all of the above.

Being Christ's ambassador isn't crazy—it's the only way to find deep-down satisfaction! Tempted to give up? Second Corinthians is just what you need.

PURPOSE:
To affirm Paul's own ministry, defend his authority as an apostle, and refute the false teachers in Corinth

AUTHOR:
Paul

TO WHOM WRITTEN:
The church in Corinth and Christians everywhere

DATE WRITTEN:
About AD 55–57, from Macedonia

SETTING:
Paul has already written three letters to the Corinthians (two are now lost). In 1 Corinthians (the second of these letters), he used strong words to correct and teach. Most of the church has responded in the right spirit. There are, however, those who are denying Paul's authority and questioning his motives.

KEY PEOPLE:
Paul, Timothy, Titus, false teachers

KEY PLACES:
Corinth, Jerusalem

SPECIAL FEATURE:
Along with 2 Timothy, 2 Corinthians is the most personal and intimate of Paul's writings.

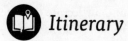 *Itinerary*

In this letter to the church at Corinth (actually his fourth), Paul responds to attacks on his character and authority. Apparently the Corinthians have been using misrepresentations of Paul as an excuse for some of their own misbehavior.

Paul Explains His Actions (1:1–2:11)
The apostle begins with an explanation of his recent actions. He has made some tough decisions about his travel plans. He is prayerfully hoping his letters will prepare the way for a future visit.

Paul Defends His Ministry (2:12–7:16)
Next Paul describes the components of genuine ministry, using his own track record as an example. He also asks them to remember how he has treated them with integrity.

Paul Defends the Collection (8:1–9:15)

Then Paul reminds the Corinthians of their connections in Christ with Christians everywhere. He defends the collection he has been accumulating to take to Jerusalem, where Christians are in dire need. He wants the Corinthians to feel a sense of duty toward those through whom they received the gospel.

Paul Defends His Authority (10:1–13:14)

Last Paul defends his authority as an apostle. He makes it clear that God's call on his life has little to do with any merit of his own. He continues to be amazed by God's grace in his life. He also recognizes in his "thorn in the flesh" God's choice to keep him humble. As the letter ends, Paul remains hopeful of a positive visit in the near future.

 Notebook

TRIALS (1:3-11; 2:1-11; 6:3-13; 12:1-10)

Paul experienced great suffering, persecution, and opposition in his ministry. He even struggled with a personal weakness—a "thorn in the flesh." Through it all Paul affirmed God's faithfulness.

God is faithful. His strength is sufficient for any trial, and trials can keep us from becoming prideful and teach us dependence on God. We must look to God for comfort during trials. As he comforts us, we can learn to comfort others.

- What are some of the feelings Paul expressed regarding his personal trials?
- What truth had Paul learned from his suffering and persecution?
- Based on Paul's example, what feelings can you expect when you encounter trials?
- What attitude does God want you to have during trials? Why?
- Describe a time when you encountered personal difficulty. How did you feel then? How do you feel about the experience now? What did you learn about God from that experience?

CHURCH DISCIPLINE (2:1-17; 5:11-21; 7:2-16; 10:1-18; 11:1-33; 12:1-21; 13:1-4)

Paul defended his role in church discipline. Neither immorality nor false teaching could be ignored. The church was to be neither too lax nor too severe in administering discipline. The church was to restore the corrected person when that person repented.

The goal of discipline in the church should be correction, not vengeance. For churches to be effective, they must confront and solve problems, not ignore them. But in everything we must act in and on behalf of God's love.

- In 2:5-11 we are given a glimpse into what church discipline should be about. What does this passage teach you about Paul?
- What was Paul's motive for seeing the person disciplined?
- What should the church's role be when dealing with members who refuse to repent of sin?
- What does this teach about how God wants you to deal with your sins?

HOPE (3:7–5:10)

Paul tried to encourage the Corinthians as they faced trials by reminding them that they would receive new bodies in heaven. This would be a great victory in contrast to their present suffering.

Knowing that we will receive new bodies gives us hope. No matter what we face, we can keep going, for our faithful service will result in triumph.

- What hope does Paul gives to the Corinthians in 5:1-10?
- Why did Paul use this part of his letter to communicate this hope to the Corinthians? (See 4:13-18.)
- Under what circumstances would you most need to be reminded of your heavenly hope?
- How should being reminded of that promise bring hope to you in your present circumstances?

GIVING (8:1–9:15)

Paul organized a collection of funds for the poor in the Jerusalem church. Many of the Asian churches gave money. Paul explained and defended his beliefs about giving, and he urged the Corinthians to follow through on their previous commitment.

We, too, should honor our financial commitments. Our giving must be generous, sacrificial, according to a plan, and based on our ability. Generosity helps the needy, enabling them to thank God. Giving is a part of our godliness.

- What benefit had Paul received from the believers' giving? What benefit had the believers themselves received as a result of their giving?
- What should Christians understand about giving money for God's work in the church? How could this be applied to giving other personal resources, such as time and service?
- In what ways do you think God wants you to continue what you are doing in your giving? How should you change what you are doing?

SOUND DOCTRINE (6:14–7:1; 13:5-13)

False teachers were challenging Paul's ministry and authority as an apostle. Paul asserted his authority to preserve correct Christian doctrine. His sincerity, love for Christ, and concern for the people were his defense.

We should share Paul's concern for correct teaching in our church. In so doing we must also share his motivation—love for Christ and people—and we should be sincere.

- Describe the common characteristics of those who were opposing Paul (chapters 10–11).
- How was Paul responding to their opposition? Why do you think he was so concerned about their influence?
- Contrast Paul's ministry with the actions of those who opposed him. What were the key differences?
- How can you avoid being deceived by teachers of false doctrine?
- We must not only know sound doctrine but also live according to its truth. What areas of your daily life reflect sound doctrine?

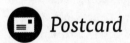 *Postcard*

Discipleship—trusting Jesus—is not just a decision; it is a lifestyle. You choose to follow daily—for a lifetime. As you read 2 Corinthians, look for ways to make decisions from the long view, not just the short view of the Christian life.

GALATIANS

 Snapshot of Galatians

Ever known a church like Matt's? Words like *different* and *strict* don't even begin to tell the story. Maybe Matt's best friend Randy gave the best description. He attended Matt's church for several months—then quit. Matt wanted to know why.

"I just don't like it, OK?" Randy finally said. "It's the 'don't church.' You guys have about 50 million rules! Don't date. Don't wear certain clothes. Don't go to the movies. Don't dance. Don't go to parties. Don't wear jewelry. Don't be friends with non-Christians. And the list just keeps going. I can't even remember all the rules, much less follow them! Besides, some people there act like they're better than people who go to other churches."

"But you said you liked our preacher—and the services."

"I guess I did—at first. But I came home feeling more and more guilty and further away from God than ever. Sorry, Matt, but if following all those rules is how I'm supposed to get close to God, I might as well forget it. Hey, I want to be a good Christian—but I'll never be that good."

Almost two thousand years ago there was another "don't church" of Christians trying to follow rules. In fact, a whole book of the Bible addresses trying to earn God's acceptance by doing "right" things.

Read Galatians. You'll find that anyone who thinks the Bible doesn't relate to modern times has never read it!

PURPOSE:
To refute the Judaizers (who taught that Gentile believers must obey the Jewish law to be saved), and to call Christians to faith and freedom in Christ

AUTHOR:
Paul

TO WHOM WRITTEN:
The churches in southern Galatia (including Iconium, Lystra, Derbe) founded on Paul's first missionary journey, and Christians everywhere

DATE WRITTEN:
About AD 49, from Antioch, prior to the Jerusalem council (AD 50)

SETTING:
The most pressing controversy of the early church is the relationship of new believers, especially Gentiles, to the Jewish laws. When this problem hit the converts and young churches Paul founded on his first missionary journey, Paul writes to correct it. Later, at the council in Jerusalem, the conflict is officially resolved by the church leaders.

KEY PEOPLE:
Paul, Peter, Barnabas, Titus, Abraham, false teachers

KEY PLACES:
Galatia, Jerusalem

SPECIAL FEATURE:
This letter is directed to the Christians in a region rather than to those in a particular church or city.

 Itinerary

Authenticity and Superiority of the Gospel (1:1–4:31)
Paul's purpose in writing this letter becomes apparent within the first few verses. After a brief introduction (1:1-5), the letter addresses those who were accepting the twisted gospel of the Judaizers (1:6-9). Paul summarizes the controversy, including his personal confrontation with Peter and other church leaders (1:10–2:16). He then demonstrates that salvation is by faith alone by alluding to his own conversion (2:17-21), appealing to his reader's experience of the gospel (3:1-5), and showing how the Old Testament teaches about grace (3:6-20). Next he explains the purpose of God's laws and the relationship between law, God's promises, and Christ (3:21–4:31).

Freedom of the Gospel (5:1–6:18)

Having laid the foundation, the letter builds Paul's case for Christian liberty: we are saved by faith, not by keeping the law (5:1-12); our freedom means that we are free to love and serve one another, not to do wrong (5:13-26); Christians should carry each other's burdens and be kind to each other (6:1-10). Paul himself (not a secretary) writes the final verses (6:11-18) to emphasize the importance of his final thoughts.

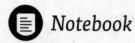 *Notebook*

LAW (1:6-8; 2:15-21; 3:1-25; 5:2-6; 6:12-16)

A group of Jewish teachers was insisting that non-Jewish believers obey Jewish laws and traditions. These teachers believed that a person was saved by following the law of Moses (with emphasis on circumcision, the sign of the covenant) in addition to faith in Christ. Paul opposed them, showing that the law can't save anyone.

The law can't save us. It wasn't ever meant to be our salvation. It was intended to be a guide, to point out our need to be forgiven. Christ fulfilled the obligations of the law for us, and we must turn to him to be saved. Christ alone can make us right with God. Then we should obey God in response to what he has done for us.

- What error had the Jewish believers made concerning the role of the law?
- What truth did Paul use to correct their error?
- Based on Galatians, why are good works not enough to bring a person salvation?
- How does the law point out our need for salvation?
- How should you respond to the law now that you have been saved through Jesus Christ?

FAITH (2:15-21; 3:6-18, 23-29)

God's gracious gift saves us from God's judgment and the penalty for sin. We receive salvation by faith—trusting in Christ, not in anything else. Becoming a Christian is in no way based on our work, wise choices, or good character. We can only be right with God by believing in Christ.

Eternal life comes only through faith in Christ. You must never add to this truth or twist it. We are saved by faith and faith alone. Have you placed your whole trust and confidence in Christ? He alone can forgive you and bring you into a relationship with God.

- What does it mean to be saved by faith?
- How would you answer a person who said, "I have been good, so I know God will let me into heaven"?
- In spite of your sin, God gave you faith. What does this reveal to you about God?
- How have you responded to God's offer of salvation?
- During this past week, how have you lived your life by faith?

FREEDOM (4:1–5:1, 13-15)

Galatians sets forth the believer's freedom in Christ. We are not under the jurisdiction of Jewish laws and traditions, nor under the authority of Jerusalem. Faith in Christ brings true freedom from sin and from the futile attempt to be right with God by keeping the law.

We are free in Christ—free to serve him—but freedom is a privilege. Let us use our freedom to love and to serve, not to do wrong.

- Finish these sentences: (a) Christian freedom means _____. (b) Christian freedom does not mean _____.
- In what ways could your freedom in Christ be misused?
- For what purpose has God given you freedom? How are you fulfilling that purpose in your life?

HOLY SPIRIT (3:14; 5:16–6:10)

We become Christians through the work of the Holy Spirit. The Spirit brings new life, and even our faith is a gift from him. The Holy Spirit instructs us, guides us, leads us, and gives us power. He ends our bondage to evil desires, brings us love, joy, and peace, and changes us into the image of Christ.

When the Holy Spirit controls us, he produces his fruit in us. Through faith we can have the Holy Spirit within us, strengthening and guarding us and helping us grow spiritually.

- According to 3:14, how does a person receive the Holy Spirit?

- According to 5:16-26, what difference does the Holy Spirit bring to a person's life? What difference has the Holy Spirit made in your life?
- Why do you need the Holy Spirit to be at work in your life?
- What can you do to continue to walk in the Spirit?

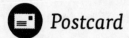 *Postcard*

As you read and study the letter to the Galatians, write out your understanding of Christian freedom. What specific guidelines will you use to help you make decisions about what you can and cannot do?

EPHESIANS

 Snapshot of Ephesians

Every event of every day underlines this fundamental fact: life is made up of relationships. We relate in a horizontal way to other people; we relate in a vertical manner to our Creator. Pretty basic stuff, right?

But here's where things get profound: our problems, individual and national, are due to broken-down relationships. It's because we fail to relate properly to God and to each other that we lie, cheat, steal, murder, drink and drive, divorce, engage in illicit sex, abort babies, fight wars, pollute, buy and sell drugs, ignore the needy, commit suicide, and do all the other wrong things we do.

So what is the remedy for ruptured relationships? In a nutshell: Jesus Christ can repair our broken-down relationships!

First Jesus pardons our sins, bringing us into a right relationship with God. (Get this—by faith in Christ we are adopted into God's family! We become his children . . . eternally!) Then Christ gives us the wisdom and the power to build stronger horizontal ties—with parents, friends, bosses . . . even enemies!

Can your relationships stand a little improving? Check out Ephesians. The first three chapters explain how Jesus has made it possible for us to know God in a personal way. The rest of the book provides practical tips for getting along with people.

Hey, it just might change your life!

PURPOSE:
To strengthen the faith of the believers in Ephesus by explaining the nature and purpose of the church, the body of Christ

AUTHOR:
Paul

TO WHOM WRITTEN:
The church at Ephesus and all believers everywhere

DATE WRITTEN:
About AD 60, from Rome, during Paul's imprisonment there

SETTING:
This letter was not written to confront any heresy or problem. Instead, it was sent with Tychicus to strengthen and encourage area churches. Paul has spent over three years with the Ephesian church; he is very close to the Ephesians. His last meeting with the Ephesian elders was at Miletus (Acts 20:17-38)—a meeting filled with great sadness because Paul was leaving them forever. There are no specific references to people or problems in the Ephesian church, so Paul may have intended this letter to be read to all the area churches.

KEY PEOPLE:
Paul, Tychicus

SPECIAL FEATURE:
Paul's letter to the Ephesians pours out positive teaching and encouragement from the apostle. He does not have to correct problems, so he concentrates on deepening their understanding of Jesus Christ.

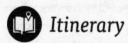 *Itinerary*

Unity in Christ (1:1–3:21)

After a warm greeting, Paul immediately affirms the nature of the church and the part of each believer in it. God has been carrying out a great plan throughout history, and that plan now includes them. This section concludes with a stirring challenge to the Ephesians to live close to Christ, and Paul breaks into spontaneous praise to God.

Unity in the Body of Christ (4:1–6:24)

As was Paul's usual practice, the second half of his letter is devoted to the practical implications of being in the body of Christ, the church. Believers should see the power of Christ's presence as they use their spiritual gifts, act with high moral standards, and allow holiness to guide their family lives. Included here is also a description of the spiritual armor that God provides to believers who are engaged in the struggle against evil in this world. The letter concludes with Paul's asking for prayer, identifying Tychicus as his chosen messenger, and giving a final word of blessing.

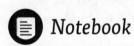 *Notebook*

GOD'S PURPOSE FOR A LIVING CHURCH (1:2–2:22; 4:4-6, 11-16)
According to God's eternal, loving plan, he directs, carries out, and sustains our salvation. When we respond to Christ's love by trusting in him, his purpose becomes our mission.

Have you committed yourself to fulfilling God's purpose? We should always be seeking to understand more of who God created us to be and what he wants us to do with our life.

- What does God want to accomplish through the working together of his children (the body of Christ)?
- What attitudes and actions are necessary for the body to function as it should? (Check Romans 12 and 1 Corinthians 12 for similar teaching on "body life.")
- In what ways can these attitudes be displayed and these actions be lived out in your church and among your Christian friends?
- What do you think God wants to accomplish through you for other believers?

CHRIST, THE CENTER (1:19-23; 2:19-22; 3:10-11, 20-21; 4:7-16)
Christ is exalted as the central meaning of the universe and the focus of history. He is the head of his body, the church.

Because Christ is central to everything, his power must be central in his people. This begins by placing all of life's priorities under his control. Your life decisions should be based on who you are as his disciple.

- According to 1:3-14, what do believers have in Christ?
- According to 2:11-22, how does Christ change human relationships?

- According to 4:11-16, what role does Christ play in the body?
- Review your responses to the previous questions. Why is it so important to make Jesus the central focus of your life, heart, and mind?
- Where is your focus today (at home, by yourself, with your best friends, at school, at church)? In what sense are you "on center" in your commitment to Christ? In what sense are you "off center"?

NEW FAMILY (1:5; 2:11-19; 3:6; 4:1-6; 5:21-23)

Because God through Christ paid our penalty for sin and forgave us, we have been reconciled and brought near to him. We are a new society, a new family. Being united with Christ means that we are to treat each other as family members.

We are one family in Christ, so there should be no barriers, no divisions, and no discrimination. Because we all belong to him, we should live in harmony with one another. We have a responsibility toward each other as brothers and sisters in Christ.

- Check out 2:11–3:13. How does God want Jews and Gentiles to relate?
- What people in your community do not relate well to each other because of differences in color, race, culture, social status, or other personal barriers?
- From what people are you most separated or alienated? What does this study teach you about those relationships? What can you do to change those relationships because of your faith in Christ?

CHRISTIAN CONDUCT (2:1-10; 3:14-19; 4:1-3, 17-32; 5:1–6:18)

Paul encouraged all Christians to make wise, dynamic Christian living a goal. God provides his Holy Spirit to enable believers to live his way. To utilize his power, we must lay aside our evil desires and draw upon the power of his new life.

Submit your will to Christ, and seek to love with his love by the power of the Spirit.

- Ephesians gives several specific commands to obey in following Christ (for instance, 4:25—tell the truth!). What are these commands?

- Now consider each item on your list in light of this question: How does doing this action relate to my loving God?
- Read 5:1-2. How does God's love become the motivation for Christian conduct?
- As you look at your list from the first question, which actions are areas of strength in your life? Which ones are weaknesses? How can you strengthen your areas of weakness so that you can walk more closely with God?

 Postcard

Becoming a Christian connects you to Jesus Christ. It also connects you to all other Christians. What regular actions in your life demonstrate those connections?

PHILIPPIANS

 Snapshot of Philippians

Time for a little daydreaming:

Scenario 1—A high-powered attorney calls to inform you that a distant relative has left you her entire estate, worth several million bucks!

Scenario 2—In the biggest game of the year, you score with one second left to give your school an upset victory.

Scenario 3—You learn that the most attractive member of the opposite sex (in your whole school!) likes you.

Some dreams, huh? So, do you think you could get excited about those situations? Okay, let's daydream some more:

Scenario 4—Your dad accidentally throws away your term paper—the one you worked on for over a month—the one that is due today.

Scenario 5—You develop a huge pimple on the end of your nose the night before the most important date of your life.

Scenario 6—Your boyfriend/girlfriend dumps you—for your best friend!

Okay, so these are more like nightmares. Is it possible to be joyful in bad situations like these? Believe it or not, it is possible to be content—even in the midst of horrible, terrible circumstances.

Facing problems or trials? Get a fresh perspective. Read Philippians, Paul's letter to the church at Philippi. The message is clear:

joy and contentment really can be ours . . . as long as we keep trusting God through life's hard times.

PURPOSE:
To thank the Philippians for the gift they had sent Paul and to strengthen them by showing that true joy comes from Jesus Christ

AUTHOR:
Paul

TO WHOM WRITTEN:
Christians at Philippi and all believers everywhere

DATE WRITTEN:
About AD 61, from Rome, during Paul's imprisonment there

SETTING:
Paul and his companions founded the church at Philippi on the second missionary journey (Acts 16:11-40). This was the first church established on the European continent. The Philippian church has sent a gift with Epaphroditus (one of the church members) to be delivered to Paul (4:18).

KEY PEOPLE:
Paul, Timothy, Epaphroditus, Euodia, Syntyche

KEY PLACE:
Philippi

SPECIAL FEATURE:
Philippians is literally filled with joy!

 Itinerary

Joy dominates this letter to the believers in Philippi. In fact, the concept of "rejoicing" or "joy" appears at least sixteen times in four chapters. Each of those chapters can be read as an encouragement to experience joy in four broad areas.

Joy in Suffering (1:1-30)
First comes the unexpected news that we can experience joy in suffering. This doesn't mean that we seek to enjoy suffering but that pain often clarifies our true source of joy.

Joy in Serving (2:1-30)
Next Paul urges us to have Christ's attitude and find joy in serving. Jesus not only gives us joy but provides the best example for us on how to live in joy.

Joy in Believing (3:1–4:1)

Third, joy deepens and grows as we participate in knowing and believing in Jesus. Compared to this, all other sources of joy fall short.

Joy in Giving (4:2-23)

Last, Paul instructs his brothers and sisters to get along in joy by giving. He recognizes personality conflicts but encourages the Philippians to focus on joy. He tells them to rejoice in the Lord always. Then he adds, "I say it again—rejoice!" (4:4).

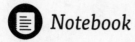 *Notebook*

HUMILITY (1:15-18; 2:5-11; 3:7-14)

Christ showed true humility when he laid aside his rights and privileges as God to become human. He poured out his life to pay the penalty we deserve. Laying aside self-interest is essential to all of our relationships.

We are to take Christ's attitude in serving others. We must not be concerned about personal recognition. When we give up the need to receive credit and praise, we will be able to serve with joy, love, and kindness.

- If a person were described to you as "humble," what would be your impression of that person? Positive or negative? Weak or strong? Unique or average?
- How did Jesus display his attitude of humility?
- If Jesus were to attend your school, how do you think people would respond to him as he humbly served others?
- What would it mean for you to display humility toward kids at school?

SELF-SACRIFICE (1:15-26; 2:4, 17, 25-30; 3:7-14; 4:14-19)

Christ suffered and died so that we might have eternal life. With courage and faithfulness, Paul sacrificed himself for the ministry, preaching the gospel even while he was in prison.

Christ gives us power to lay aside our personal needs and concerns. To utilize his power, we must imitate those leaders who deny themselves and serve others. We dare not be self-centered in view of such a self-sacrificing Savior.

- What are the differences between a self-sacrificing person and a self-centered one?
- What makes it difficult for a person to be self-sacrificing?
- What was the connection between the self-sacrifice of Jesus and the self-sacrifice of Paul?
- How could you overcome areas of self-centeredness through the help of Christ and the work of his Spirit? What will you do to begin this work?

UNITY (1:15-18, 27-30; 2:1-4, 14-16; 4:2-3)
In every church, in every generation, certain problems divide people (issues, loyalties, conflicts). It is easy to turn against each other. Paul encouraged the Philippians to agree with one another, to stop complaining, and to work together.

Believers should fight against a common enemy, not against each other. United in love, we become aware of Christ's strength. Always remember teamwork, consideration, and unselfishness. Keep your focus on the model of Jesus Christ.

- What things cause anger, hurt, and division among God's people?
- What principles do you find in Philippians that could prevent or help resolve such conflict?
- As you examine these principles, what truth is the key to maintaining unity in the body of believers?
- What can you do to apply these principles in relationships with your Christian friends—specifically those in your church?

CHRISTIAN LIVING (1:6, 9-11, 21-29; 2:12-13; 3:12-21; 4:4-13)
Paul shows how to live a successful Christian life. We can become mature by being so identified with Christ that his attitude of humility and sacrifice rules us. Christ is both our source of power and our guide.

Developing character begins with God's work in us, but it also requires discipline, obedience, and continual concentration on our part.

- Read 3:1-16. If you had never heard of Paul before, what would be your impression of him after reading these verses?

- Do you agree or disagree with this statement? Paul thought the Christian life was basically easy. Explain your response based on Philippians.
- Summarize the key points you find in Paul's testimony of himself and of his life in Christ. What can you do to develop godly character?
- Describe your life as a Christian. In what ways is your experience similar to Paul's? In what ways is it different?

JOY (1:3-6, 12-26; 2:1-4, 17-18; 3:1; 4:4-13)

Believers can have profound contentment, serenity, and peace no matter what happens. This joy comes from knowing Christ personally and from depending on his strength rather than on our own.

Joy does not come from outward circumstances but from inner strength. We Christians should not rely on what we have or what we experience to give us joy but on Christ within us. His joy is greater than life's trials.

- Based on Paul's circumstances and the content of his letter to the Philippians, how do you think Paul would have described being joyful?
- How can a Christian find joy in apparently unhappy circumstances?
- If a Christian friend were to say to you, "How can I possibly find joy in the Lord when life seems so unfair?" what would you say?
- How will you find joy in Jesus this week?

◼ Postcard

You need a joy checkup today. In what ways have you separated joy from happiness? What is the source of your joy?

COLOSSIANS

 Snapshot of Colossians

Will the real Jesus please stand up?

Sometimes it's hard to know what to think about Jesus Christ. Christians say he is God with skin on—the second person of the Trinity and the carpenter from Nazareth all rolled into one. Others insist he never even existed. Still others regard Jesus as a troublesome politician with a Messiah complex who ended up being executed. Then there is the Hollywood Jesus—weak, wishy-washy, misguided, filled with contradictions, and surrounded by controversy.

How about the increasingly popular New Age Jesus who is but one of many ways to God? And don't forget some cults who claim that Christ is now living on the earth in the person of their leader!

So, was Jesus just a good man and great moral teacher? Or was he, as Islam teaches, a prophet like Moses, Buddha, and Muhammad? Was he just one of many gods? Was he truly divine, was he just superhuman, or was he simply one manifestation of a divine, universal force?

Hundreds of conflicting ideas circulate about who Jesus is. But only one of the views can be true—which makes the others wrong . . . and extremely dangerous!

Don't fall for lies about Christ. Meet him as he really is. See for yourself how superior he is to everything and everyone else in the universe. See what it means to know him in a personal way. See all of this and more in the book of Colossians.

PURPOSE:
To combat errors in the church and to show that believers have everything they need in Christ

AUTHOR:
Paul

TO WHOM WRITTEN:
The church at Colosse, a city in Asia Minor, and all believers everywhere

DATE WRITTEN:
About AD 60, during Paul's imprisonment in Rome

SETTING:
Paul has never visited Colosse—evidently the church was founded by Epaphras and other converts from Paul's missionary travels. The church, however, has been infiltrated by religious relativism, with some believers attempting to combine elements of heathenism and secular philosophy with Christian doctrine. Paul confronts these false teachings and affirms the sufficiency of Christ.

KEY PEOPLE:
Paul, Timothy, Tychicus, Onesimus, Aristarchus, Mark, Epaphras

KEY PLACES:
Colosse, Laodicea (4:15-16)

SPECIAL FEATURES:
Colossians offers a clear and compelling view of Jesus' full identity as God coming to his creation as a human being. The beginning and end of this letter also offer an example of Paul's habit of praying for those he loved and then asking them to pray for him.

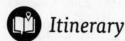 *Itinerary*

Typical of Paul, this letter devotes its first half to teaching and its second half to practical application. Paul wants his readers to understand in a fresh way the awesome truth about Jesus. But he also wants them to actively live out that truth in their daily lives.

What Christ Has Done (1:1–2:23)
The teaching part of this letter centers on what Jesus Christ has done. Jesus is essential to the Christian faith. He is ultimate truth. Any substitute is false.

What Christians Should Do (3:1–4:18)

The application section of this letter answers the question, What should Christians do? Our personal life and relationships will be affected if we are living for Christ. Jesus is Lord of every part of life: home, work, and worship.

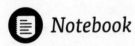 *Notebook*

CHRIST IS GOD (1:15-20; 3:15-17, 23-24)

Jesus Christ is God in the flesh, Lord of all creation, and Lord of the new creation. He is the exact reflection of the invisible God. He is eternal, preexistent, all-powerful, and equal with the Father. Christ is supreme and complete.

Because Christ is supreme, our life must be Christ centered. To recognize Jesus as God means to regard our relationship with him as most vital and to make his interests our top priority. He must become the navigator of life's voyage.

- What words and phrases are used to describe Jesus Christ in chapters 1 and 2? What do you learn about Christ as God in these descriptions?
- Why is it important to understand that Christ is both God and man?
- Based on the fact that Christ is truly God, how should you respond to his lordship (control and leadership)?
- How are you responding to Christ's lordship in your life at the present? What can you do to be more submissive to Christ's role as your Lord?

CHRIST IS THE HEAD OF THE CHURCH (1:15-20; 3:15-17, 23-24)

Because Jesus is God, he is the head of the church, his true believers. Christ is the founder and leader of the church and the highest authority on earth. He requires first place in all our thoughts and activities.

To acknowledge Christ as leader, we must welcome his leadership in all we do or think. No person, group, or church should have more loyalty from us than Jesus Christ.

- What does this phrase mean? Christ is the head of the church.

- If you were starting a local church, what kinds of things would you insist on in order to keep Christ as the central leader of that church?
- Write a statement for yourself and other young people that challenges them to respond to Christ's headship of your local church.

UNION WITH CHRIST (1:13, 21-23; 2:6-15, 20; 3:1-4, 11, 15-17)

Because our sins have been forgiven and we have been reconciled to God, we have a union with Christ that can never be broken. In our faith connection with Christ, we identify with his death, burial, and resurrection.

We should live in constant contact and communication with God. When we do, we will be unified with Christ and with our fellow believers. We are a part of each other's spiritual life-support system.

- Read 2:6-15. What were you called to be and do when you were united to Christ?
- Read 3:1-17. What does it mean to have new life in Christ?
- From what things were you set free when you were united with Christ?
- In what specific ways has your union with Christ made a difference in your past? in your present? in your future?

HUMAN-MADE RELIGION (2:8, 16-23)

False teachers were promoting a heresy that stressed human-made rules (legalism). They also sought spiritual growth by denying themselves personal contacts and by following mysterious rules. This search created pride in their self-centered efforts.

We must not hold on to our own ideas and try to blend them into Christianity. Nor should we let our hunger for a more fulfilling Christian experience cause us to trust in a teacher, group, or system of thought more than in Christ himself. Christ is our hope and our true source of wisdom. We must reject any teacher whose message is not based absolutely on the truth of Christ.

- What lie was behind the legalism that the false teachers taught to the Colossians?

- What is the danger of promoting a religion that is based on people's responsibility to save themselves with good works?
- What are some current examples of the false teachings of legalism? Why are these harmful? How does this hinder non-Christians from understanding and accepting the gospel?
- What can you do to make sure you don't get trapped by false teachings such as legalism?

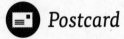 *Postcard*

How well can you put into words the basics of what you believe? Beginning with Jesus Christ himself, what else follows as central to your faith?

1 THESSALONIANS

 Snapshot of 1 Thessalonians

Phobias are "phascinating" phenomena. Psychiatrists and psychologists have catalogued hundreds of them. Check out this short list:

Anthophobia—the fear of flowers
Decidophobia—the fear of making decisions
Mysophobia—the fear of dirt
Trichophobia—the fear of hair

Would you believe that some people are even terrified about peanut butter sticking to the roof of their mouth? That's called arachibutyrophobia.

You may not struggle with such odd fears, but you probably do worry about more common stuff. Every day the media spotlights a different concern: Is the environment damaged beyond repair? Will researchers ever find a cure for AIDS? How many people are infected without knowing it? Are we on the brink of a worldwide economic collapse? How are we going to deal with a generation of drug-addicted babies? Can we confront and correct our country's epidemic of violent crimes? How has war affected our life?

These are scary issues, but the Christian has real hope and genuine peace—even in uncertain times.

That's the message of this book: be comforted, for no matter what happens, God is with us. Rest in the reassuring truth that Jesus Christ is coming back soon to . . .

Aw, that's enough blabbering. Read it yourself. You won't believe your eyes.

PURPOSE:
To strengthen the Thessalonian Christians in their faith and give them assurance of Christ's return

AUTHOR:
Paul

TO WHOM WRITTEN:
The church at Thessalonica and all believers everywhere

DATE WRITTEN:
About AD 51, from Corinth; one of Paul's earliest letters

SETTING:
The church at Thessalonica was established only two or three years before this letter was written. The Christians need to mature in their faith. Also, there is a misunderstanding about Christ's second coming—some think he will return immediately; others wonder if the dead will experience a bodily resurrection at his return.

KEY PEOPLE:
Paul, Timothy, Silas

KEY PLACE:
Thessalonica

SPECIAL FEATURE:
Although 1 Thessalonians was written after Paul had received a good report from Timothy about the church, Paul felt he had to correct some misconceptions of the Thessalonians regarding the resurrection and the return of Christ.

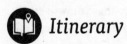 *Itinerary*

Faithfulness to the Lord (1:1–3:13)
The first half of this letter offers an extended note of affirmation to Paul's Thessalonian friends, recalling their response to the gospel and expressing joy over their continued faithfulness. Paul is glad about Timothy's glowing report of their spiritual growth.

Watchfulness for the Lord (4:1–5:28)
The letter then turns to the core of Paul's message—challenging encouragement. The apostle reminds the Thessalonian believers

that faithfulness to Christ must be exercised in daily living. Lastly, this brief epistle offers some extended teaching to help fill the gaps in the Thessalonian understanding of the Resurrection and Christ's second coming (4:13–5:28). Those who have died in Christ are just as available to greet the Lord's arrival as those who are still alive. No one who trusts Jesus will be left out.

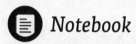 *Notebook*

PERSECUTION (1:6; 2:1-2, 14-16; 3:3-8)
Paul and the new Christians at Thessalonica experienced persecution because of their faith in Christ. Believers today can also expect trials and troubles. We need to stand firm in our faith during our trials, being strengthened by the Holy Spirit.

The Holy Spirit helps us to remain strong in faith; he enables us to show genuine love to others and to maintain our moral character even when we are being persecuted, slandered, or oppressed.

- How did the Thessalonians respond to pressure and opposition that came because of their faith in Christ?
- During this persecution, where did they get their strength?
- What pressures or opposition have you faced as a Christian? How did you feel when that happened? How have you responded to such situations?
- What does it mean to "stand firm" when you are persecuted?
- What can you do to prepare yourself so that you will stand firm throughout your life, even during intense persecution?

PAUL'S MINISTRY (1:5-6; 2:1-20; 3:1-8)
Paul expressed his concern for this church even while he was being slandered. Paul's commitment to share the gospel in spite of difficult circumstances is an example that believers today should follow.

Paul not only gave his message, he also gave himself. In our ministries we must become like Paul—faithful and bold yet sensitive and self-sacrificing. Achieving such maturity results from years of commitment to God's will—the younger you begin, the deeper will be your growth.

- What qualities do you see in Paul's wonderful example of godly ministry that enabled his message to be so powerful?
- If you were Paul's companion in ministry, what would you most want to learn from him?
- Who are the people closest to you who need to hear God's message? How will you follow Paul's example and tell them about Christ?
- What thoughts, attitudes, or actions do you have as a result of the hope that is within you in Christ? What can you do to comfort and encourage others with this truth?

BEING PREPARED (1:3, 9-10; 2:19-20; 3:13–4:12; 5:1-28)
No one knows when Christ will return. In the meantime believers are to live moral and holy lives, ever watching for his coming. Believers must not neglect their daily responsibilities but must always work and live as unto the Lord.

The gospel tells us not only what we should believe, but also how we must live. The Holy Spirit leads us in faithfulness, so we can avoid lust and fraud. Live as though you expect Christ's return at any time. Don't be caught unprepared.

- According to 1 Thessalonians, what events will precede Christ's return?
- What does it mean to be prepared for these events? Why is this so important? (Check Matthew 25 for Jesus' teaching.)
- What are you doing to be ready for Christ's return?

Postcard

When you spend time with other Christians, what goals do you have in mind? Do you expect them to have a positive effect on you or the other way around? As you study 1 Thessalonians, keep track of all the ways you can encourage other Christians with your life and your words.

2 THESSALONIANS

 Snapshot of 2 Thessalonians

A bestselling new book has predicted that Christ is coming back in a few days.

Anne: "It's supposed to happen this weekend."

Sandra: "I guess I'm ready. But if it does happen, I'll never get my license—and I'll never get to . . . well, you know." (Everyone but Pam giggles.)

Karen: "I think it's great. I've got a huge algebra test on Monday that I can't possibly pass. Now I can just relax and forget about it."

Sandra: "Right, and no more abuse from Steve Hampton and his atheist friends!"

Anne: "Ah! I never even thought about that. That will be the best!"

Pam: "You guys cannot be serious! You talk like you actually believe that stuff!"

Anne: "Of course we do! It all fits together, and it's in the Bible, Pam. You'd better get ready."

Jesus is coming back. And his return will radically change things. It will be great, just as the girls imagine. But that doesn't mean we should start picking dates and sit around waiting. The prospect of Christ's return should motivate us to action, not laziness. He is coming back, so let's live for him—and encourage others to do the same.

That's the message of 2 Thessalonians. So keep watching, waiting—and working.

(And by all means study for your algebra exam!)

PURPOSE:
To clear up the confusion about the second coming of Christ

AUTHOR:
Paul

TO WHOM WRITTEN:
The church at Thessalonica and all believers everywhere

DATE WRITTEN:
About AD 51 or 52, a few months after 1 Thessalonians, from Corinth

SETTING:
Many in the Thessalonian church are confused about the timing of Christ's return. Because of increasing persecution, they think the Lord must be returning soon, so they interpret Paul's first letter to say that the Second Coming will be at any moment. In light of this misunderstanding, some have become lazy and disorderly.

KEY PEOPLE:
Paul, Silas, Timothy

KEY PLACE:
Thessalonica

SPECIAL FEATURE:
This is a follow-up letter to 1 Thessalonians. In this epistle Paul writes of various events that must precede the second coming of Christ.

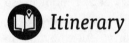 *Itinerary*

The Bright Hope of Christ's Return (1:1–2:17)

When Paul wrote in 1 Thessalonians about his confidence in the return of Christ, he did not expect the believers to apply the message the way that some of them have. They have decided that waiting means doing nothing else. Already facing growing persecution for being Christians, they think that surely the Second Coming must be near. Paul begins this second letter with greetings and immediate correction of their behavior. They are to allow neither persecution nor "delay" to keep them from living faithfully.

Living in the Light of Christ's Return (3:1-18)

Then Paul presents guidelines for life during the waiting time, however long that might turn out to be. Paul emphasizes busy waiting and warns that idleness is not holiness. Those who are doing nothing must be encouraged to once again add their energy to the work of Christ.

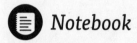

Notebook

PERSECUTION (1:4-12; 3:1-5)

Paul encouraged the church to have patience despite their troubles and hardships. God would bring victory to his faithful followers, and he would judge those who were persecuting them.

God promises to reward our faith with his power and to help us bear persecution. Suffering for our faith will strengthen us to serve Christ. God never will allow us to experience suffering apart from his power and presence.

- How did the Thessalonians respond to persecution?
- What did Paul say to encourage them?
- What was the basis of Paul's belief that the Thessalonians could stand firm in their faith in spite of these painful experiences?
- In what ways have Paul's words helped you?

CHRIST'S RETURN (1:5-7; 2:1-12)

Paul had said that Christ would come back at any moment, so some of the Thessalonian believers had stopped work to wait.

Christ will return and bring total victory to all who trust in him. If we stand firm and keep working, we will be ready. If we are ready, we won't have to be concerned about when he will return. Our life is already eternally secure in Christ.

- What concerns did Paul express in chapter 3? What false ideas had developed about what it means to prepare for Christ's coming?
- How did the promise of Christ's ultimate reign affect Paul's attitude toward life? How did he challenge the Thessalonians to live in light of Christ's coming?
- How does thinking about the promise of Christ's ultimate reign affect your feelings? Thoughts? Actions?
- What is your plan of preparation for the Second Coming? How does this relate to Paul's prayer request in 3:5?

GREAT REBELLION (2:7-12)

Before Christ's return, there will be a great rebellion against God led by the man of lawlessness (the Antichrist). God will remove all the restraints on evil before he brings judgment on the rebels. The Antichrist will attempt to deceive many.

We should not be afraid when we see evil increase. God is in control no matter how evil the world becomes. God guards us from satanic attack. We can have victory over evil by remaining faithful to God. Satan and all evils are subject to him.

- What is the danger of the Antichrist?
- In light of the fact that the Antichrist will impact the world and that evil is already present, how should we live?
- How should you live in an evil world? How can this give you the confidence to endure even the dangers of the Antichrist?

PERSISTENCE (1:4, 11-12; 2:13-17; 3:1-15)

Because some church members had quit working and had become disorderly and disobedient, Paul criticized them for their laziness. He told them to show courage and to live as Christians should.

We must never get so tired of doing right that we quit. We can be persistent by making the most of our time and talent. Our endurance will be rewarded.

- Why is laziness so negative for a Christian?
- In what areas do you struggle most with laziness? What does this tell you about the root of laziness?
- Developing self-discipline is a learned quality. It is easy and natural to do only what we want to do. What does it take to develop self-discipline?
- Outline a plan for developing self-discipline in one specific weak area of your life.

⬛ *Postcard*

For the faithful disciple, the question that must be answered each day is not, Will Christ return today? but, If Christ returns today, will he find me faithful? In what ways have you denied or applied yourself today that could be called examples of endurance?

1 TIMOTHY

 Snapshot of 1 Timothy

What does it take to be a leader? Brains? Good looks? A magnetic personality? The ability to speak persuasively? A ruthless obsession for power? That's what the world says.

The world is wrong. Leadership is not about being tall, tan, and telegenic. Leadership has nothing to do with impressive résumés or rousing speeches. Leadership is far more than being wellborn or highly educated or multitalented. Jesus defined leadership as servanthood. It involves compassion, courage, and conviction.

So here's the shocker: anyone who takes the time to develop those qualities can be a leader. Even you.

"Who? Me?! You must be kidding. I don't have any special talents. Besides, I'm young and kind of shy. I could never lead anyone."

A young man by the name of Timothy once felt the exact same way. He found himself facing big responsibilities and even bigger challenges. He wondered what to do and whether he had what leadership requires. Then he got a letter from his friend and mentor, Paul. More than a letter, 1 Timothy is also an essay on leadership.

Hey, you may never be a major politician or the president of a big company, but you'll always have friends, relatives, neighbors, and acquaintances who need to be influenced. People you can (and should) influence for Christ.

So read about the character, compassion, courage, and conviction that leadership involves. Then give it a try. Be a leader.

PURPOSE:
To encourage and instruct Timothy

AUTHOR:
Paul

TO WHOM WRITTEN:
Timothy, young church leaders, and all believers everywhere

DATE WRITTEN:
About AD 64, from Rome or Macedonia (possibly Philippi), probably just prior to Paul's final imprisonment in Rome

SETTING:
Timothy is one of Paul's closest companions. Paul sent him to the church at Ephesus to counter the false teaching that has arisen there (1:3-4). Timothy probably served for a time as a leader in the church there. Paul hopes to visit Timothy (3:14-15; 4:13), but in the meantime, he is writing this letter to give Timothy practical advice for the ministry.

KEY PEOPLE:
Paul, Timothy

KEY PLACE:
Ephesus

SPECIAL FEATURES:
First Timothy reveals the kind of long-term relationship that can develop between younger and older Christians. It also offers basic insights into church leadership and discipline.

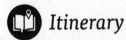 *Itinerary*

Instructions on Right Belief (1:1-20)
Written like a follow-up memo, 1 Timothy includes expressions of intimate encouragement alongside reminders of specific instructions that Paul has delegated to his protégé, Timothy. The letter begins with an overview of basic beliefs, with Paul's assuring Timothy that he has what it takes if he will practice and live it.

Instructions for the Church (2:1–3:16)
Next come guidelines for church life. Paul wants to advise Timothy on how to handle various groups as well as opinions that might surface in the Ephesian church.

Instructions for Elders (4:1–6:21)

Last, the apostle gives Timothy directives for elders in the church. He expects Timothy to be an example of these instructions even as he passes them on to others.

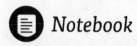 *Notebook*

SOUND DOCTRINE (1:3-11; 4:1-10; 6:3-5)

Paul instructed Timothy to preserve the Christian faith by teaching sound doctrine and modeling right living. Timothy had to oppose false teachers who were leading church members away from belief in salvation by faith in Jesus Christ alone.

We must know the truth to defend it. And the truth is that Christ came to save us. We should stay away from those who twist the words of the Bible for their own purposes. Therefore, we must study and know the Bible ourselves.

- What do you consider to be the main points in the Bible concerning God and people, sin and salvation, life and death?
- Why are these truths so important to the Bible's message?
- Paul greatly opposed those who taught against the truth of the gospel. What did Paul tell Timothy to do about false teachers?
- Based on this study, how should you respond to the message of a false teacher? What can you do to be able to discern the truth from error?

PUBLIC WORSHIP (2:1-15; 4:11-16)

In public worship, prayer must be done with a proper attitude toward God and fellow believers.

Christian character must be evident in every aspect of worship. We must rid ourselves of any anger, resentment, and offensive attire that might disrupt worship or damage church unity. Christian unity begins with your own attitude and actions toward others.

- What instructions did Paul give Timothy about worship?
- What aspects of public, congregational worship do you most enjoy? Least enjoy? How do you feel about worship overall?

- What should be a Christian's attitude in worship? What actions should be a part of worship services?
- What steps can you take to deepen your worship as well as to encourage others in your church to do the same?

CHURCH LEADERSHIP (3:1-16; 4:1-16)

Paul gave specific instructions concerning the qualifications for church leaders so that the church might honor God and run smoothly.

Church leaders must be wholly committed to Christ. If you are a new or young Christian, don't be anxious to become a leader in your church. Develop your Christian character first. Be sure to consider God, not your own ambition.

- According to 3:1-16, what should be the overall character of the persons who are qualified to serve in church leadership?
- In what specific ways did Paul challenge Timothy to mature and develop personally?
- How can a young person who is a Christian prepare now to be a man or woman of God later, as he or she matures?
- Praise God for your areas of personal strength. Design a plan to work on your personal weaknesses so that, by his grace, you will be a godly leader throughout your life.

PERSONAL DISCIPLINE (4:11-16; 5:21-25; 6:6-16, 20-21)

It takes discipline to be a leader in the church. Timothy, like all church leaders, had to guard his motives, minister faithfully, and live right. Any pastor must keep morally and spiritually fit.

To stay in good spiritual shape, you must discipline yourself to study God's Word and to live a godly life. Put your spiritual abilities to work!

- What areas of personal discipline would Timothy have to develop as a result of what Paul told him?
- How do you think Timothy felt as he read this letter? Read chapters 4 and 6, and describe how you would have felt if this letter had been written to you.
- What beginning steps can you take to deepen your faith?
- How will the Holy Spirit of God help you to deal with the personal difficulties you may face as you attempt to step out?

CARING CHURCH (5:1-20; 6:1-2, 17-19)

The church has a responsibility to care for the needs of all its members, especially the sick, the poor, and the widowed.

Caring for the family of believers demonstrates our Christlike attitude and genuine love. We are Christ's touch of love in each other's lives.

- What did Paul think about the church's responsibility for reaching out to others?
- Why is this so important for the church as Christ's body?
- On a scale of A-B-C-D-F, give your church a grade in terms of Paul's descriptions of what it means to serve those in need.
- Grade yourself on the above scale. What can you do to improve your grade?
- What can you do to get involved with your church to improve its grade?

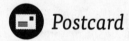 *Postcard*

Read 1 Timothy as a Bible book written specifically to you as a young person. Use a verse like 4:12 as a personal guideline in living for Christ.

2 TIMOTHY

 Snapshot of 2 Timothy

Trivia means "unimportant matters." It's all that information that's often interesting but doesn't really matter much. For instance, did you know that:

Grasshoppers are approximately three times more nutritious than rib-eye steak.

Kangaroos can't jump when their tails are lifted off the ground.

It's impossible to sneeze with your eyes open.

Benjamin Franklin invented swim fins and the rocking chair.

Nine hundred twenty-eight average-sized fleas will fit inside a Ping-Pong ball.

Though amusing—and helpful for filling the silence in an awkward conversation—the facts just cited are worthless. They won't change your life. They're trivia. Trivial trivia.

Not so the book of 2 Timothy.

The apostle Paul's second letter to Timothy is serious stuff. History says that these were Paul's last words; he died shortly after penning them.

Perhaps the aged saint recognized that his time was running out. If so, it's not surprising that he talked about important matters. Consider carefully Paul's final thoughts. He is, after all, one of the most influential individuals in history.

And Paul's challenge to Timothy is just as appropriate two thousand years later.

The bottom line? Second Timothy is no trivial pursuit!

PURPOSE:
To give final instructions and encouragement to Timothy, a leader of the church at Ephesus

AUTHOR:
Paul

TO WHOM WRITTEN:
Timothy and all Christians everywhere

DATE WRITTEN:
About AD 66 or 67, from prison in Rome. After a year or two of freedom, Paul was arrested again and eventually executed under Emperor Nero.

SETTING:
Paul is virtually alone in prison; only Luke is with him. He writes this letter to pass the torch to the new generation of church leaders. He also asks for visits from his friends, for his books, and especially for the parchments—possibly parts of the Old Testament, the Gospels, and other biblical manuscripts.

KEY PEOPLE:
Paul, Timothy, Luke, Mark, and others

KEY PLACES:
Rome, Ephesus

SPECIAL FEATURE:
Holds a place of honor as most likely Paul's last letter

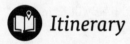 *Itinerary*

Foundations of Christian Service (1:1–2:26)
Paul's first letter to Timothy exudes an easygoing, well-worn companionship. His second flows with tenderness. The letter begins with the kind of insightful encouragement that comes from really knowing someone else. Paul reminds Timothy of the basics of teaching and modeling the Christian life. Service to Christ should always be the central purpose of each believer.

Difficult Times for Christian Service (3:1–4:22)
As much as Paul is sensitive to Timothy's past struggles, he doesn't hesitate to tell him that things will get worse. He reminds Timothy

of his own experience—life has gotten harder, and faith has gotten deeper. His last words to Timothy ring with affirmation in the God who has remained faithful all the way!

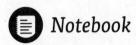 *Notebook*

BOLDNESS (1:5-12; 4:1-5)
In the face of opposition and persecution, Timothy was told to carry out his ministry unashamed and unafraid of the earthly consequences. Paul urged Timothy to use the gifts of preaching and teaching that the Holy Spirit had given him.

God honors our confident testimony even when we suffer. To get over our fear of what people might say or do, we must take our eyes off people and look only to God. People will disappoint us; God will always be faithful.

- Why was boldness important in Timothy's ministry? How did Paul challenge Timothy to find this boldness?
- At what time did you feel bold in your faith? When did you feel timid about your faith?
- What caused the difference between the time of boldness and the time of timidity?
- What is your level of boldness for Christ at church? In your neighborhood? At home? In school? At social activities? Where is it most difficult for you to be boldly honest about your faith and lifestyle?

FAITHFULNESS (1:13-14; 2:1, 3-13; 3:14-15)
Jesus was faithful to all of us when he died for our sins. Paul was a faithful minister even when he was in prison. Paul urged Timothy to maintain not only sound doctrine but also loyalty, diligence, and endurance.

We can count on opposition, suffering, and hardship as we serve Christ. But that will show that our faithfulness is having an effect on others. As we trust Christ, he counts us worthy to suffer and will give us the strength we need to be steadfast.

- How did Paul challenge Timothy to live out his faithfulness to God?

- What reasons do you have for being faithful to God? What struggles do you face in trying to be faithful?
- When you find yourself drifting away from God, what can you do to remember your commitment of faithfulness to God?
- How are you being faithful today?

PREACHING AND TEACHING (2:2, 22-26; 3:16-17; 4:1-5)
Paul and Timothy were active in preaching and teaching the Good News about Jesus Christ. Paul encouraged Timothy not only to carry the torch of truth but also to train others, passing on to them sound doctrine and enthusiasm for Christ's mission.

We must prepare people to pass on God's Word to others. Does your church carefully train others to teach? Each of us should look for ways to become better equipped to serve, as well as for ways to teach others what we have learned.

- Why do you think Paul stressed to Timothy the importance of training others to carry out preaching and teaching?
- How was Paul a good example of this?
- Who are the preachers and teachers in your church? How are they training others? (Are they training others?)
- What type of ministry training would you want to receive? Who could provide this training?

ERROR (2:14-21; 3:1-17; 4:9-18)
In the final days before Christ returns, there will be false teachers, spiritual dropouts, and heresy. The remedy for error is to have a solid program for teaching Christians.

Because of deception and false teaching, we must be disciplined and ready to reject error by knowing God's Word. Knowing the Bible is your sure defense against error and confusion.

- What are the dangers of deceptive teachers?
- According to 3:14-17, how does God use his Word to prevent his people from being deceived?
- Based on this study, how should you respond to Bible teaching?
- What can you do to improve yourself as a student of God's Word?

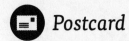 *Postcard*

You probably have several older Christian friends who have been your mentors—your Pauls. Have you thanked them for their faithfulness? Have you expressed how grateful you are for their consistent example and encouragement to you? This would be a good time to do that.

TITUS

 Snapshot of Titus

In many of life's situations—whether from natural instinct, repeated instruction, or unpleasant experience—you know precisely what to do. For instance:

> In case of emergency, call 9-1-1.
> Never stare at the sun during an eclipse.
> On a romantic first date, never order pizza with extra garlic and onions.
> Don't run while carrying sharp objects.
> Never swim right after eating.
> When attacked by a bear, fall facedown and play dead.
> Look both ways before crossing a street.
> Make certain you know the price of an object before you agree to buy it.
> Never sign anything until you read the fine print.

You've probably heard these rules before; no doubt you could handle each situation with ease. But what about the millions of other life circumstances where it's really difficult to know what to do?

That's why the next book of the Bible is so important. The apostle Paul's epistle to Titus gives plenty of practical advice for living a pure life in an impure world. Commitment, discipline, self-control, moral purity, solid relationships, civic duties—you'll learn about all those important topics and more. By the way, as you prepare to dive into this dynamite little letter, here's a reminder of one more famous rule of life (it's one that Mom pounded into our head!): never cross your eyes while reading; they might get stuck that way.

PURPOSE:
To advise Titus in his responsibility of supervising the churches on the island of Crete

AUTHOR:
Paul

TO WHOM WRITTEN:
Titus, a Greek convert, who had become Paul's special representative to the island of Crete

DATE WRITTEN:
About AD 64, around the same time 1 Timothy was written; probably from Macedonia when Paul traveled during the time between his Roman imprisonments

SETTING:
Paul had sent Titus to organize and oversee the churches on the island of Crete. This letter tells him how to do this job.

KEY PEOPLE:
Paul, Titus

KEY PLACES:
Crete, Nicopolis

SPECIAL FEATURE:
Titus is very similar to 1 Timothy with its instructions to church leaders.

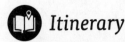 *Itinerary*

Leadership in the Church (1:1-16)
Though Titus is written to an individual, it is meant for group teaching. Paul offers Titus an open outline to use in instructing the Cretan Christians. After briefly identifying himself and the recipient of the letter, Paul launches into a description of leadership qualities in the church.

Right Living in the Church (2:1-15)
Next Paul highlights several types of people (older women, youth, slaves) to illustrate how their lives as Christians ought to stand

apart from typical society. Every Christian is to be a living advertisement for the gospel of Jesus Christ.

Right Living in Society (3:1-15)

Last, Paul gives directions regarding the relationship of Christians to social structures. They are to be good citizens. After all, Paul reminds them, "we will inherit eternal life" (3:7). That fact ought to make a big difference in how we live!

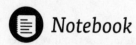

Notebook

A GOOD LIFE (3:3-8, 12-15)

The Good News of salvation is that a person can't be saved by living a good life; people are saved only by faith in Jesus Christ. But the gospel transforms people's lives, so they eventually perform good works. Our service won't save us, but we are saved to serve.

A good life bears witness to the gospel's power. Christians must have commitment and discipline to serve. Every believer should be a living servant; no one should consider himself or herself inactive.

- Why is it important for a Christian to live a good and pure life even though this is not the basis of salvation?
- What kind of life is pleasing to God?
- What areas of your life do you think are pleasing to God? In what areas of your life do you need to make changes in order to be more like the life you described in the previous question?
- What will be your personal plan for improving these areas for God's glory?

CHARACTER (1:5-16)

Titus's responsibility on Crete was to appoint church leaders (elders) to maintain proper organization and discipline, so Paul listed the qualities that elders should have. Their conduct in their homes revealed their fitness for service in the church.

It's not enough to be educated or have a following to be Christ's kind of leader. You must have self-control, spiritual and moral fitness, and Christian character. Who you are is just as important as what you can do.

- Summarize Paul's description of those who are qualified to serve as church leaders.
- Describe the person you want to be when you are older. What will be your personal qualities? What will be your priorities? What will be the impact of your life? How will you be serving God?
- What choices are you making now that will help you eventually fulfill the above description?

CHURCH RELATIONSHIPS (2:1-10, 15; 3:9-11)

Church teaching was supposed to relate to various groups. Older Christians were to teach and be examples to younger men and women. Every age and group has a lesson to learn and a role to play.

Right living and right relationships go along with right doctrine. Treat relationships with other believers as important parts of your relationship with God.

- Summarize Paul's teaching on church relationships in 2:1-15.
- What groups in your church seem to be the most "distant" in their personal relationships (young/old, wealthy/average/poor, liberal/conservative, traditional/nontraditional, etc.)?
- What would Paul say to those groups if he were to write a letter to your church leaders about this distance? From your perspective, how could this gap be bridged?
- What might you do to be a "bridge builder" in your church?

CITIZENSHIP (2:11–3:14)

Christians must be good citizens in society, not just in church. Believers must obey the government and work honestly.

How you fulfill your civic duties is a witness to the watching world. Your community life should reflect Christ's love as much as your church life does. You must guard against trying to separate your walk with God from the way you live each day.

- Why is it important for Christians to obey the government?
- Do you agree or disagree with this statement? Being a good citizen involves more than just not breaking the law. Explain your response.

- What are the biggest issues facing your community? How would you apply this study to your role as a member of the community?
- How can a Christian have an impact for Christ by simply being a citizen who contributes positively? How can you provide this impact in your community?

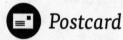 *Postcard*

As you read Titus, you probably will be thinking seriously about the church in which you participate—not in a critical way but with a desire to understand. Can you explain how your church functions? What specific roles have you found, and how are you doing in fulfilling them?

PHILEMON

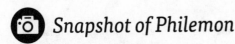 *Snapshot of Philemon*

"I could never forgive her!"

"He'll never get serious about God!"

"I wish things would work out, but they won't. My situation is impossible!"

Ever heard—or made—statements like those? If so, take this hint! Never say never. Many of the hard-to-believe things we declare "Impossible!" eventually do come to pass . . . right before our embarrassed eyes.

Consider the Munich elementary school teacher who told ten-year-old Albert Einstein, "You will never amount to very much." Or the misguided executive with the Decca Recording Company in the early sixties who decided not to offer a contract to an obscure musical group called the Beatles.

Never say never. Don't end that friendship or relationship just because you've been wronged. Don't give up on that friend who claims to be an atheist. Don't throw in the towel on your dream. Don't write off your future just because you've made some bad choices in the past.

Never say never. The Gospel of Matthew states that same principle ("With God everything is possible"—Matthew 19:26), and the book of Philemon illustrates it, describing how a poor slave and his rich master ended up as Christian brothers. You are about to read a story of betrayal and forgiveness and of how Jesus Christ breaks down all barriers.

So before you say "That's impossible!" or "That could never happen!" take five minutes to read Paul's postcard to Philemon.

PURPOSE:
To convince Philemon to forgive his runaway slave, Onesimus, and accept him as a brother in the faith

AUTHOR:
Paul

TO WHOM WRITTEN:
Philemon, who probably was a wealthy member of the Colossian church

DATE WRITTEN:
About AD 60, during Paul's first imprisonment in Rome, at about the same time the books of Ephesians and Colossians were written

SETTING:
Slavery is very common in the Roman Empire. Evidently some Christians have slaves. Paul makes a radical statement by calling this slave Philemon's brother in Christ.

KEY PEOPLE:
Paul, Philemon, Onesimus

KEY PLACES:
Colosse, Rome

SPECIAL FEATURE:
This is Paul's shortest letter.

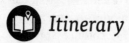 *Itinerary*

Paul's Appreciation of Philemon (1:1-7)
Paul begins his brief letter by expressing his special appreciation for Philemon.

Paul's Appeal for Onesimus (1:8-25)
Having established his high regard for his Christian brother and leader in the Colossian church, Paul then makes a special request on behalf of Onesimus, a slave who has run away from his owner. Onesimus has become a Christian with Paul in Rome, and the old apostle feels compelled to send the slave back home. Paul closes the letter by assuring Philemon that if there is any further unfinished business between them over Onesimus, they can discuss it when Paul arrives.

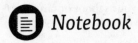

Notebook

FORGIVENESS (1:17-21)

Philemon was Paul's friend and Onesimus's owner. Paul asked Philemon not to punish Onesimus but to forgive and restore him as a new Christian brother.

Christian relationships must be full of forgiveness and acceptance. Forgiving those who have wronged you is the appropriate response to Christ's forgiveness of you.

- If you were Philemon, how would you have felt before you received the letter? How would Paul's letter have changed your attitude? What verses in the letter would have had the most impact on your thinking?
- How is Paul's request for Onesimus in 1:18-20 a reflection of what Christ has done for all of us?
- As you think about this study, what do you learn about the importance of forgiveness in Christian relationships? What is the basis of this forgiveness? How is this forgiveness lived out when someone has been wronged?
- What difference does it make whether or not you forgive a Christian friend who wrongs you? If there is a wrong that you have not forgiven, how can you go to that friend and make things right?

BARRIERS (1:10-16)

Slavery was widespread in the Roman Empire. Slavery was a thick barrier, but God can break through anything that divides people. Christian love and fellowship should overcome such barriers.

In Christ we are one family. No walls of race, economic status, or political differences should separate believers. Let Christ work through you to remove barriers between Christian brothers and sisters. Take steps to act out the love of Christ in you.

- What differences and prejudices separate and alienate people from one another?
- Why are such conflicts offensive to God?
- In your community, what groups of people do not relate to each other simply because of external differences?

- What can you do to demonstrate to your school or church that God is greater than all barriers?

RESPECT (1:4-9, 21-25)

Paul was a friend of both Philemon and Onesimus. He had the authority as an apostle to tell Philemon what to do (1:8). Yet Paul chose to appeal to his friend in Christian love rather than order him to do what he wished.

When dealing with people, tactful persuasion accomplishes a great deal more than commands. Remember to exhibit courtesy and respect in dealing with people.

- What do you think it means to respect a person?
- Who are the people you most respect? What qualities lead you to respect them?
- Which of these qualities do you most want to develop as you grow into an adult who can be respected by others?
- What about now? What leads others to respect you as a young person?

📧 Postcard

What barriers to peace are in your home, neighborhood, and church? What separates you from fellow believers? Is it race? Status? Wealth? Education? Personality? What have you done this week to promote peace?

HEBREWS

 Snapshot of Hebrews

Four Very Uncool Activities You Can Do:

1. Wear a diaper to school, and suck on a pacifier during all your classes.
2. Treat yourself to a lunch of baby food: strained carrots, creamed spinach, and milk (out of a baby bottle, of course).
3. Drool all over yourself and cry uncontrollably.
4. Crawl from class to class.

Such behavior is uncool for a teenager—it's immature, the kind of thing we expect babies to do. We would never tolerate such immaturity in an older person. So why do we tolerate it in the spiritual realm?

The church has far too many "baby Christians." Some have only been believers in Christ a short time, so it's understandable that they might do silly or immature things. But for those who have been Christians for years and still act like infants—well, there's just no excuse.

In the same way that little kids grow up physically, baby Christians need to grow up in their relationship with Christ. That's what Hebrews is all about—growing up spiritually. You should know up front that Hebrews contains some tough statements and some sobering challenges. It's a risky book to read—and apply.

Neglect its powerful message, and you face an even greater risk—remaining a spiritual infant. You can't get more uncool than that.

PURPOSE:

To present Christ's sufficiency and superiority

AUTHOR:

Unknown. Paul, Luke, Barnabas, Apollos, Silas, Philip, Priscilla, and others have been suggested. Whoever the author was speaks of Timothy as "brother" (13:23).

TO WHOM WRITTEN:

Hebrew Christians who may have been considering a return to Judaism, perhaps because of immaturity due to their lack of understanding of biblical truths—they seem to be "second-generation" Christians (2:3)— and to all believers everywhere.

DATE WRITTEN:

Probably before the destruction of the Temple in Jerusalem in AD 70; the religious sacrifices and ceremonies are referred to, but not the Temple's destruction

SETTING:

These Jewish Christians are probably undergoing fierce persecution, socially and physically, from both Jews and Romans. They need to be reassured that Christianity is true and that Jesus is the Messiah.

KEY PEOPLE:

Old Testament men and women of faith (11:1-40)

SPECIAL FEATURE:

Hebrews serves as the key to understanding how the Old Testament is fulfilled in Jesus.

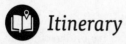 *Itinerary*

The Superiority of Christ (1:1–10:18)

The message of Hebrews is that Jesus is better and that faith connects us to Christ. From the opening verses, the book emphasizes that both Judaism and Christianity are part of God's full revelation. The teaching section that follows shows how Jesus is superior to angels (1:4–2:18), superior to human leaders (3:1–4:13), and superior to priests (4:14–7:28). Christianity fulfills Judaism because it has a better covenant (8:1-13), a better sanctuary (9:1-10), and a complete sacrifice for sins (9:11–10:18).

The Superiority of Faith (10:19–13:25)

Having established the superiority of Christ, the book moves to the practical implications of following Christ. This section includes the great "Faith Hall of Fame" (11:1-40), which catalogs the great men and women of faith in the Old Testament. The writer wants believers to see themselves cheered on by those who have been faithful before them (12:1-2). It's our turn, today, to endure in Jesus Christ.

 Notebook

CHRIST IS SUPERIOR (1:1-14; 2:5–3:6; 4:14–5:10; 6:13–10:18)

Hebrews reveals Jesus' true identity as God. Christ is the ultimate authority. He is greater than any religion or any angel and superior to any Jewish leader (such as Abraham, Moses, or Joshua) or priest. Christ is the complete revelation of God.

Jesus alone can forgive your sin. He has secured your forgiveness and salvation by his death on the cross. With Christ you can find peace with God and real meaning for life. Without him there is no hope for true life.

- What was unique about Jesus Christ?
- Why did the first-century Jews have difficulty accepting these truths about Jesus?
- How do the majority of people in your school feel about being a Christian? What are their misconceptions about Jesus?
- If you could explain one thing about Christ to those who do not understand him, what would you tell them?

HIGH PRIEST (3:1; 4:14–5:10; 6:19–8:6; 9:6–10:22; 13:11-13)

In the Old Testament, the high priest represented the Jews before God. Jesus Christ links us with God. There is no other way to reach God. Because Jesus Christ lived a sinless life, he is the perfect substitute to die for our sin. Christ is our perfect representative with God.

Jesus guarantees believers access to God the Father. He intercedes for us so that we can boldly come to the Father with our needs. When we are weak, we can come confidently to God for forgiveness and help. He never shuts us out or refuses to respond to our requests.

- In Hebrews, what do you learn about the role of a high priest?
- Based on 4:14-16 and 7:19-28, what are the ways that Jesus is the perfect High Priest?
- What benefits do you have because Jesus is your High Priest?
- What hurts, needs, and desires do you want to bring to God, your Father?
- How does Jesus, your High Priest, provide the way for you to present these to God? Express your needs to God, and share with him your feelings about the perfect High Priest he has provided in Jesus.

SACRIFICE (1:3; 2:9; 7:27; 9:12-14, 24-28; 10:5-22)

Christ's sacrifice was the ultimate fulfillment of all that the Old Testament sacrifices represented—God's forgiveness for sin. Because Christ was the perfect sacrifice, believers' sins have been completely forgiven—past, present, and future.

Christ removed the sin that kept us from God's presence and fellowship. But we must accept Christ's sacrifice for us. By believing in him, we are declared not guilty, cleansed, and made whole. Christ's sacrifice provided the way for us to have eternal life.

- What qualified Jesus to be the perfect, once-and-for-all fulfillment of the Old Testament sacrificial requirements?
- What blessings do you have as a result of Jesus' sacrifice?
- What is the difference for those who reject Christ's sacrifice and those who accept it (check 10:26-39)?
- What have you personally received from the one who sacrificed himself for your sins? What difference has Jesus' sacrifice made in your life?

FAITH (11:1-40; 13:1-21)

Faith is confident trust in God. The salvation God offers is through his Son, Jesus, who is the only one who can save us from sin.

If you trust in Jesus Christ for your salvation, he will transform you completely. Then you should live a life of faith.

- Rewrite 11:3 in your own words.
- What does this statement mean? Faith is not just knowing; it is doing.
- Read 11:1-40. What do you learn about the life of faith from the great men and women listed there?
- If someone were to write a paragraph describing your life of faith, what would they include?
- In what ways would you like to see your faith grow? How can you develop this growth in faith?

MATURITY THROUGH ENDURANCE (2:11-13; 5:11–6:3)
Faith enables Christians to face trials. Genuine faith includes the commitment to stay true to God when we are under fire. Endurance builds character and leads to victory.

You can have victory in your trials if you don't give up or turn your back on Christ. Stay true to Christ, and pray for endurance. He will never grow tired of supporting you.

- Hebrews 12 describes what it means to grow through endurance and discipline. Why is discipline necessary for growth?
- Based on 12:1-5, what are the keys to endurance? How can you apply these principles to where you are in "the race" at this point in your life?
- What are the main points of Hebrews's teaching concerning God's discipline?
- If someone were to ask you, "Why should I take obedience to God so seriously?" how would you respond?

Postcard

Use your reading and study of Hebrews to answer the following personal question: How will I know I have become an adult Christian?

JAMES

 Snapshot of James

You've been feeling strange all week. At first you had trouble sleeping. Then came the headaches. Yesterday your teeth began hurting, and your fingernails turned blue for several hours. This morning you realized it was time to consult your family doctor when, after a morning jog, your mom asked if you had been sprayed by a skunk.

The doctor tries to hold her breath as she asks you questions. She nods knowingly as you tick off your symptoms. After looking in your eyes and noting your swollen eardrums, she orders some lab work.

A few hours later she returns to tell you, "Just what I suspected—you have an extremely high number of antibiomolecularsucrothyamin microbes in your liver. But don't worry. You have a common ailment we call odoramonia. We'll put you on an antibiotic and get you eating a balanced diet, and you'll be fine."

Aren't doctors amazing? By examining us and noting our symptoms, they usually are able to diagnose our physical ailments and prescribe the proper treatments.

God does the same thing in the spiritual realm. By looking at our actions (or lack of action), God can tell us exactly what attitudes and desires need healing. His Word gives detailed prescriptions for curing wrong behavior patterns.

Is your spiritual life on the sick side? Are you fighting worldly infections or possibly even the disease of disobedience? Follow the advice of the Great Physician. No matter what your ailment, the Epistle of James has the cure.

PURPOSE:
To expose unethical practices and to teach right Christian behavior

AUTHOR:
James, Jesus' half brother, a leader in the Jerusalem church

TO WHOM WRITTEN:
First-century Jewish Christians residing in Gentile communities outside Palestine, and all Christians everywhere

DATE WRITTEN:
Probably AD 49, prior to the Jerusalem council held in AD 50

SETTING:
This letter expresses James's concern for persecuted Christians who were once part of the Jerusalem church.

SPECIAL FEATURE:
James insists that a believer's relationship with God should have an effective balance between deep faith and practical action. Neither stands alone.

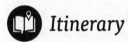 *Itinerary*

Genuine Religion (1:1-27)
James knows that his readers are facing difficulties. He doesn't just sympathize; he challenges them to turn their sufferings into opportunities for growth. James's letter begins with an explanation of how every single part of life relates to a believer's relationship with God.

Genuine Faith (2:1–3:12)
The next section confronts the attitude that faith is an "internal" action unrelated to the rest of life. James points out that claimed faith is empty faith without external evidence. Believing leads to transformed living.

Genuine Wisdom (3:13–5:20)
The final section of the epistle is all about wisdom. Those who believe in Christ and who live for Christ must also be involved in constantly thinking about the next step of obedience. Believers can expect to suffer and to be tempted as long as they live in this

world. Godly wisdom prepares believers to face these aspects of life
with humility and prayer.

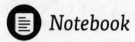 *Notebook*

LIVING FAITH (1:19–2:26)

James wanted believers to hear the truth and to do it. He contrasted empty faith (claims without conduct) with faith that
works. Commitment to love and to serve is evidence of true faith.

Living faith makes a difference. Make sure that your faith results
in action. Be alert to ways of putting your faith to work. Be certain
that you not only "talk" the gospel, but that you "walk" the gospel
as well.

- What's the difference between "living faith" and "dead faith"?
- What would it mean to have dead faith in your school? What
  would it mean to have living faith in that environment?
- How are your vital signs? Identify evidence of life in your
  faith.
- In what ways can you become more alive as a doer of
  God's Word in your school? With your friends? In your
  relationships at church? In response to the needy in your
  community?

TRIALS (1:2-18; 5:7-11)

The Christian life has trials and temptations. Successfully overcoming these adversities produces maturity and strong character.

Don't resent troubles when they come; pray for wisdom. God
will supply all you need to face persecution or adversity. He will
give you patience and keep you strong.

- What attitude does James teach believers to have concerning their trials?
- What trials and problems have you recently experienced?
- How did you feel when you were facing these trials and
  problems? How did you feel toward God?
- Describe how you can choose to respond with an appropriate attitude the next time you face a trial or problem. Why is
  developing such responses important for a Christian? (Check
  the results of enduring trials in chapter 1.)

LAW OF LOVE (1:27; 2:8-17; 3:17-18; 4:11-12; 5:19-20)
Believers are saved by God's gracious mercy, not by keeping the law. But Christ gave a special command: "Love your neighbor as yourself" (Matthew 19:19). We are to love and serve those around us.

Keeping the law of love shows that our faith is vital and real. To show love to others, we must root out our own selfishness. This begins by acting on what we know to be true about God's will in our life.

- What does James teach in chapter 2 about the life of faith?
- What would happen if every Christian in your community lived with the attitude and actions described in 2:2-16?
- Why are the acts of giving to those in need and not showing favoritism important expressions of living faith?
- What does it mean in your life (home, school, church) not to show favoritism? Who are the needy who can benefit from your resources (time, love, food, money, work)?

WISE SPEECH (1:19, 26; 3:1-18; 4:11-16; 5:9, 12)
Wisdom shows itself in speech. We are responsible for the destructive results of our talk. The wisdom of God that helps control the tongue can help control all our actions.

Accepting God's wisdom will affect your speech because your words will reveal their godly source. Think of God and others before you speak, and allow God to strengthen your self-control.

- Why did James devote so much of this book to the issue of controlling the tongue?
- When did someone's words hurt you or a person you really care about? How did you feel? What were the results?
- When did your words hurt another person? How did you feel? What were the results?
- Taking the principles from James, what could have been done differently in those situations that would have led to positive communication?

WEALTH (1:9-12; 2:1-7; 5:1-6)
James teaches Christians not to adopt worldly attitudes about wealth. Because the glory of wealth fades, Christians should store up God's treasures through sincere service. Christians must not show partiality to the wealthy or be prejudiced against the poor.

We all are accountable for how we use what we have. We should be generous toward others. We are to see one another as God sees us—created as equals in his image.

- What did James think about rich people? What was it about these wealthy men in chapter 5 that caused James to react so strongly?
- After studying chapters 2 and 5, what do you think should be the Christian lifestyle of a person who is blessed with great wealth?
- How can you make your possessions a part of your life of faith? Why is it important that you not separate what you have from your responsibility to God?

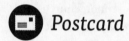 *Postcard*

Probably the most application-oriented book in the Bible, James invites you to put almost every verse into practice. Keep a list of how many practical actions you are directed to take as you study this book.

1 PETER

Snapshot of 1 Peter

Each year a few individuals compete in what may be the most grueling athletic competition of all: a bicycle race across the continental United States. Consider the obstacles: blazing deserts, towering mountain ranges, inclement weather, eighteen- to twenty-hour stretches of pedaling, flat tires, potholes, skin-scraping spills, inconsiderate motorists, and sheer fatigue. It's amazing that anyone ever finishes. The fact that some complete the two-thousand-plus mile trip in just over a week is downright unbelievable!

How do they do it? With the help of carefully trained support teams. These support teams follow the cyclists in specially equipped recreational vehicles, providing whatever the riders need—food, drink, a repair job, a replacement bike, medical attention, a rubdown, a short nap, coaching, or a few shouts of encouragement. These support teams make an otherwise impossible trip very possible.

The Christian life is similar to that grueling bicycle marathon. The occasional joys of gliding downhill are obscured by the more frequent times of having to churn our way up steep mountain peaks. We get weary. We feel like quitting. The finish line seems far, far away.

Fortunately, God has given us a first-rate support team to help us go the distance. With the Holy Spirit, the Word of God, and other believers to encourage us, we can not only finish the race, we can win!

Find out more about your spiritual support team in the book called 1 Peter. (But don't wait too long. The race has already begun!)

PURPOSE:
To offer encouragement to suffering Christians

AUTHOR:
Peter

TO WHOM WRITTEN:
Jewish Christians who had been driven out of Jerusalem and scattered throughout Asia Minor, and all believers everywhere

DATE WRITTEN:
About AD 62–64, from Rome

SETTING:
Peter is probably in Rome when the great persecution under Emperor Nero begins (Peter is eventually executed during the persecution). Throughout the Roman Empire, Christians are being tortured and killed for their faith, and the church in Jerusalem is being scattered throughout the Mediterranean world.

KEY PEOPLE:
Peter, Silas, Mark

KEY PLACES:
Jerusalem, Rome, and the regions of Pontus, Galatia, Cappadocia, Asia Minor, and Bithynia

SPECIAL FEATURES:
Some echoes of Peter's own intimate relationship with Jesus can be found in this book. Jesus called Peter "rock" (Matthew 16:18) and also left him with a final challenge to "feed my lambs" (John 21:15). It isn't surprising that Peter would use terms like "living stones" and "sheep" in describing the church.

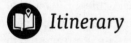 *Itinerary*

God's Great Blessings to His People (1:1–2:10)
Since his purpose is to encourage suffering Christians, Peter begins with the big picture. He describes God's great blessings to his people. Although facing difficulties, they must not forget that God is in control and that the privileges of eternal life far outweigh the discomforts of this life.

The Conduct of God's People in the Midst of Suffering
(2:11–4:19)
Moving from general encouragement, 1 Peter then focuses on specific instructions for believers in the midst of suffering. They are to exhibit noticeable hopefulness. Their behavior ought to be described as holy—centered on God.

The Shepherding of God's People in the Midst of Suffering
(5:1-14)
Last, Peter has some counsel for those responsible for leadership during suffering. Leaders are to care, to remain alert, and to set a personal example of Christlikeness.

 Notebook

SALVATION (1:1-5, 10-12, 18-20; 2:4, 6, 21-25; 3:18-22; 5:4)
Salvation is a gracious gift from God. God chose us out of his love for us, Jesus died to pay the penalty for our sin, and the Holy Spirit cleansed us from sin when we believed. Eternal life is a wonderful gift to those who trust in Christ.

Our safety and security are in God. If we experience joy in our relationship with Christ now, how much greater will our joy be when he returns and we see him face-to-face! Such a hope should motivate us to serve Christ even more.

- What are the blessings of our salvation that have been revealed to us through Jesus?
- Why would this be such an important message for Jewish Christians who had been suffering for their faith?
- What does it mean to you to be saved? Include your feelings, the present benefits, and your hope for the future.
- How can you communicate this through your life to someone who is without Christ? Why is it important that others come to know Christ?

PERSECUTION (1:6-9; 2:19-21; 3:14-17; 4:12-19; 5:10)
Peter offers faithful believers comfort and hope. We should expect ridicule, rejection, and suffering because we are Christians. Persecution makes us stronger because it refines our faith. We can face persecution victoriously, as Christ did, if we rely on him.

We don't have to be terrified by persecution. The fact that we will live eternally with Christ should give us the confidence, patience, and hope to stand firm even when we are persecuted. Suffering can glorify God.

- Read 2:21-25. How did Jesus respond to suffering?
- How does Jesus' example provide encouragement and inspiration during suffering?
- How do fellow believers provide encouragement and inspiration during suffering?
- When you face ridicule or oppression for your faith, what can you do to cope with this suffering?

GOD'S FAMILY (1:14, 22; 2:4-10; 3:8; 5:12-14)

We are privileged to belong to God's family, a community with Christ as Founder and Foundation. Everyone in this community is related—we are all brothers and sisters loved equally by God.

We must be devoted, loyal, and faithful to Christ, the foundation of our family. Through obedience we show that we are his children. We must live differently from the society around us. Our relationships are to be patterned by what we see in Christ, not by what we see in the world.

- What specific teachings concerning Christian fellowship do you find in 4:7-11?
- Who are the people who have ministered Christ's love and grace to you? In what ways have they provided this love and grace?
- Why is it necessary for you and other believers to be providers of his love to each other?
- This week, in what two ways will you become a part of God's love and grace in the life of fellow believers?

FAMILY LIFE (3:1-7)

Peter encouraged the wives of unbelievers to submit to the authority of their husband as a means of winning them to Christ. He urged all family members to treat others with sympathy, love, tenderness, and humility.

We must treat our families lovingly. Though it may be difficult, willing service is the best way to influence our loved ones. To gain the needed strength, we must pray for God's help. Relationships with parents, brothers, sisters, and spouses are important aspects of Christian discipleship.

- In chapter 1 what principles do you find for a godly marriage?
- How could 3:6 be misused by a domineering husband? What corrective does God's Word provide against misusing this husband-wife relationship? (Also check Ephesians 5.)
- What qualities do you want in a marriage partner?
- What qualities do you think your mate will desire in you? How can you develop those qualities so that you will bring godliness and maturity to your marriage?

JUDGMENT (1:17; 3:18-22; 4:7, 17-18; 5:4)

God will judge everyone with perfect justice. He will punish evildoers and those who persecute his people; he will reward those who love God with life forever in his presence.

Because all people are accountable to God, we can leave judgment of others to him. We must not hate or resent those who persecute us, and we should realize that we will be held responsible for how we live each day.

- What will happen to those without Christ when they face God's judgment?
- What difference will having Jesus as your Lord make when you face God's judgment?
- Review 1:14-25. If you will not be condemned because of Jesus, why should God's holiness continue to be your motivation for living a holy life?
- What specific areas of your life still need to become holy through obedience to Christ? How can this be accomplished?

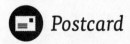 *Postcard*

Imagine someone actually putting you in the position described in 3:15 and asking you to explain why you live with hope. What answer would you give? Take some time to formulate a response. It will probably come in handy!

2 PETER

 Snapshot of 2 Peter

Every person comes face-to-face with life's ironies. One man, noting the regularity (and certainty) of these quirks, decided to make a list. The result? The famous "Murphy's Laws." Some of Murphy's more interesting observations:

> If anything can go wrong, it will.
> "Broken" gadgets will operate perfectly in the presence of a repairman.
> Saying "Watch this!" guarantees that the behavior you want others to witness will not happen.
> A poorly thrown Frisbee will always come to rest under the exact center of a parked car.
> The other line always moves faster.
> If you put a napkin in your lap, you will not spill; failure to use a napkin ensures spillage.

We nod and smile at those "laws" because we've lived them. They're amazingly true to life. How about some other laws of life? Perhaps not as humorous, but just as true—and much more life-changing:

> Spiritual growth only happens when we get to know God and make the effort to serve him.
> The world is full of people who will try to lead you astray.
> Jesus Christ is coming back.

Would you like to know more about these critical principles? They're all contained in the Bible book we call 2 Peter.

PURPOSE:
To warn Christians about false teachers and to exhort them to grow in their faith and knowledge of Christ

AUTHOR:
Peter

TO WHOM WRITTEN:
The church at large

DATE WRITTEN:
About AD 67, three years after 1 Peter was written, possibly from Rome

SETTING:
Peter knows that his time on earth is limited (1:13-14), so he writes about what is on his heart, warning believers of what will happen when he is gone—especially about false teachers. He reminds believers of the unchanging truth of the gospel.

KEY PEOPLE:
Peter, Paul

SPECIAL FEATURES:
The date and destination are uncertain, and the authorship has been disputed. Because of this, 2 Peter was the last epistle admitted to the canon of the New Testament Scripture. Also, there are similarities between 2 Peter and Jude.

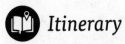 *Itinerary*

Guidance for Growing Christians (1:1-21)
This letter begins with warnings for growing Christians, pointing out that Christians don't stay in the same place—we're either moving forward or losing ground. Peter notes that his own remaining time will shortly be over. He expects his readers, however, to keep the faith.

Danger to Growing Christians (2:1-22)
To that end Peter offers some serious warnings about false teachers. They will be prevalent and persistent. The letter includes several distinguishing features of these untrustworthy guides: they are lovers of money, rejecters of the things of God, self-centered, and proud. He promises God's judgment on them.

Hope for Growing Christians (3:1-18)

This letter closes with a review of hopeful benefits that God offers to those who continue to grow in the faith.

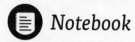 *Notebook*

DILIGENCE (1:5-11, 19-21; 3:14-18)

If our faith is real, it will be evident in our faithful behavior. If people are diligent in Christian growth, they won't backslide or be deceived by false teachers.

Growth is essential. It begins with faith and culminates in love for others. To keep growing we need to know God, keep on following him, and remember what he taught us. It may not always be easy, but it will always be worthwhile.

- According to chapter 1, what are the attitudes and actions that lead to maturity?
- If a Christian friend were to ask you, "How are you growing?" what would be your response?
- Based on this study, what are five practical steps to personal spiritual growth?
- How and when will you apply these five steps to your relationship with God?

FALSE TEACHERS (2:1-22; 3:3-5, 17)

Peter warned the church to beware of false teachers. These teachers were proud of their position, promoted sexual sin, and advised against keeping the Ten Commandments. Peter countered by pointing to the Spirit-inspired Scriptures as the only authority.

Christians need discernment to resist false teachers. God can rescue us from their lies if we stay true to his Word, the Bible, and reject those who twist the truth. The truth is our best defense because it exposes the lies of those who try to deceive us.

- How do the lives of the false teachers compare with the lives of those who follow God's truth?
- Why can God's Word be trusted more than all teachers?
- What false teaching have you heard about God and Jesus?
- What would you say to someone who wanted to be certain not to fall for the deception of a false teacher?

CHRIST'S RETURN (3:3-14)

One day Christ will create a new heaven and earth where we will live forever. As Christians, our hope is in this promise. But with Christ's return comes his judgment on all who refuse to believe.

The cure for complacency, lawlessness, and heresy is found in the confident assurance that Christ will return. God is still giving unbelievers time to repent. To be ready, Christians must keep on trusting Christ and resisting the pressure to give up waiting for his return.

- What reason does Peter give for Christ's patience in waiting to return?
- How does Peter say we should live in light of Christ's expected return?
- How do most Christians view Christ's eventual return?
- What difference does Christ's expected return make in your life?

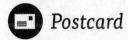 *Postcard*

Describe what growth you would like to have in your relationship with Jesus Christ over the next five years. What spiritual disciplines do you want to have significantly improved? Now, what smaller steps can you take to get there?

1 JOHN

Snapshot of 1 John

Love. We can't touch it, count it, bottle it, or even see it. But who among us would argue that love isn't real?

Love. It makes sane people do and say crazy things. It prompts snobby, selfish people to do noble things. It turns boring people into exciting, unpredictable creatures. What else on earth has that kind of power?

Love. It can hurt like nothing else in the world. And yet, paradoxically, not loving is much more painful.

Love. The most talked-about and sung-about and thought-about theme in all the world. And also the most misunderstood.

Love. Would you like to know more about it and see it in a brand-new light? Then read 1 John, the most eloquent description of love ever penned.

Love. It's not everything you think it is. It's more . . . much, much more.

PURPOSE:
To reassure Christians in their faith and to counter false teachings

AUTHOR:
The apostle John

TO WHOM WRITTEN:
The letter is untitled and was written to no particular church. It was sent as a pastoral letter to several Gentile congregations. It was also written to all believers everywhere.

DATE WRITTEN:
Probably between AD 85 and 90, from Ephesus

SETTING:
John is an older man and perhaps the only surviving apostle at this time. He has not yet been banished to the island of Patmos, where he will live in exile. As an eyewitness of Christ, he writes authoritatively to give this new generation of believers assurance and confidence in God and in their faith.

KEY PEOPLE:
John, Jesus

SPECIAL FEATURES:
John is called the apostle of love, and love is mentioned throughout this letter. There are a number of similarities in vocabulary, style, and main ideas between this letter and John's Gospel. John writes with brief statements and simple words, and his writing features sharp contrasts: light and darkness, truth and error, God and Satan, life and death, love and hate.

 Itinerary

God Is Light (1:1–2:29)
First John demonstrates how the most essential things around us and about us can teach us about God. This letter uses three of these core ideas as an outline. To begin, John reviews the fact that God is light. God's light allows people to see their own sinfulness. God's light shines brightly in forgiveness (1:9).

God Is Love (3:1–4:21)
Second, John moves to a subject that he has experienced perhaps more than any other person in his relationship with Jesus—love. He writes that God is love. God's love touches everything. God wants to love us, and he wants us to pass his love on to others.

God Is Life (5:1-21)
Third, John concluded his thoughts by stating that God is life. The particular life that John wants us to find in God is eternal life. That is God's gift to us through Jesus Christ.

 Notebook

SIN (1:5-10; 2:1-2, 12-17; 3:4-9; 5:16-21)
Even Christians sin. Sin requires God's forgiveness, which Christ's death provides. Determining to live according to God's biblical

standards shows that we are forgiven and that our life is being transformed.

We cannot deny our sinful nature or minimize the consequences of sin in our relationship with God. We must resist the attraction of sin, yet we must confess when we do sin. Sin is our fault; Christ is our Redeemer.

- What happened when the sinless Christ entered the sinful world?
- What happens when the sinless Christ enters the life of a sinful person?
- What does John say we should do about our sins?
- What is happening in your life in terms of dealing with sin? Are you dealing with your sin with the action and attitude of 1:9? Explain.

LOVE (2:7-11; 3:10-11, 14-16, 23; 4:7-21; 5:1-3)

Christ commands his people to love others as he did. This love is evidence of those who are truly saved. God is the Creator of love, and he wants his children to love each other.

Love means putting others first. Love is action—showing others we care, not just saying it. To show love we must give our time and money to meet the needs of others.

- Describe God's love for you as described in 1 John.
- Why is knowing and experiencing God's love essential to living a full life?
- Who are the people you love most? How does your love life compare to your description of God's love? What are your strengths and weaknesses?
- Whom do you have difficulty loving? How can you apply God's love to those relationships? Why should you do this?

FAMILY OF GOD (1:1-4; 2:18-21, 24-25, 28-29; 3:1-3, 10-20; 4:20-21)

People become God's children by believing in Christ. God's life in his children enables them to love fellow family members.

How a person treats others reveals his or her true Father. Live as a faithful, loving family member. Remember whose child you are!

- Who are the children of God?
- What privileges do these children have? What responsibilities?
- Complete this statement with specific responses from your own life: "Being a child of God enables me to _____ _____."
- How would those who know you describe your Father based on their knowledge of you as his child?

TRUTH AND ERROR (2:4-6, 18-23, 26-27; 3:7-9; 4:1-6)

Teaching that the body does not matter, false teachers encouraged believers to throw off moral restraints. They also taught that Christ wasn't really a man and that we must be saved by having some special mystical knowledge. As a result people became indifferent to sin.

God is truth and light, so the more we get to know him, the better we can keep focused on the truth. Don't be led astray by any teaching that denies Christ's deity or humanity. Check the message; test the claims.

- What false teachings was John correcting in his letter?
- What are our resources for discerning and dealing with false teachings?
- How can you live so that others can see the difference between God's truth and the false messages in the world?
- How would you describe your commitment to God's truth? What will you do this week? Put into action what you answered for the previous question.

ASSURANCE (2:3-6; 3:19-24; 5:1-15, 19-20)

God rules over heaven and earth. Because God's Word is true, we can have assurance of eternal life and victory over sin. By faith we can be certain of our eternal destiny with Christ.

- Assurance of our relationship with God is a promise, but it is also a way of life. We build our confidence by trusting in God's Word and in Christ's provision for our sin. If a young Christian were to ask you, "How can I be that sure I am saved?" what would be your response?
- How could you use 3:12-16 in your answer?

- How do you know that you are saved? What impact does this assurance have on the way you are currently living?

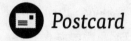 ## Postcard

The Gospel of John demonstrates that Jesus is the Son of God, and John's first letter shows how to live confidently in a relationship with Jesus. What are you presently finding most challenging about living as a Christian? You will probably find a practical solution in this short letter.

2 JOHN

 Snapshot of 2 John

Practical jokes have been around a long time. Just read through the Old Testament; it's full of sneaky characters. There's Abraham, trying to pass off his wife, Sarah, as his sister—twice. There's Jacob, donning a goatskin disguise to snatch his big brother's blessing. (And that's just in the first half of the first book—Genesis!)

Most people have tried shocking or embarrassing someone with a joy buzzer or a whoopee cushion. Others have short-sheeted beds or done various phone pranks. Perhaps you have attempted a more complicated stunt—turning a friend's dresser drawers upside down, freezing your brother's underwear, toilet-papering a house. (It's reported that some university pals lined a dormmate's room with plastic and turned it into a giant aquarium—complete with a shark!)

As long as no one gets hurt, no laws are broken, and no property is damaged, pranks are no big deal. It's fun to fool people—or even to be fooled.

Except in the spiritual dimension. There we can't afford to be deceived, because our enemy, the devil, packs his pranks with disaster!

One of Satan's favorite methods of suckering us is to get us to listen to false teaching. This can come in many different forms, some very pleasing. But no matter how pleasant it may seem, false teaching is always deadly.

The book of 2 John warns against false teaching. That's a warning we need to heed because the enemy's tricks aren't just for amusement—they're meant for destruction!

PURPOSE:
To emphasize the basics of following Christ—truth and love—and to warn against false teachers

AUTHOR:
The apostle John

TO WHOM WRITTEN:
To "the chosen lady" and her children (this may refer to a local church) and to Christians everywhere

DATE WRITTEN:
About the same time as 1 John, around AD 90, from Ephesus

SETTING:
Evidently this woman and her family have been involved in one of the churches that John is overseeing—they have developed a strong friendship. John is warning her of the false teachers that are becoming prevalent in some of the churches.

KEY PEOPLE:
John, the chosen lady, the lady's children

SPECIAL FEATURE:
This is the only New Testament book addressed specifically to a woman.

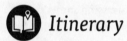 *Itinerary*

Watch Out for False Teachers (1:1-11)
More like a brief memo than a letter, 2 John gets right to its point. John is concerned about the temptation to stray from the truth. He assures his readers that faithfulness and obedience to the word of Christ are the only ways to maintain fellowship with God.

John's Final Words (1:12-13)
Having issued his warning, John adds that he will have more to say when he arrives. John is confident that his visit will result in joy.

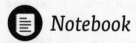 *Notebook*

TRUTH (1:1-5)
Following God's Word, the Bible, is essential to Christian living because God is truth. Christ's true followers consistently obey his truth.

To be loyal to Christ's teachings, we must know the Bible, but we must never twist the Bible's message to our own needs or purposes nor encourage others who misuse it. We should be servants to the truth of the Word.

- Why is truth important?
- How can we know what the truth is?
- Who are the enemies of the truth? What should be our response to these enemies?
- How does your life compare with the enemies of the truth in your world?

LOVE (1:3-6)
Christ commands Christians to love one another. This is the basic ingredient of true Christianity.

To obey Christ fully, we must believe his command to love others. Helping, giving, and meeting needs put love into practice. Love in deed is love indeed.

- How does John connect love for one another with love for God?
- What seems to be the connection between love and truth?
- Identify the people in your life who do not know Christ and his love. What can you do for them that will be a witness concerning the reality of the truth and God's love?

FALSE LEADERS (1:7-11)
We must be wary of religious leaders who are not true to Christ's teachings. We should not give them a platform to spread false teachings.

Don't encourage those who are contrary to Christ. Politely remove yourself from association with false leaders. Be aware of what's being taught in the church.

- How can you tell who is a false teacher?
- What do you see as the main dangers of false teachings?
- What passages of Scripture would you use to correct the error of these false teachers?
- Why is it important, based on this study, to be a student of God's Word?
- What steps are you taking to be led by the truth and to avoid error?

✉ *Postcard*

When you are living on your own, you will probably have to go through the process of finding a church in which to serve and worship. What are some of the major guidelines you can note even in this short letter that, hopefully, will help you with that decision?

3 JOHN

 Snapshot of 3 John

"It was over before it got started!" "Blink, and you'll miss it." "Short, sweet, and to the point."

Those are just some of the expressions you might use to describe:
The 1896 war between the United Kingdom and Zanzibar. (It lasted a mere 38 minutes!)
Boxer Al Couture's 1946 knockout of opponent Ralph Walton in only ten seconds (and that included a ten-second count by the referee)!
The twenty-minute reign of King Dom Luis III of Portugal in 1908.
Montana's Roe River. (Its length? A measly 201 feet!)
The ten-yard-long (or should we say "ten-yard-short") McKinley Street in Bellefontaine, Ohio.

But just because things are brief or small or short doesn't mean they're unimportant.

Take 3 John, for instance. With only fifteen verses it is one of the shortest books of the Bible—a quick contrast between godly living and worldly behavior.

In fact, this introduction is about as long as the book itself! So go ahead and read this warm, personal note from the apostle John to his friend Gaius.

When you do, another familiar expression may come to mind: "Good things come in small packages."

PURPOSE:
To commend Gaius for his hospitality and to encourage him in his Christian life

AUTHOR:
The apostle John

TO WHOM WRITTEN:
Gaius, a prominent Christian in one of the churches known to John, and all Christians everywhere

DATE WRITTEN:
About AD 90, from Ephesus

SETTING:
Church leaders are traveling from town to town to help establish new congregations. They depend on the hospitality of fellow believers. Gaius is one who welcomes them into his home.

KEY PEOPLE:
John, Gaius, Diotrephes, Demetrius

SPECIAL FEATURE:
Third John takes the form of a brief thank-you note to Gaius for his gift of hospitality.

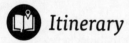 *Itinerary*

God's Children Live by the Standards of the Gospel (1:1-12)
John writes to commend Gaius, who is taking care of traveling teachers and missionaries. He adds some warnings about people like Diotrephes, who is proud and refuses to listen to spiritual leaders.

John's Final Words (1:13-15)
This brief letter closes with some personal notes and John's hope for a future visit.

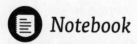 *Notebook*

HOSPITALITY (1:5-10)
John wrote to encourage those who were kind to others. Genuine hospitality for traveling Christian workers was needed then and is still important.

Faithful Christian teachers and missionaries need our support. Whenever you can extend hospitality to others, it will make you a partner in their ministry.

- Why is Christian hospitality important?
- In what specific ways can you and your friends at church extend Christian hospitality?
- How might your actions of hospitality enable you to become partners in God's work in and through others?
- What attitudes are required in order to be truly hospitable? How are you doing in terms of these attitudes?
- Develop a hospitality plan of action based on this study.

PRIDE (1:9-11)

Diotrephes not only refused to offer hospitality, but he also set himself up as a church boss. Pride disqualified him from being a real leader.

Christian leaders must shun pride and its effects on them. Be careful not to misuse your position of leadership. The best leaders are always the best servants.

- What were Diotrephes's sinful actions?
- Why does John label Diotrephes as proud?
- How can a person who is proud learn to be more humble?
- Do you struggle with sinful pride? If so, how can you apply your responses to the previous question to your pride?

FAITHFULNESS (1:1-5, 12)

Gaius and Demetrius were commended for their faithful work in the church. They were held up as examples of faithful, selfless servants.

Don't take for granted Christian workers who serve faithfully. Be sure to encourage these workers so they won't grow weary of serving.

- What do you learn about Gaius in this short book?
- What Christians do you know who live faithfully in their relationship with God? What qualities do you see in them that reflect faithfulness to God? How could you encourage them in their ministry and leadership?
- Why is faithfulness such an essential quality in the Christian life?

- Currently, what reflects faithfulness in your life? Identify the ways that your faithfulness, like that of Gaius and those you listed in the second question, makes a difference to others.

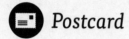 *Postcard*

One of the most impressive habits a young person can develop is expressing thanks to others for their help and generosity. How are you doing in showing gratitude?

JUDE

 Snapshot of Jude

Is your faith fit for a (spiritual) fight?

What would you say if the school agnostic called the resurrection of Christ a myth? Or if a minister you respect admitted that he believes the Bible contains errors and contradictions?

What if your favorite teacher announced, "It is insensitive and downright wrong for one group of people to try to force its views on another group! Right and wrong is a relative concept, and we cannot legislate morality"?

Imagine meeting someone full of joy and peace, a person seemingly very much in touch with God. As you converse, this person tells you that she is content and fulfilled because of daily yoga exercises, meditation, and also because of an experience she recently had in which she journeyed back through her previous incarnations. She nods when you mention Jesus Christ and says, "If that works for you, great! But I found the truth another way."

If you haven't already had encounters like the ones just described, then just wait. Your time is definitely coming!

The fact is that our world is full of confused people who are eagerly spreading their confusing ideas.

Don't get caught off guard! Get your Christian beliefs and behavior ready for spiritual battle by understanding what you believe and why. There's no better place to start your Bible boot camp training than in Jude.

PURPOSE:
To remind the church of the need for constant vigilance—keeping strong in the faith and defending it against heresy

AUTHOR:
Jude, James's brother and Jesus' half brother

TO WHOM WRITTEN:
Jewish Christians and all believers everywhere

DATE WRITTEN:
About AD 65

SETTING:
From the first century on, the church has been threatened by heresy and false teaching—we must always be on our guard.

KEY PEOPLE:
Jude, James, Jesus

SPECIAL FEATURE:
One of only two books written by half brothers of Jesus (the other is James)

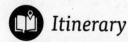 Itinerary

The Danger of False Teachers (1:1-16)
Jude begins his letter by noting that his original purpose in writing has changed. Instead of a letter of encouragement, he has to write a letter of warning. Those to whom he is writing are being overrun by false teachers. They are in danger of giving attention to those who can lead them from the faith.

The Duty to Fight for God's Truth (1:17-25)
Having given his warning, Jude next gives some orders. If his readers will remember the apostolic teaching they have received and will speak out boldly, they will preserve their own faith and encourage the wavering faith of others.

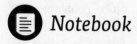 Notebook

FALSE TEACHERS (1:4, 8, 10-19)
Jude warned against false teachers and leaders who were rejecting the lordship of Christ, undermining the faith of others, and

leading people astray. These leaders and any who follow them would be punished.

We must stoutly defend Christian truth. Make sure that you avoid leaders and teachers who change the Bible to suit their own purposes. Genuine servants of God will faithfully portray Christ in their words and conduct.

- How does Jude describe the false teachers?
- What were the negative results of their teachings?
- How were the Christians supposed to respond to erroneous teachings?
- What safeguards can you build into your life to insure that you are not deceived by false teachings?
- What are you doing to serve as a living testimony of the truth of God?

APOSTASY (1:4-9, 10-11, 14-19, 22-25)

Jude warned against apostasy—turning away from Christ. Believers are to remember that God punishes rebellion against him. They must be careful not to drift away from a firm commitment to Christ.

Those who do not study God's Word are susceptible to apostasy. Christians must guard against any false teachings that would distract them from the truth preached by the apostles and written in God's Word.

- How do those who are led by God compare with those who are living in rebellion?
- What are the principles found in 1:20-23 for dealing with the rebellious?
- How would you apply those principles to your life at school? In church? In your social life?
- What confidence do you find in 1:24-25 that tells you God will remain faithful to you as you follow him? Take time to praise God for who he is and for how he keeps you in his love.

📧 Postcard

Review the last few times you spoke up for Christ in a less-than-friendly environment. What did you learn from those experiences? What will you try to do better next time?

REVELATION

 Snapshot of Revelation

Fairy tales always end perfectly. The frog turns into a prince, the unloved stepsister becomes a beloved bride, and mean and greedy people get paid back for the rotten things they've done.

Unfortunately, fairy tales aren't true. "Happily ever after"? No way! The real world doesn't work that way.

Or does it?

We are near the end of the Bible. One book left to read: Revelation. This wild vision is one of the most discussed, mysterious, and controversial books ever written. It's labeled "prophecy" and "theology." And it's like a fairy tale.

A fairy tale?!

That's right. According to Revelation, those who have become God's children by faith in Christ will have the happiest of all endings: being in the very presence of God, enjoying an existence untouched by sorrow or death.

And every bad and wicked creature (including the devil himself) will face the music. All injustices will be righted; all unforgiven sin will be judged. That is a concise summary of the message of Revelation: happiness and reward for the good, punishment and justice for all the guilty. A picture-perfect ending.

You must admit that it does sound like a fairy tale. There is, however, one important difference: this too-good-to-be-true story is truer than anything that ever existed. It is going to happen.

You can count on it.

PURPOSE:
To reveal the full identity of Christ and to give warning and hope to believers

AUTHOR:
The apostle John

TO WHOM WRITTEN:
Seven Asian churches and all believers everywhere

DATE WRITTEN:
About AD 95, from the island of Patmos

SETTING:
Most scholars believe that the seven churches of Asia to whom John is writing were experiencing the persecution that took place under Emperor Domitian (AD 90–95). Apparently the Roman authorities have exiled John to the island of Patmos (off the coast of Asia). John, an eyewitness of the incarnate Christ, has a vision of the glorified Christ. God also reveals to him what will take place in the future—judgment and the ultimate triumph of God over evil.

KEY PEOPLE:
John, Jesus

KEY PLACES:
Island of Patmos, the seven churches, the new Jerusalem

SPECIAL FEATURES:
Revelation begins and ends with the theme of Christ's return. It includes more references to Old Testament books than any other New Testament book.

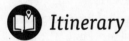 *Itinerary*

Letters to the Churches (1:1–3:22)
Revelation begins with John's explanation of how he received this revelation from God. John then records specific messages from Jesus to the seven churches in Asia.

Message for the Church (4:1–22:21)
Suddenly, the scene shifts as a kaleidoscope of dramatic and majestic images burst into view before John's eyes. This series of visions portrays the future rise of evil, culminating in the rule of the Antichrist. Then follows John's recounting of the triumph of the King of kings, the wedding of the Lamb, the final judgment, and the coming of the new Jerusalem.

Revelation concludes with the promise of Christ's imminent return (22:6-21), and John breathes a prayer that has been echoed by Christians through the centuries. "Amen! Come, Lord Jesus!"

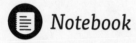 Notebook

GOD'S SOVEREIGNTY (1:4-20; 4:1–5:14; 11:15-19; 15:1-4; 19:1-16)

God is sovereign. He is greater than any power in the universe and not to be compared with any leader, government, or religion. He controls history for the purpose of uniting true believers in loving fellowship with him.

Though Satan's power may temporarily increase, we are not to be led astray. God is all-powerful. Satan is not equivalent to God. God is supreme, in control, and will safely bring his family into eternal life. God cares for us; we can trust him with our life.

- In what ways is God revealed as sovereign in Revelation?
- How does God's sovereignty offer security to you?
- Based on your security in God, what plans, dreams, worries, and problems can you bring to him today? How does trusting God with both hopes and fears enable you to experience his sovereignty?

CHRIST'S RETURN (1:7-8; 19:11-21; 22:7-21)

Christ came to earth as a "Lamb," the symbol of his perfect sacrifice for our sin. He will return as the triumphant "Lion," the rightful ruler and conqueror. Christ will defeat Satan, settle accounts with all those who rejected him, and bring his faithful people into eternity.

Assurance of Christ's return gives suffering Christians the strength to endure. We can look forward to Christ's return as King and Judge. Because no one knows the time when Christ will appear, we must be ready at all times by keeping our faith strong.

- How does Christ's first coming compare with his second coming?
- What impact did Christ's first coming have on the world? On you?

- What impact will Christ's second coming have on the world? On you?
- How can the reality of Christ's second coming have a positive impact on you now?

GOD'S FAITHFUL PEOPLE (1:1-3; 2:1-3:22; 7:1-17; 11:1-12; 14:1-13; 19:1-10)

John wrote to encourage the church not to worship the Roman emperor. His warning is for all God's people to be devoted only to Christ. Revelation identifies the faithful people and what they should be doing until Christ returns.

Take your place in the ranks of God's faithful people; believe in Christ. Victory is sure for those who resist temptation and make loyalty to Christ their top priority.

- What were some of the problems facing the churches in chapters 2 and 3? How were they to correct those problems?
- With which of these churches can you identify? How would you apply the command for correction?
- What is the reward of those who endure faithfully?
- Why is the cost of being a Christian worth it? Explain how this motivates you to grow in Christ rather than just surrendering to your weaknesses.

JUDGMENT (6:1-17; 8:1-10:11; 11:15-13:18; 14:14-18:24; 20:1-15)

One day God's anger toward sin will be fully and completely unleashed. Satan will be defeated; false religion will be destroyed. God will reward the faithful with eternal life, but all who refuse to believe in him will face eternal punishment.

God's final judgment will put an end to evil and injustice. We must be certain of our commitment to Christ if we want to escape this great final judgment. No one who is uncommitted to Christ will escape God's punishment. All who belong to Christ will receive their full reward based on what Christ has done.

- What will happen in the final judgment (chapter 20)?
- Whose names are written in the Book of Life?
- How does the knowledge of this final judgment affect the way you live? The way you view death?

- What would you like to communicate to your friends about the final judgment? How can you do this?

HOPE (1:1-8; 21:1–22:21)

One day God will create a new heaven and a new earth. All believers will live with God forever in perfect peace and security. Those who have already died will be raised to life. These promises for the future bring us hope.

Our greatest hope is that what Christ promises will be true. When we have confidence in our final destination, we will be able to follow Christ with unwavering dedication no matter what we must face. Because we belong to him, there is no room for despair.

- What will God do after the final judgment?
- What is your ultimate hope in Christ?
- When do you find yourself most needing to rely on this ultimate hope? How does your "final hope" provide hope in the present?
- What would you like to communicate to your friends about the final hope? How can you do this?

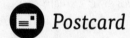 **Postcard**

Most people want to apply the book of Revelation without ever reading it. God, however, promises a blessing to those who do read it! (See 1:3.) Make it a point to take several hours to simply read the book humbly, attentively, and openly, letting God give you a vivid, life-shaping image of his greatness.

BIBLE READING PLAN

INTRODUCTION

We usually think of the Bible as one book. That's logical because it looks like one book and claims to come from one Author. We also speak of it as God's Word. But when we read and study the Bible, we discover that it is actually an entire library between two covers. Not one book, but 66 (39 in the Old Testament; 27 in the New Testament)! Each book has its own style and uniqueness—yet each book contributes to the message God wants to get across with the whole Bible. What's more, though we use the word *book*, some parts of the Bible are letters (like Paul's letter to the Romans) or collections (like the Psalms). Still, the overall message of the Bible is one because it has one main author—God. The reason the styles throughout the Bible vary is because God teamed up with dozens of people to write his Word.

HOW THIS PLAN IS DIFFERENT

There are many plans to help you read through the Bible library. You can even start at page one and read straight through. The approach taken here, however, is designed to help you get a flavor of the whole Bible by reading selections from it throughout a year. You will be reading the best-known stories and many important lessons. Some parts of the Bible offer so much help that they can be read every day. Among these are the Gospels, Psalms, and Proverbs. One way or another, you need to read God's Word!

BEFORE YOU BEGIN

Notice that each day's reading has a title and a question. These are important application questions that will help you as you read. Always pray before you read and ask God to help you understand, obey, and apply his Word to your life. And remember, this is only the start of the great adventure of reading God's Word and getting to know him.

Old Testament

Genesis 1:1–2:3 How It All Started
Why do human beings have value and worth?

Genesis 2:15–3:24 Adam and Eve
In what ways are you like those first humans?

Genesis 4:1-16 Cain and Abel
How do you handle anger?

Genesis 6:9-22 Noah Gets to Build a Boat
What is the most difficult act that God has asked you to do?

Genesis 7:1-24 All Aboard!
If you were alive at this time, what reasons would Noah have to invite you on the boat?

Genesis 8:1-22 A Long Wait
How would you have spent your time on the boat?

Genesis 9:1-17 Rules and Rainbows
What could you do the next time you see a rainbow?

Genesis 11:1-9 The Tower of Babel
Who do you trust more than God?

Genesis 12:1-9; 17:1-8 God's Promises to Abraham
How does God affect the way you make decisions?

Genesis 18:1-15 Unusual Visitors
What is your basic attitude toward strangers?

Genesis 19:15-29 Destruction of Sodom and Gomorrah
How does God feel about sin?

Genesis 21:8-21 Hagar and Ishmael
How does God deal with the messes in your life?

Genesis 22:1-19 Abraham's Painful Decision
What do you have trouble giving up to God?

Genesis 24:1-27 Abraham's Resourceful Servant
How do you approach difficult tasks?

Genesis 24:28-67 Isaac and Rebekah
What unexpected good thing has God done for you recently?

Genesis 25:19-34 Jacob and Esau
How do you treat your brothers or sisters?

Genesis 27:1-40 Jacob Tricks His Father
How honestly have you treated your parents?

Genesis 28:10-22 Jacob Meets God
In what places in your life has God been the most real?

Genesis 29:14-30 Jacob's Marriages
What qualities make up the way you love others?

Genesis 32:1–33:16 Jacob Returns Home
What happens inside you when you try to avoid a problem?

Genesis 37:1-36 Jacob's Children
How are disagreements settled in your family?

Genesis 39:1-23 Joseph in Trouble
How do you feel about getting in trouble for doing right?

Genesis 40:1-23 Dreams in Prison
When have you helped someone even though you had your own problems?

Genesis 41:1-36 Dreams in the Palace
Whom has God used to give you guidance?

Genesis 41:37-57 Joseph in Charge
How well do you handle big responsibilities?

Genesis 42:1-38 Joseph Sees His Brothers Again
What would you do with a chance for revenge?

Genesis 43:1-34 Back to Joseph
How well do you know how to forgive?

Genesis 44:1-34 Crisis in the Palace
How do you react when someone points out a mistake you've made?

Genesis 45:1-28 Finding a Lost Son
When did you last let your parents know you appreciate them?

Genesis 49:1-33 Jacob's Final Words
What's the strongest impression you've made on your parents?

Exodus 1:8–2:10 Moses Is Born
How have you appreciated the gift of birth?

Exodus 2:11-25 Moses on the Run
When was the last time you found yourself running from God?

Exodus 3:1-22 God's Burning Bush
In what ways has God made himself known to you?

Exodus 4:1-17 Moses Isn't Sure
How much self-confidence do you have when it comes to God?

Exodus 5:1-23 Resistance
What have people said when you've tried to obey God?

Exodus 6:1-13 Rejection
What would it cost you to do what God wants?

Exodus 7:1-14 A Stubborn Ruler
How does stubbornness affect your relationship with God?

Exodus 7:15–9:7 Five out of Ten Plagues
When do you try to bargain with God?

Exodus 9:8–10:29 Four More Plagues
What has God used to get your attention?

Exodus 11:1-10; 12:29-36 The Ultimate Plague
What does it mean to fear God in your life?

Exodus 13:17–14:31 A Narrow Escape
When have you experienced God's protection?

Exodus 15:22-27; 17:1-7 God Provides Water
What do you complain about to God?

Exodus 16:1-36 God's Unusual Food Supply
For what specific gift did you last say thanks to God?

Exodus 18:1-27 Helpful Advice
Who are the dependable advisers in your life?

Exodus 19:1-25 An Appointment with God
How would you prepare to meet with God?

Exodus 20:1-22 The Ten Commandments
How often do you think about God's standards?

Exodus 32:1-29 The Gold Calf
What distracts you from obeying God?

Exodus 40 Instructions about God's Tent
When are you most aware of God's presence in your life?

Numbers 12:1-16 Moses under Fire
What do you do when you find yourself jealous of someone else?

Numbers 13:1–14:4 Spying on the Promised Land I
How does God affect the word impossible *in your mind?*

Numbers 14:5-45 A Majority That Was Wrong
How often are your decisions based on peer pressure?

Numbers 21:4-9 Another Hard Lesson
What can you do to avoid repeating mistakes?

Numbers 22:5-38 Balaam and His Donkey
What happens when you do what you know you shouldn't do?

Deuteronomy 29:1-29 Moses Reviews God's Actions
How do you keep track of what God has done for you?

Deuteronomy 30:1-20 Moses Challenges the People
How do you show that you love God?

Deuteronomy 31:1-8 Moses Appoints New Leaders
If you were Joshua, who would be "Moses" in your life?

Deuteronomy 34:1-12 The Death of Moses
How would you most like to be remembered?

Joshua 1:1-18 God Takes Over
Which of these qualities would you most need to be like Joshua?

Joshua 2:1-24 Spying on the Promised Land II
What unexpected persons has God used in your life?

Joshua 3:1-17 The Invasion of Canaan
How would you illustrate God's guidance in your life?

Joshua 5:13–6:27 The Battle of Jericho
How serious are you about having God use you?

Joshua 7:1-26 Ultimate Consequences
What consequences have you experienced?

Joshua 10:1-15 The Longest Day
How do you know God is powerful?

Joshua 23:1-16 Joshua Warns the Leaders
Which of Joshua's warnings do you most need to obey?

Joshua 24:1-31 Joshua's Last Words
How can you get hope from history?

Judges 4:4-24 Judge Deborah
How do people know that you care about them?

Judges 6:1-40 Gideon Becomes a Judge
What examples of obedience can be found in your life?

Judges 7:1-25 Gideon and the Midianites
In what area of your life do you need to trust God more?

Judges 13:1-25 The Birth of Samson
What part of your life needs more discipline?

Judges 14:1-20 Samson's Riddle
How carefully do you consider the wisdom of your parents?

Judges 15:1-20 Samson and the Jawbone
How do you know that mistakes usually don't correct themselves?

Judges 16:1-21 Samson and Delilah
In what situations do you find yourself flirting with disaster?

Judges 16:22-31 Samson's Death
How well do you understand God's patience?

Ruth 1:1-22 Ruth and Naomi—A Friendship
How do difficulties affect your friendships?

Ruth 2:1-23 Ruth Meets Boaz
When have you found your reputation to be an advantage?

Ruth 3:1-18 Ruth Finds a Husband
What unexpected methods has God used in your life?

Ruth 4:1-22 A Happy Ending
What future reasons could there be for obeying God today?

1 Samuel 1:1-28 A Serious Prayer
What promises have you made to God lately that you have kept?

1 Samuel 3:1-21 God Calls Samuel
When you open God's Word, what do you expect him to say to you?

1 Samuel 8:1-22 The People Demand a King
What has God taught you about responsibility for your own choices?

1 Samuel 9:1-21 Saul and the Lost Donkeys
What is God's part in your daily decisions?

1 Samuel 10:1-27 Saul Becomes King
How do you evaluate people?

1 Samuel 13:1-18 Saul's Big Mistake
How do you respond when between a rock and a hard place?

1 Samuel 14:1-23 A Son to Make a Father Proud
What would it mean to have a friend like Jonathan?

1 Samuel 16:1-13 Samuel Anoints David
What people do you appreciate for something other than how they look?

1 Samuel 17:1-31 David and Goliath's Challenge
How does your confidence in God affect your decision to accept challenges?

1 Samuel 17:32-58 David Kills Goliath
What "giants" need to be defeated in your life?

1 Samuel 18:1-30 Trouble between Saul and David
How do you treat your friends who succeed?

1 Samuel 20:1-42 David and Jonathan
How far can your friends trust you?

1 Samuel 24:1-22 David Spares Saul's Life
Do you treat others the way you want to be treated?

1 Samuel 25:1-42 David and Abigail
How does God keep you from making big mistakes?

1 Samuel 28:1-25 Saul and the Occult
What would God's attitude be toward your involvement in any occult practices?

2 Samuel 5:1-12 David Becomes King over All Israel
How could you become a person who is more pleasing to God, as David was?

2 Samuel 9:1-13 The King's Kindness
What promises need to be kept in your life?

2 Samuel 11:1-27 David and Bathsheba
How often are you tempted to correct one sin by committing another?

2 Samuel 12:1-25 David and Nathan
What friends do you have who love you enough to correct you?

2 Samuel 13:1-19 Family Consequences of Sin
What actions do you take to avoid temptation?

2 Samuel 13:20-39 Family Revenge
Are you more likely to have committed David's or Absalom's sin?

2 Samuel 15:1-37 Family Betrayal
Who helps you keep your motives clear?

2 Samuel 18:1-18 The Death of Absalom
In what situations are you most likely to lose control?

1 Kings 1:5-27 Conflict over the Throne
What happens in your life when you don't make good decisions?

1 Kings 1:28-53 David Gives Solomon the Crown
When things in your world get confusing, how do you know God is still in control?

1 Kings 3:1-15 Solomon's Wisdom
Which of Solomon's choices would you have made?

1 Kings 3:16-28 Solomon Solves a Problem
In what situation in your life do you presently need God's wisdom?

1 Kings 6:1-38 Solomon Builds the Temple
What can you learn from Solomon about making and carrying out plans?

1 Kings 10:1-13 Solomon and the Queen of Sheba
When are you tempted to try to impress people?

1 Kings 12:1-24 Solomon's Unwise Son
Who are the people you know who will give you good advice?

1 Kings 17:1-24 God Takes Care of Elijah
How do obeying and trusting God go together in your life?

1 Kings 18:16-46 Elijah versus the Priests of Baal
How would you describe your attitude toward God's power today?

1 Kings 19:1-21 Spiritual Burnout
When was the last time you felt sorry for yourself?

1 Kings 21:1-29 The Stolen Vineyard
How important is justice in your life?

1 Kings 22:29-40 The Death of King Ahab
When are you tempted to think that you can hide from God?

2 Kings 2:1-12 Elijah's Chariot
When you make a commitment, how far will you go to carry it out?

2 Kings 2:13-25 Elisha's Miracles
How would someone else know that you have a deep respect for God?

2 Kings 5:1-27 The Healing of Naaman
What "small" things have you refused to do for God?

2 Kings 11:1-21 The King Who Was Seven Years Old
Who were your best examples in childhood?

2 Kings 22:1–23:3 Discovery of the Lost Book
What happens in your life when the Bible is a "lost book"?

Ezra 3:7-13 Rebuilding the Temple
How do you feel when you're working on a large, important project?

Nehemiah 2:1-20 Nehemiah Returns to Jerusalem
What relationships in your past need to be rebuilt?

Nehemiah 5:1-19 Nehemiah's Concern for the Poor
How do you express your concern for the poor?

Nehemiah 8:1-18 Reading God's Word
What are your expectations when you open God's Word?

Esther 1:1-22 The Fall of a Queen
How often do you take the important people in your life for granted?

Esther 2:1-23 A Strange Way to Become Queen
When have difficult or confusing events in your life actually been a preparation for something you would later experience?

Esther 3:1-15 The Jews in Danger
In what situations are you tempted to compromise your faith?

Esther 4:1-17 The Queen Decides to Help
In what ways has your faith cost you?

Esther 5:1-14 Esther Risks Her Life
When was the last time you did something scary to obey God?

Esther 6:1–7:10 God Protects His People
When is it helpful to remember that God is still in control of the world?

Job 1:1-22 The Testing of Job
In what situations do you most quickly question God's care?

Job 2:1-13 Job and His Friends
How do you normally respond to someone else's pain? How should you respond?

Job 38:1-41 God Speaks to Job
What things around you remind you of God's greatness?

Job 42:1-17 The Rest of Job's Story
What difference does it make to know and remember that God always has the last word?

Psalm 1:1-6 Two Kinds of Lives
What kind of person do you really want to be?

Psalm 8:1-9 The Value of Humans
How do you know you have worth?

Psalm 23:1-6 A Sheep's Song
What is the most comforting phrase to you in this psalm?

Psalm 51:1-19 A Confession
What examples of repentance have been part of your life?

Psalm 103:1-22 What God Is Like
Which picture in this psalm helps you understand God better?

Psalm 139:1-24 How Well God Knows Us
What emotions does this psalm bring out in you?

Psalm 145:1-21 God for All People and Time
Which of God's qualities do you most need today?

Proverbs 4:1-27 Wise Words about Life
What priority does getting wisdom have for you?

Proverbs 5:1-23 Wise Words about Sex
How do these words match what you hear around you every day?

Ecclesiastes 12:1-14 A Summary of Life
In what way can you remember your Creator today?

Isaiah 6:1-13 God Chooses Isaiah
When did you last realize your regular need for God's forgiveness?

Isaiah 53 The Suffering Servant
How would you describe what Jesus did for you?

Jeremiah 1:1-9 God Calls a Prophet
What is your reaction to the possibility of God using your life?

Jeremiah 36 The Book Burning
How much risk is involved in your relationship with God?

Jeremiah 38:1-13 Jeremiah in the Well
What part of your life compares in any way with Jeremiah's time in the well?

Ezekiel 37:1-14 A Valley of Dry Bones
What can you do to help you understand God's plan for the world?

Daniel 1:1-21 Coping with Pressure to Conform
How might Daniel react to the pressure situations in your life?

Daniel 2:1-24 A King's Dream
What do you do in seemingly hopeless situations?

Daniel 2:25-49 The Meaning of the Dream
Who gets the credit when things go right in your life?

Daniel 3:1-30 Three Friends in a Furnace
What examples can you give of God's protection in your life?

Daniel 5:1-30 The Writing on the Wall
What reasons would God have for passing judgment on the society in which you live?

Daniel 6:1-28 Daniel and the Lions
Do you pray regularly?

Jonah 1:1–2:10 Bending God's Directions
When did you last try to avoid doing what you knew God wanted you to do?

Jonah 3:1–4:11 Wrong Motives
What do you complain to God about?

New Testament

You will be reading various parts of the four Gospels in order to have a fairly chronological biography of Jesus' life.

Luke 1:1-4; John 1:1-18 Beginnings
Have you personally received Jesus as your Savior and become a child of God?

Luke 1:5-25 The Angel and Zechariah
How would you react to an angel's visit?

Luke 1:26-56 Mary and Elizabeth
What does joy do in your life?

Luke 1:57-80 John the Baptist Is Born
When did you last say thank you to your parents?

Matthew 1:1-25 A Family Tree
Which of these people have you read about in the Old Testament?

Luke 2:1-20 Jesus Is Born!
What does Christmas mean to you?

Luke 2:21-39 Jesus' First Trip to Church
How would you react to holding Jesus when he was a baby?

Matthew 2:1-12 Foreign Visitors
What gifts have you ever given Christ?

Matthew 2:13-23 Escape and Return
How has knowing God brought excitement into your life?

Luke 2:41-52 Jesus in the Temple Again
What four words would summarize your teenage years?

Mark 1:1-13 Baptism and Temptation
What are your most difficult temptations? Compare them to Jesus' temptations.

John 1:19-34 John the Baptist and Jesus
Who did you last talk to about Christ?

John 1:35-51 Jesus' First Disciples
How would someone know that you're a disciple of Jesus?

John 2:1-25 Jesus and Surprises
How has Christ been unpredictable in your life?

John 3:1-21 Jesus and Nicodemus
When did you first meet Jesus? How?

John 3:22-36; Luke 3:19-20 John Gets into Trouble
When has knowing Christ ever gotten you into trouble?

John 4:1-42 Jesus Changes a Town
In what ways has Jesus affected your town?

John 4:43-54 Jesus Preaching and Healing
Why do you believe in Christ?

Luke 4:16-30 Jesus Rejected
How would Jesus be received in your church next Sunday?

Mark 1:16-39 Jesus Calls People to Follow
What specific things have you left behind to follow Christ?

Luke 5:1-39 Miracles and Questions
How do Jesus' miracles affect you today?

John 5:1-47 Jesus Demonstrates He Is God's Son
What do you find most attractive about Jesus?

Mark 2:23–3:19 Jesus and Disciples
How would Jesus treat your personal traditions?

Matthew 5:1-16 Jesus Gives the Beatitudes
Which of these attitudes most needs to be in your life today?

Matthew 5:17-30 Jesus on Law, Anger, and Lust
How do Jesus' views compare with yours?

Matthew 5:31-48 Jesus on Relationships
What part of your life could be most radically changed by these words?

Matthew 6:1-18 Jesus on Doing Good Things
How do your public and private lives compare?

Matthew 6:19-34 Jesus on Money and Worry
In what ways are money and worry related in your life?

Matthew 7:1-12 Jesus on Criticizing and Praying
Which one are you most persistent in doing? Why?

Matthew 7:13-29 How Jesus Looks at Us
What is your foundation in life?

Luke 7:1-17 Jesus and Foreigners
What is your attitude toward foreigners? How can you show them God's love?

Matthew 11:1-30 Jesus Describes John
How would you want Jesus to summarize your life?

Luke 7:36–8:3 Jesus and Women
How would you have fit into the group that followed Jesus?

Matthew 12:22-50 Troubles for Jesus
When are you tempted to have Jesus prove himself to you?

Mark 4:1-29 Jesus Seeks, Seeds, and Weeds
What kind of soil is your life right now?

Matthew 13:24-43 More of Jesus' Parables
How concerned are you about the eternal fate of the people you know?

Matthew 13:44-52 Even More Parables
How and where did you find the hidden treasure?

Luke 8:22-56 Jesus in Control
Which of these examples gives you greatest comfort?

Matthew 9:27-38 The Concerns of Jesus
How do you picture Jesus caring for you?

Mark 6:1-13 Some Don't Listen; Some Need to Hear
How clear an idea do you have of what God wants you to do?

Matthew 10:16-42 Jesus Prepares His Disciples
In what ways do Jesus' words speak to the fears you have?

Mark 6:14-29 Herod Kills John the Baptist
How do you most want to be like John the Baptist?

Matthew 14:13-36 Jesus: Cook, Water Walker, Healer
Would you have been more likely to step out with Peter or to stay in the boat? Why?

John 6:22-40 Jesus Is the Bread from Heaven
How is Jesus "bread" to you?

John 6:41-71 Jesus Criticized and Deserted
How do you react when you hear critical or derogatory comments about Jesus?

Mark 7:1-37 Jesus Teaches and Defines Purity
What would God have to do to improve the purity of your life?

Matthew 15:32–16:12 Jesus Feeds and Warns
How do you evaluate what you hear?

Mark 8:22–9:1 Peter Identifies Jesus
In what specific ways have you come to understand Jesus better in the last few weeks?

Luke 9:28-45 Jesus Is Transfigured
Would you rather leave the world and be with Christ or be with Christ in the world?

Matthew 17:24–18:6 Who's the Greatest?
When do you worry about status?

Mark 9:38-50 Who's on Our Side?
How do you respond to the beliefs of others?

Matthew 18:10-35 Jesus Teaches Forgiveness
How do you react to the failures of others?

John 7:1-31 Jesus Out in the Open
What parts of Jesus' teachings do you struggle to accept?

John 7:32-53 A Warrant for Jesus' Arrest
What does it mean to have rivers of living water flowing from within you?

John 8:1-20 Jesus: Forgiveness and Light
Who is the last person you have had to forgive?

John 8:21-59 Jesus: Giver of Freedom
How has Christ made you free?

Luke 10:1-24 Jesus Sends out Seventy Messengers
What would have been most exciting about this trip for you?

Luke 10:25-42 Jesus Tells a Story and Visits Friends
Who has been a Good Samaritan to you?

Luke 11:1-13 Jesus Teaches about Prayer
How could your prayer habits be improved?

Luke 11:14-32 Accusations and Unbelief
What are your strongest reasons for being a faithful follower of Christ?

Luke 11:33-54 Real Spirituality versus Unreal Spirituality
Who has noticed light in your life recently?

Luke 12:1-21 Religious and Rich Fools
In what situations do you get too caught up in the goals of this world?

Luke 12:22-48 Jesus Warns about Worry
Does thinking about the future create worry or hope in you? Why?

Luke 12:49-59 Jesus Warns about Troubles
What examples have you seen of the problems Jesus is warning about?

Luke 13:1-21 Jesus and the Kingdom of God
When in your life would Jesus have to call for repentance?

John 9:1-41 Jesus and a Blind Man
What different stages of "seeing" have been part of your life?

John 10:1-18 Jesus Is the Good Shepherd
How have you experienced God's guidance in your life?

Luke:13:22-35 Jesus: The King Who Grieves
How do you feel about those around you who don't know Christ?

Luke 14:1-14 Jesus on Seeking Honor
When would others say that you look out for yourself too much?

Luke 14:15-35 Jesus Teaches about Being His Disciple
What is it going to cost you to be a follower of Jesus? Are you willing to pay the price?

Luke 15:1-10 Two Parables of Losing and Finding
How do these stories help you understand God's love for you?

Luke 15:11-32 A Son Who Was Found
In what ways is this story like your life?

Luke 16:1-18 The Parable of the Shrewd Manager
What does it mean to be an honest person?

Luke 16:19-31 The Rich Man and the Beggar
Where are the poor people in your community? Whom do you know who is poor?

John 11:1-36 Lazarus Dies
In what situations have you been disappointed with God?

John 11:37-57 Jesus Raises Lazarus
How would you have felt watching Lazarus walk out of the tomb?

Luke 17:1-19 Jesus and Ten Lepers
For what are you thankful to God?

Luke 17:20-37 Jesus and the Kingdom of God
What difference would it make in your life if Jesus returned today?

Luke 18:1-14 Jesus Teaches about Prayer
What is the attitude of your prayers?

Mark 10:1-16 Jesus on Family Matters
How far will you go to keep your word?

Mark 10:17-31 Jesus and the Rich Man
What is the most difficult thing Jesus could ask you to give up?

Matthew 20:1-19 A Parable about Equal Pay
How often are you jealous of what God has given to someone else?

Mark 10:35-52 Jesus on Serving Others
In what ways are you learning to be a servant?

Luke 19:1-27 Jesus and Zacchaeus
What personal physical characteristic has most affected how you feel about yourself?

John 12:1-11 A Woman Anoints Jesus
What have you ever "wasted" as an expression of love for Christ?

Matthew 21:1-17 Jesus Rides into Jerusalem
If you had been part of the crowd that day, what would have been your most lasting memory?

John 12:20-36 Jesus Explains Why He Must Die
How would you explain to someone why Jesus had to die on the cross?

John 12:37-50 Jesus and His Message
What kinds of pressures make you hesitant to tell others about your belief in Christ?

Mark 11:20-33 Permission to Pray for Anything
How bold is your prayer life?

Matthew 21:28-46 Two Parables
Which son are you most like?

Matthew 22:1-14 Jesus Tells about the Wedding Feasts
At what point in your life did you realize that you were invited? How did you respond?

Luke 20:20-40 Jesus Answers Questions
How do you really feel about living forever?

Mark 12:28-37 Questions Given and Taken
Whom do you know who is not far from the Kingdom of God?

Matthew 23:1-39 Jesus: Warnings and Grieving
Which of these seven warnings most directly relate to your life?

Luke 21:1-24 Jesus Talks about the Future
What do your giving habits say about your level of trust in God?

Luke 21:25-38 Jesus on Being Prepared
What does your schedule today say about your watchfulness?

Matthew 25:1-30 Parables about Being Prepared
With which of the people in these two stories do you identify most?

Matthew 25:31-46 Jesus on the Final Judgment
What people in your life are you treating like you would want to treat Christ?

Luke 22:1-13 Preparing the Last Supper
What do you do to prepare yourself for Communion?

John 13:1-20 Jesus Washes His Disciples' Feet
What is the greatest example of service someone has done for you? How do you serve others?

John 13:21-38 A Sad Prediction
How well do you feel Christ knows you?

John 14:1-14 Jesus Is the Way
How would you rate your present level of understanding of Christ and his teaching?

John 14:15-31 Jesus Promises the Comforter
How have you experienced the Comforter?

John 15:1-16 Jesus on the Vine and the Branches
What kind of fruit has the Gardener produced in you?

John 15:17–16:4 Jesus Warns about Troubles
What have you learned recently about loving others?

John 16:5-33 Jesus on the Holy Spirit and Prayer
Where in these verses do you find peace of heart and mind?

John 17:1-26 Jesus Prays
Where do you find yourself in this prayer?

Mark 14:26-52 A Repeated Prediction
What practical prayer problems do you need to work on?

John 18:1-24 Jesus Betrayed and Abandoned
How close have you come to Peter's denial of Christ?

Matthew 26:57-75 Trial and Denial
In what ways has being a follower of Jesus complicated your life?

Matthew 27:1-10 The Religious Trial and Judas's Death
When you think of sin's consequences, what personal examples come to mind?

Luke 23:1-12 Two Political Trials
In what ways did your childhood and background prepare you to respond to Jesus?

Mark 15:6-24 Sentencing and Torture
Was there a time you chose to do the wrong thing on purpose? Why? What happened?

Luke 23:32-49 Jesus Crucified
What do you feel when you read the description of the Crucifixion?

Matthew 27:57-66 Jesus Body Laid in a Guarded Tomb
What have you seen people do in their resistance to Christ?

John 20:1-18 Jesus Is Alive!
What makes Easter an important celebration in your life?

Matthew 28:8-15 Reactions to the Resurrection
What would be your first words to Jesus if he appeared to you?

Luke 24:13-43 Appearances of Jesus
Would you recognize Jesus if you saw him today? How?

John 20:24–21:14 More Appearances of Jesus
How has Christ answered your doubts?

John 21:15-25 Jesus Talks with Peter
What difference would it make to you to read these verses with your name in the place of Simon Peter's?

Matthew 28:16-20 Jesus Gives the Great Commission
What are you doing specifically to obey Christ's words?

Luke 24:44-53 Jesus Says Farewell
How do you find Christ opening your mind as you read the Bible?

Acts 1:1-11 The Departure of Jesus
What one thing would you be sure to do if you knew Jesus was coming back today?

Acts 1:12-26 First Things First
What is your idea of the right amount of time for prayer?

Acts 2:1-13 An Amazing Gift
What is the main purpose of any gift God might have given you?

Acts 2:14-40 Peter's First Sermon
How would you put this sermon into your own words?

Acts 2:41–3:11 Daily Life in the Early Church
What part of these early days would you have enjoyed the most?

Acts 3:12–4:4 Peter's Second Sermon
If you were given three minutes to tell the story of your spiritual life, what would you say?

Acts 4:5-22 Hostile Reactions
What excuses are you most likely to use to keep from sharing your faith?

Acts 4:23-37 Praying and Sharing
When was the last time you shared something that was yours with someone else?

Acts 5:1-16 Strange Events
How often are you tempted to take God lightly?

Acts 5:17-42 Arrested!
How do you react when you are treated unfairly?

Acts 6:1-15 Stephen: Special Servant
What specific responsibilities do you have in your local church?

Acts 7:1-29 History Review I
How familiar are you becoming with "his story" in history?

Acts 7:30-60 History Review II
In what ways would you want to be more like Stephen?

Acts 8:1-25 Benefits of Persecution
What difficulties in your life has God used to help you grow spiritually?

Acts 8:26-40 Unexpected Appointment
What have you done about baptism?

Acts 9:1-19 Paul Meets Jesus
What unusual events has God used to catch your attention?

Acts 9:20-31 Paul's New Life
How has Christ changed your life?

Acts 9:32-42 God Uses Peter
This past week, what special ability did you use to meet someone's need?

Acts 10:1-23 Peter Sees a Lesson
What lessons has God had to repeat in your life?

Acts 10:24-48 Peter Learns a Lesson
How has God helped you change your mind about some attitudes?

Acts 11:1-18 Gentiles Get a Chance
What prejudices of yours is God still working on?

Acts 11:19-29 Christians Helping One Another
What do you do when you hear stories of extreme poverty or hardship among Christians in other parts of the world?

Acts 12:1-25 A Great Escape and Capital Punishment
How do you react when God answers your prayers?

Acts 13:1-12 Paul and Barnabas: Travel Preaching
What Christians do you know who might help you discover more clearly how God wants you to invest your time and abilities?

Acts 14:1-28 Response and Reaction
How does the gospel act like Good News in your life?

Acts 15:1-21 A Church Conference
How important is it for you to talk problems over with other Christians?

Acts 15:22-41 The Gentiles Are Accepted
In what ways is God affecting the way you live and plan?

Acts 16:1-15 Paul, Silas, and Timothy
How would you describe the spiritual team of which you are part?

Acts 16:16-40 Adventures in Jail
How would you react to God using a difficult situation of yours to help another person discover him?

Acts 17:1-15 Different Responses from Two Cities
What part does the Bible play in your evaluation of what you hear and read?

Acts 17:16-34 Paul in Athens
What unconscious symbols of God's presence do you see around you in society?

Acts 19:1-20 Paul in Ephesus
In what situations are you most likely to become discouraged?

Acts 19:21-41 The Riot
When are you most likely to forget that God is in control?

Acts 20:1-12 Sleeping in Church
How does God respond to your human weaknesses?

Acts 20:13-38 Saying Good-Bye to Ephesus
When have painful good-byes worked for the best in your life?

Acts 21:1-17 Difficult Decision
What hard decisions do you have to make?

Acts 21:18-36 Paul in Jerusalem
How important is it to respect the consciences of others?

Acts 21:37–22:29 Paul Speaks
What difference has God made in your life?

Acts 22:30–23:22 A Plan to Kill Paul
How well do you know your rights and fulfill your responsibilities as a citizen of your country?

Acts 23:23–24:27 Paul in Prison
What would be harder for you, the pressure or the prison?

Acts 25:1-27 Paul Speaks to Festus
If Christianity were outlawed, what evidence could be brought against you to prove you are a Christian?

Acts 26:1-32 Paul Speaks to Agrippa
How comfortable are you in explaining your faith?

Acts 27:1-26 The Storm at Sea
What is your attitude when you are going through difficulties as part of a group?

Acts 27:27-44 The Shipwreck
What disasters in your life has God used to teach you?

Acts 28:1-14 The Winter on Malta
How often are you aware of God in everyday occurrences?

Acts 28:15-31 Paul in Rome
What would you most like to be doing when your time on this earth is over?

Romans 5:1-11 Faith Brings Joy
When was the last time you thanked God for all he has done for you?

Romans 8:1-18 Truly Free from Sin
In what areas are you still struggling with your sinful nature?

Romans 8:19-39 How God Loves
What things do you sometimes feel might be able to separate you from the love of Christ?

Romans 12:1-21 Living Sacrifice
What act of living sacrifice might God allow you to do today?

1 Corinthians 13:1-13 Real Love
Which quality of real love do you most need to ask God to increase in your life?

1 Corinthians 15:1-20 The Basic Gospel
What parts of the gospel are especially helpful to you in times of doubt or stress?

1 Corinthians 15:42-58 Destiny!
How much are you looking forward to all Christ has planned for you?

2 Corinthians 4:1-18 Weak Containers; Strong Contents
Which of the four difficult situations Paul mentions in these verses do you identify with most clearly?

Galatians 5:13-26 Two Radically Different Lives
What person comes to mind as someone whom you need to love as you love yourself?

Ephesians 1:3-23 God's Action
In what ways has God marked your life?

Ephesians 2:1-22 God's Plan
When have you recently reminded yourself and God that you want your life to be used for his purposes?

Ephesians 4:1-16 Picture of the Church
What is your role in the body of Christ?

Ephesians 6:10-20 Armor of God
Which of these weapons do you need to learn to use better?

Philippians 2:1-18 The Mind of Jesus
In what ways would having Christ's attitude make you face this day differently?

Philippians 3:1-21 Learning Joy
What areas of your life could God be using to teach you joy?

Colossians 2:1-15 What We Have in Christ
What dangerous philosophy is present in your environment that could affect your relationship with Christ?

Colossians 3:1-17 Christian Relationships
What do you see when you think about heaven?

1 Thessalonians 1:1-10 Spiritual Reputation
How do you think others would evaluate your spiritual life?

1 Thessalonians 4:1-18 Living for God
What specific action could you take today simply out of obedience to God?

2 Thessalonians 1:1-12 Encouragement
What other Christians could you encourage today?

2 Thessalonians 3:1-18 Final Requests
How aware and involved are you in the worldwide spread of the gospel?

1 Timothy 4:1-16 Always Going Forward
Which of the positive commands in these verses need to be a higher priority in your life?

1 Timothy 6:3-21 A Friend's Final Words
How does your attitude toward money match Paul's advice?

2 Timothy 1:1-18 The Importance of Examples
Who has been a good spiritual example for you? How can you thank him or her?

2 Timothy 3:1-17 Last Days
How many of these characteristics are part of your world today?

Titus 3:1-11; Philemon 1:4-7 Good Counsel
Which of these commands applies directly to your life?

Hebrews 10:19-39 The New Life
What do your prayer habits and church habits say about the real importance of faith in your life?

Hebrews 11:1-40 A Review of Faith
How deep is your commitment to Christ?

Hebrews 12:1-13 Our Turn
Which of these directions would have a significant impact on your faith?

James 1:2-27 Tough Times, Happy People
In what difficulty could you use the "James plan" right now?

James 2:1-13 Valuing Other People
What tendencies do you have to watch for in how you treat other people?

James 3:1-12 Words as Weapons
How sharp would others consider your tongue?

1 Peter 2:1-25 Living Stones
Which would you choose as the biggest personal challenge in these verses?

1 Peter 3:1-22 Relationships and Pain
How willing are you to carry out your relationships God's way, even when there are difficulties?

2 Peter 1:2-21 Knowing God
How would you answer someone who asked you what it means to know God?

1 John 1:1-10 The Way of Forgiveness
What part does confession have in your life?

1 John 3:1-24 God Is Love
How can you tell if your love is growing?

1 John 5:1-21 The Life God Gives
How do you know that you have eternal life?

2 John 1:4-6; 3 John 1:5-8; Jude 1:17-25 Family Matters
How often do you go out of your way to meet the needs of other Christians?

Revelation 1:1-20 Jesus the King
How would you describe your mental picture of Jesus?

Revelation 21:1-27 Everything Made New
What difference do you think you will most notice between the new world and the old?

Revelation 22:1-21 Life in the New City
How excited are you about heaven?

"WHERE TO FIND IT" INDEX

STORY

Jesus is the Bread of Life. *John 6:35*
Jesus is the Gate for the sheep. *John 10:7*
Jesus is the Good Shepherd. *John 10:11*
Jesus is the Light of the World. *John 8:12*
Jesus is the Vine. *John 15:1*
Jesus is the Way, Truth, and Life. *John 14:6*
Jesus' baptism. *Matthew 3:13-17*
Jesus' birth. *Luke 2:1-20*
Jesus' temptation by Satan. *Matthew 4:1-11*
Jesus' transfiguration. *Luke 9:28-36*
John the Baptist killed. *Mark 6:14-29*
Jonah and the fish. *Jonah 1:1–2:10*
Jordan River parts. *Joshua 3:1-17*
Joseph sent to Egypt. *Genesis 37:1-36*
Lazarus raised from the dead. *John 11:1-44*
Lord's Prayer. *Matthew 6:9-13*
Lot's wife turns to salt. *Genesis 19:15-26*
Love chapter. *1 Corinthians 13*
Moses protected as a baby. *Exodus 2:1-10*
Naaman is healed of leprosy. *2 Kings 5:1-19*
Nicodemus talks with Jesus. *John 3:1-21*
Noah and the ark. *Genesis 6:1–9:17*
Passover in Egypt. *Exodus 12:1-30*
Paul and Silas sing in prison. *Acts 16:16-40*
Paul's conversion. *Acts 9:1-19*
Paul's shipwreck. *Acts 27:13–28:10*
Pentecost. *Acts 2:1-13*
Peter's escape from prison. *Acts 12:1-19*
Plagues on Egypt. *Exodus 7–11*
Rainbow after the Flood. *Genesis 9:8-17*
Red Sea parts. *Exodus 14:5-31*
Samson and Delilah. *Judges 16:4-22*
Sermon on the Mount. *Matthew 5–7*
Sodom and Gomorrah. *Genesis 19:1-28*
Stoning of Stephen. *Acts 7:54-60*
Sun stands still. *Joshua 10:1-15*
Ten Commandments. *Exodus 20:1-17*
Tower of Babel. *Genesis 11:1-9*
Water from the rock. *Numbers 20:1-13*
Wise men visit Jesus. *Matthew 2:1-12*
Zacchaeus meets Jesus. *Luke 19:1-10*

TEACHING PARABLES
About the Kingdom of God
The Soils. *Matthew 13:3-8; Mark 4:4-8; Luke 8:5-8*
The Thistles (Tares). *Matthew 13:24-30*

JESUS' MIRACLES

Five thousand people are fed. *Matthew 14:15-21; Mark 6:35-44; Luke 9:12-17; John 6:5-14*

Stilling the storm. *Matthew 8:23-27; Mark 4:35-41; Luke 8:22-25*

Demons sent into the pigs. *Matthew 8:28-34; Mark 5:1-20; Luke 8:26-39*

Jairus's daughter raised from dead. *Matthew 9:18-26; Mark 5:22-24, 35-43; Luke 8:41-42, 49-56*

Diseased woman healed. *Matthew 9:20-22; Mark 5:25-34; Luke 8:43-48*

Jesus heals a paralyzed man. *Matthew 9:1-8; Mark 2:1-12; Luke 5:17-26*

A leper is healed at Gennesaret. *Matthew 8:1-4; Mark 1:40-45; Luke 5:12-15*

Peter's mother-in-law healed. *Matthew 8:14-17; Mark 1:29-31; Luke 4:38-39*

A withered hand is restored. *Matthew 12:9-13; Mark 3:1-5; Luke 6:6-11*

A demon-possessed boy is cured. *Matthew 17:14-21; Mark 9:14-29; Luke 9:37-42*

Jesus walks on the sea. *Matthew 14:22-33; Mark 6:45-52; John 6:17-21*

Blind Bartimaeus receives sight. *Matthew 20:29-34; Mark 10:46-52; Luke 18:35-43*

A girl is freed from a demon. *Matthew 15:21-28; Mark 7:24-30*

Four thousand are fed. *Matthew 15:32-38; Mark 8:1-9*

Cursing the fig tree. *Matthew 21:18-22; Mark 11:12-14, 20-24*

A centurion's servant is healed. *Matthew 8:5-13; Luke 7:1-10*

A demon is sent out of a man. *Mark 1:23-27; Luke 4:33-36*

A dumb demoniac is healed. *Matthew 12:22; Luke 11:14*

Two blind men find sight. *Matthew 9:27-31*

Jesus heals the mute man. *Matthew 9:32-33*

A coin in a fish's mouth. *Matthew 17:24-27*

A deaf and dumb man is healed. *Mark 7:31-37*

A blind man sees at Bethsaida. *Mark 8:22-26*

The first miraculous catch of fish. *Luke 5:1-11*

A widow's son is raised from the dead. *Luke 7:11-16*

A handicapped woman is healed. *Luke 13:10-17*

Jesus cures a sick man. *Luke 14:1-6*

Ten lepers are cured. *Luke 17:11-19*

Jesus restores a man's ear. *Luke 22:49-51*

Jesus turns water into wine. *John 2:1-11*

A nobleman's son is healed at Cana. *John 4:46-54*

A lame man is cured. *John 5:1-16*

Jesus heals a man born blind. *John 9:1-7*

Lazarus is raised from the dead. *John 11:1-45*

The second miraculous catch of fish. *John 21:1-14*

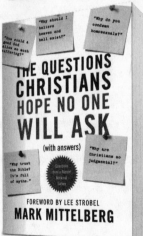